Ants and Orioles

Showing

the Art of

Pima Poetry

THE UNIVERSITY OF UTAH PRESS
SALT LAKE CITY

Ants and Orioles

Donald Bahr

Lloyd Paul

Vincent Joseph

LIBRARY OF CONGRESS CATALOGING-IN-PUBLICATION DATA

Bahr, Donald M.
    Ants and Orioles : showing the art of Pima poetry / Donald Bahr, Lloyd Paul,
Vincent Joseph.
        p.   cm.
    Includes bibliographical references.
    ISBN 0-87480-549-X (alk. paper)
    1. Pima poetry. 2. Tohono O'Odham poetry. 3. Pima poetry—Translations into
English. 4. Tohono O'Odham poetry—Translations into English.   I. Paul, Lloyd,
1919–   . II. Joseph, Vincent. III. Title.
    PM2174.A2B34   1997
    879'.45—dc21   97-29657

Contents

PAUL ZOLBROD

Foreword

As Donald Bahr suggests at the outset, this volume asserts a claim all too seldom made: there is poetry in Native American oral discourse. In it resides the artistry of language conceptually framed and meticulously patterned—artistry drawn from that secular past conventionally called history; from that sacred, mythic past commonly understood as religion; from that creative faculty sometimes identified as imagination; and from that shared reality that induces a culture to articulate its visions and values.

By offering as an example a sheath of Pima songs, Professor Bahr pursues more fully than anyone the poetic range of two tribes sharing a single language. His earlier contribution to *Rainhouse and Ocean: Speeches for the Papago Year* places dramatic oratory of poetic proportions on exhibit. More recently, his edition of *The Short Swift Time of Gods on Earth* reveals the rich narrative tradition the Pimas and Papagos have inherited from their common Hohokam ancestors. And with the publication of this volume, he demonstrates how that single language community fills the poetic spectrum as colorfully as any written European tradition can.

The method he has devised for placing the songs on a page, makes evident a lyric precision that surpasses other efforts to represent a body of Native American poetry in "the quiet language," as he calls conventional print. He produces a veritable sound spectrograph for each song, so that readers unexperienced at hearing them can visualize how individual syllables are strung together from line to line according to the key metered zones he has recognized. The statements he and his Pima colleagues make reawaken awareness of lyric's great importance not only to this people, but throughout the broader human community. Together they set a precedent for understanding the communal function of a living tribe's song, and the relationship lyric poetry can establish between individuals and sacred tradition—in this case a tradition that speaks through dreams of "mythic persons." And in so doing, they rightly secure "the poetry of small nations" in the large arena of great literature.

Today's editors of old, alphabetically preserved works rarely if ever listen to or consult with actual singers the way Professor Bahr has done. Nor can they bring his ethnographer's experience to the matrix culture. Thus, his rendering of these Pima songs reminds us that in spite of the silence of print, poetry is a living art that articulates what is at once universal and particular. The relationship he draws between Pima songs and the fundamental myths of that tribe ushers the reader into a unique cultural mind-set—exotic yet somehow familiar—fascinating in and of itself for what it reveals about a people seen from a cultural distance while renewing what we know most deeply about ourselves. And because it provokes reflection on the way mythology and song combine to reconcile sacred and secular thought, it gives old European works unexpected new life.

Products of a living tradition, these songs explain how great lyrics can compel an audience to listen, much as Coleridge's ancient mariner held the wedding guest spellbound. As a wellspring of poetry created not by authorial invention but transacted first while dreaming and then in performance, these songs invite speculation about inspiration more immediate than standard written poems allow. Originating during dreams or dream-like visitations, they remind us that dream-poems, ranging from the modest "Caedmon's Hymn" or Keats's magical "Belle Dame Sans Merci" to majestic allegories like Langland's *Piers Plowman* and Dante's *Commedia*, demand verbal expression of the highest order. With their lyric precision, they invoke the fleetingness of sharply-felt experience expressed in sonnets; and as works to be sequenced they move readers closer to the remote sequences of Philip Sidney and Edmund Spenser. And in light of Bahr's broadened conception of literature beyond the printed word to include any means by which a people preserve the meaningful, they make works such as the Childe ballads, recovered from a so-called folk, literary creations of a high order.

In gathering this material so patiently, Donald Bahr reinforces a paradigm I outlined in *Reading and Writing: Native American Oral Poetry on the Written Page* (Utah 1995). In it I argued that Native American poetry deserves an attention it has yet to receive. First, however, editors must recognize that poetry originates orally, while readers should learn to distinguish between the dual modes of narrative and dramatic poetry rendered either in a lyrical or a colloquial voice. In his work overall Professor Bahr has essentially done that without necessarily employing

my exact terms, which require his kind of amplification anyhow. And
what he offers here represents a giant step towards fully acknowledging
Native North America as a source of serious poetry in its purest form—
the unwritten lyric, with its carefully orchestrated units of syntax and
sound.

Thanks to his metrical analyses of these songs, coupled with his pre-
cise orthographic method of arranging the texts—his "line-writing the-
ory," as he calls it—Donald Bahr helps close the gap between the sound
of lyric poetry and the technique of transferring it onto the stubbornly
silent page. To the best of my knowledge, nobody who has attempted to
do so has so fully merged the out-loud language of lyric outcry and the
silent language of print. The result is a text to be read carefully and sa-
vored in an effort to reconstruct its pure sound in the mind's ear, and to
discover how carefully arrayed components of speech advance meaning.
Reading and listening are thus reunited, reminding us that in this elec-
tronic age, too, we live in a world of song and hence of lyric poetry; that
for us as for the Pimas "song was part of the original order of things;" and
that in bringing the lyric poetry of a little nation to light, the term *litera-
ture* takes on new clarity, and the literary heritage of the mainstream An-
glo-European community emerges from the darkness of misguided
abandon.

INTRODUCTION

Purpose of the Book

The second part of this book's title is borrowed from James Liu's *The Art of Chinese Poetry*, published in 1962. The borrowing is motivated by a desire to apply to the Pimas the same two questions that Liu applied to Chinese poetry: what is poetry in this tradition and what makes some poems good? The questions are simple but open and ever refinable. The Native literatures of the New World, including Pima literature, have not yet yielded refined answers to these questions, but many could. There is a chance that the yield will be good for the Native poetries, if it is true that they exist to be noticed, if their makers wanted them to be carefully thought through.

The first part of the title designates the two pieces of Pima poetry whose quality we will examine, one sing—that is, a performance—of thirty-one Ant songs and another sing of forty-seven Oriole songs. To those performances will be brought what has been learned to date about the art of social dance singing, which is the use of the songs.

The Pimas live in southern Arizona. The dances are held for pleasure and celebration, hence they are called social dances. In Pima they are called "*cu:dk*," "stomping," for the step used in performing them, a light-footed stomp. Men and women hold hands in a line and stomp lightly around a circle through the night.

The art of the sing, to take up Liu's first question, is in stringing thirty to forty individual songs together in a manner that suggests a story. This art is not merely of the single song but of the whole string of them. What makes some sequences good poetry can be stated in three steps. First, it is unlikely that any full sequence is ever repeated. The individual songs are perfectly memorized, but the sequence is improvised both in selection and ordering. Second, the improvisation is subject to rules. Third, strings are considered good when the rules are obeyed and when the chosen combination seems appropriate to the time, place, and occasion. The credit for that appropriateness goes to the singer, the artist, who is the master of rules and selector of songs. Criticism in this case, the appreciation of goodness, comes down to knowing, or thinking that one knows, how the singer conveys an ephemeral appropriateness, in other words, to knowing the artist's skilled mind.

The individual songs are lovely. Surely they, too, can be subjected to Liu's two questions. They can and will be, but of course then the answers about them will be different, being concerned with isolated short poems rather than sequences of many. Furthermore, although one might dispute them in this, the Pimas do not think that they are the authors of the poems. They hold that the poems originate in dreams and are sung to dreamers by spirits during great, fantastic journeys. Humans learn the song poems, for example, from Ant spirits and Oriole spirits. Then they teach them to each other and combine and recombine them artfully in sings.

A few people have now begun to make up songs that resemble those that the old-timers acquired from spirits. These could be compared with the old ones, and the whole could be a topic for study, the study of the short poem. This, however, will not be our emphasis, which will be on the performed sequence, or string. It emerges that the string is more interesting than the single song, although of course dependent on the latter. In any case, the rules of wholes are different from those of the parts.

If every song comes from a past dream, it does not follow that all of the songs in a performance come from a single dream of the present singer. Singers learn from each other, and they reshuffle their texts from performance to performance. But the central illusion of sings is that the songs *could* be one dream. The illusion is that the string sung for the present occasion corresponds to a past dream in which the singer was taken on a journey by a spirit, a journey blessed with precisely these same songs, and that the dancers are now having the same dream. The singer is like their magical poet guide. This is the illusion that the strung songs continuously play on—not insist on, but play on pro and con.

Thus, the interpretive tasks of the study are four:

To inquire into the expressive qualities of the individual songs that are put into combination so as to learn how they lend themselves to that illusion

To inquire into the principles of the whole that singers use to order their combinations

To follow the suggestions of story, and the ambiguities and contradictions that mock those suggestions, through two actual sings, one derived from Ant spirits or Ant-persons, as they will be called, and the other from Oriole-persons

To understand what we can of the use of these works in dancing and their genesis in dreaming—history on the one hand and spiritual life on the other.

Necessary for those tasks and prior to them are the writing and translating of the texts. After the performances were recorded on tape, the texts were first written as they sounded in singing, then as they would be said in ordinary spoken Pima. Then they were put through two stages of English translation. These steps, arduous, technical, and lonely, are the bookworm's equivalent to poetic creation. Whoever does not want to know about them can read the final translations only, for the interpretations proceed from those versions. Whoever distrusts translation will find the earlier steps essential and interesting. And why, the greatest distruster of translation may ask, was this book not written in Pima? The answer is that there are very few people who read that language, and probably no one except Bahr, who is white, would gladly read a Pima language book on songs; and his Pima is too poor to write such a book. Therefore the book is in English, and the songs are translated.

In sum, the book is a literary and cultural study of two works of poetic song sequence improvisation. Because great care will be taken with these sings, and because they are esoteric even to Pimas, it is important to state that they should not be considered as the very best that these singers or this people could do. Rather, they should be taken as good works which embody the rules and yet have their own individuality. They are not the first to be studied, but they are meant to be a kind of benchmark. More care will be taken with them than was, or could, be taken before. Naturally we hope that the sings and interpretation will bring credit to the Pimas and that the world will be richer from knowing them.

To return now to the issue of improvisation, it is easy to establish that the sings we will study changed in sequence, for we have a few successive recordings of the singers as testimony. It is not so easy to establish the reasons for the changes: whether in search of new effects; or to augment an existing effect or theme; or to include newly learned songs; or to accomodate an audience or place; or from sheer absent-minded chance. Each of those reasons will be invoked as we proceed. Each makes sense given what is known of Pima social dance singing in general, and more than one reason could apply to any particular, observed change. Real, particular changes are probably caused by several factors conjointly.

Actually this study will pay more attention to constancies between sings than to changes, or innovations. But most likely constancy and innovation are two sides of the same coin, or, better said, two moments in the same process. Innovations are bondings of songs that a singer temporarily favors. They appear as retentions over a few sings, but over a longer run they, too, have a beginning and end, when they give way to more innovations. The constancies that we will attend to, then, are probably ephemeral, but we cannot prove this because the successive runs of sings that we have are too few to know. We have only two sings of Ants and three of Orioles.

Now, some final remarks on spirits and dreams as a preview of what the poetry says. On the evidence of these sings, spirits are ambiguously alluded to rather than clearly delineated. Thus, the reader who hopes for clear pictures of ants or Ant spirits, or Oriole spirits, will be disappointed. The songs are very pictorial, or "filmic" as will be said, but the pictures resemble the American news documentaries in which the characters' faces and other identifying features have been electronically blurred. This blurring is typical of Pima verbal culture on spirits. Those immaterial beings are vividly felt, and everyone is interested in them, but they are always reported ambiguously.

The language itself—the lexicon, the dictionary of everyday usage—makes it difficult to speak of spirits directly. Thus, the same word, i:bdag, means both the physical heart and the spiritual soul, as if it would be presumptuous to clearly single out "soul"; and the word for "to cure," the achievement of which ultimately involves spirits, is the same as "to blow," as if the curer's breath were all that is involved. Indeed there is no word for "spirit" apart from heart or breath, or "spiritual" apart from that which is wished, or "spirituality" apart from way of life.

What do dreamers tell about their experiences with spirits, that is, with sleep-met people? Pimas are interested in telling about their "ordinary" dreams, but none is happy to tell the details of a dream in which spirits sing, for example to tell what the spirit looked like, what the scene looked like, and what one felt as the spirit sang. To tell that would be impolite, would be too open about something mysterious. The only testimony on these important dreams, then, is from what the *spirits* say, that is, from the songs; or to be more exact, from what the spirits *seem* to say. For the central illusion in dance singing hinges on the "I's" of the song texts, and while these "I's" mean "I-the-spirit" in the first place, they have overtones of "I-the-dreamer" and "I-the-dancer." The ambiguity of spirits plays out even here, indeed here above all, as the voices of the spirits are manipulated by dance singers.

The Ant songs were sung around 1972 by Andy Stepp and Claire Seota of the Salt River Indian Community, and the Oriole songs were alternatingly sung and summarized in ordinary speaking in 1983 by Vincent Joseph of The Gila River Indian Community. Bahr, the author of this introduction, did not meet Stepp and Seota, but he knew Joseph. Bahr would like to thank N. Allen, A. Bahr., J. Bierhorst, L. Cameron, G. Clyde, E. Diaz, J. Ehlers, J. Grathwohl, A. Krupat, F. Lewis, P. Lopez, S. Pablo, E. Ray, M. Schweitzer, C. Sherry, B. and E. Stone, B. Swann, S. Vaughn, E. White, and P. Zolbrod for their help in this work.

PART ONE

Ant Songs

CHAPTER ONE

Background:
Working on the Texts,
the History of Salt River,
and Pima Mythology

TEXTUAL MATTERS

Thirty-one "Ant songs" are transcribed, translated, and interpreted in these chapters. In their home use, the texts are sung poems whose melody and pitch, and some of whose articulated sounds, are different from ordinary talking speech. Unlike Europeans, the Pimas have no verse meant for the normal speaking voice, and they also have practically no music without words. Their songs are beautiful, provocative, short tellings of things—song poems.

The songs are enough removed from ordinary speech to make understanding them somewhat difficult. Some Pimas truthfully say that they don't understand the sung words at all, but more say that although they understand most of the words of a song, one or two short, difficult passages elude them. The problem with those spots is not that they yield to no interpretation, but that they resist a fully satisfactory one. People will have ideas about a particular difficult passage, but no idea fits perfectly both with the sounds of the passage and the known meanings of the rest of the words of the song. Some of these will yield after mulling, but some never do, at least not without the help of a singer who has known the song for years.[1] Alas, the singer may prefer to talk *about* what a song says,

---

[1] The Pimas believe the original singer to be a mythic person (see chapter three) who sang the song to a dreaming Pima, perhaps long ago. They do not claim to know who first dreamed the Ant songs or whether they were all dreamed by the same person. Probably they were not, since one of the songs also appears in the Oriole sing. Thus, someone did

for example, about a mountain that a song mentions, rather than to talk *the song*, that is, to reduce each of its forty to sixty syllables to something in plain Pima.

Bahr, a white anthropolgist, and Paul, a Pima singer, have reduced the Ant songs to plain Pima. Paul is a nephew of Andy Stepp, who sang the songs with Claire Seota for a home recording around 1972. Bahr took the lead in translating the songs word for word into English (Paul does not endorse every word choice), and he wrote most of the commentaries, including this text. "I" therefore means "Bahr" except in the songs, where it primarily means "I, an Ant-person," a mythic being.

The songs lose part of their poetry in their reduction to spoken Pima. In this process, Paul and I were concerned with how to render the singing into plain speech, not with making the plain speech beautiful. Accordingly, the reduction costs the songs their beautiful sounds. That loss is not made up in the first stage of translation. There the task is to match each plain Pima word with an English equivalent, either a word or short phrase. The result is a choppy, raw English.

Not all of the poetry is lost in those stages. Regardless of how they sound, the plain Pima and the raw English still convey pictures, and those pictures—verbal images—are part of the songs' poetry. Thus, reduction and literal translation cost the poems their sonorousness, but not their imagery.

A final step into freer translation provides a kind of sonorousness, but not that of the original songs. With their quick beat, syncopation, and floweriness[2], the Pima originals have a sound meant for dancing.[3] In contrast, the free English translations make slight, smoothing changes upon the first English versions so as to produce a form suitable for quiet read-

---

some mixing and exchanging. The principal Ant singer of the generation before the songs were recorded was a man named Miguel. The songs seem to be concentrated on the Salt River reservation, but this is not to say that they originated or were confined there.

Once a kind of song has entered circulation, others may dream it, that is, may receive songs of the same kind. This phenomenon is obscure because people are reluctant to say that they have dreamed songs. They prefer to say that they learned them from other Pimas. What is true of acquiring new songs is true of clarifying old ones. The normal way to do this is to ask another singer what a difficult passage means, not, so far as we know, to dream a clarification from a mythic person.

[2] Sung words have more syllables than the same words as said in ordinary speech. The additions are mainly reduplications and the addition of the vowel "e" to the ends of ordinary language words that end in a consonant, changing ordinary language *mad*, "child," to *mamade*. I consider these changes to be flourishes, therefore flowery.

[3] The sound is also meant for, or at least has the effect of, assuring memorization. Any stumble or slur in the execution of a song is immediately apparent. It it much easier to "get away" with an error in reciting ordinary speech than in reciting—singing—a song.

Andy Stepp, with family, at a wedding reception.

ing or telling, a form of quiet free verse. (The Oriole songs of the next part are translated into a loud, actually cacophonic, English, that is, an English that bends itself to match the syllable count and stress and pitch of the originals).

THE TAPES

As I stated above, the songs are from tapes of Stepp and Seota made by unknown Pimas sometime in the early 1970s. We don't know the details of the recording. Since there are no sounds of a crowd, the recording must have been of a private event, possibly to preserve the songs for one of the families. Copies of the tapes were eventually given to Fr. James O'Brien, the priest of the Catholic church at Salt River, who was known for his belief that songs such as these, which preceded the local church, could beautify and support Christianity. But being unsure of what the songs actually said, he lent me the tapes to copy in 1981 in the hope that I would help him understand them. Unfortunately, I did not try to do this until 1994 when I met a young singer named Earl Ray who introduced me to Lloyd Paul. O'Brien had died in 1993, and Stepp and Seota had died earlier. Before meeting Ray and Paul, I did not know anyone with a knowledge of songs at Salt River.

SALT RIVER

The community, formally called the Salt River Pima-Maricopa Indian Community, is bordered on the west and south by the cities of Scottsdale and Mesa, and is open to pristine land under federal and other Indian (Yavapai) control to the east and north. It was settled around 1875[4] by Pimas and Maricopas who journeyed to this place from the Gila River, twenty-five miles to the south. For the previous 200 years this part of the Salt River val-

---

[4] Paul thinks the Pimas moved to the Salt River sooner, perhaps in the 1850s, perhaps long before then. He and all Pimas think the Hohokam spoke Pima, and like many, he thinks the Hohokam were conquered by Pimas. There may have been practically no interruption in Pima occupancy after that conquest, if it occurred. The mythology states that the conquerers continued westward past the Colorado River after dealing with the Hohokam, and then they returned to the former Hohokam territory and spread out there. No one knows the date of the conquest according to white reckoning, only that it would have been before the coming of the whites (Esteban and Marcos de Niza in 1538 and 1539), Paul knows where his grandparents lived (they were born in the 1870s, some of them at Salt River), but not his great grandparents. Phoenix was first settled by whites around 1868 and was first surveyed in 1871 (Salt River Project, 1970:23, 37). Mesa was first settled around 1877 and surveyed in 1878 (Mesa Public Schools, 1978:1, 14).

ley had been an uninhabited no-man's land between the Pimas and Maricopas to the south and west and the Yavapais and Apaches to the north and east. From around A.D.1 to 1400, the land was inhabited by a prehistoric people called the Hohokam by Pimas (archaeologists use the same word for this culture). The Pimas believe that these people spoke Pima. No other tribe contradicts them, so they may well be correct, although archaeology cannot confirm this. (The Hohokam did not write, and their history seems to have stopped shortly before the first whites arrived.)

The 1875 Pima and Maricopa migration was contemporary with the founding of the white towns of Mesa, Tempe, and Phoenix (Scottsdale came later), all downstream from the Indian settlement. No whites settled upstream from the Indians on the Salt, hence their almost pristine view today to the north and east. Although politically autonomous, the Salt River Indian community developed as a rural district of the Phoenix metropolitan area. Thus, the community's roads were laid out, beginning in 1909, as part of a single valley-wide grid with east-west-running roads named the likes of Indian School (located in Phoenix), Camelback (a mountain), Apache Trail, and University (in Tempe); and north-south roads named, for example, Pima, Alma School (from the Book of Mormon), 92nd Street (calculated east from Central Avenue in Phoenix), and Country Club (of Mesa). All of the above pass through or close to the community. The Indians therefore share streets with the rest of the metropolis. Their houses are on generous lots interspersed with farmed fields and scrub. Street signs stand at the main corners, but these are often decapitated as if to say, "corner of Nowhere and Nothing You Know."

In Paul's youth, in the 1930s, nearly every Salt River family farmed. His people thought that they had been farmers somewhere in the river-crossed desert since the beginning of time. Indeed, their mythology says that as soon as the Pimas were created, their creator gave them seeds to farm with.[5] Moreover, because the Salt River Pimas lived upstream from the whites and in the path of the canals that watered the white settlements, Paul's people did not suffer the fate of their relatives back on the Gila, who lost their water to whites living upstream. In fact that loss, which started in the 1870s, was probably one of the reasons for the migration to the Salt. Other reasons would include curiosity, quarrels, and invitations from whites.

---

[5] Almost. The mythology that is followed in this book (discussed below) holds that the *Hohokam* were given seeds immediately after their creation (Bahr, et al., 1994:79–85), but an earlier creation, who may have been ancestral to the Pimas, received a wild plant, malva, for their vegetable food (1994: 49 and the rest of the story).

Here is Paul on the history of the community:

Hema jijiwia g Milgan, i:ya ñ-kii am.

A Whiteman was coming, here at my house.

G O'odham ha-himdag oidceg, g hekihu himdag oidceg, s-ma:cim ha'icu ab amjed. Wud si s-has ha'icu, am ge'ecu mascamakudc ed.

The Pimas' way he seeks after, the old way he seeks after, he wants to learn something about it. He's somebody important in higher education.

Am iñ-kaiyam c am o iñ-ta:ñ, mañ s am b o cei man p has masma s-ma:c, mas has masma i dada i:ya, iyab uliñig.

He asked me, he requested me, that I could say whatever I know, [about] how they [Pimas] came here, [so that] they are here.

Ñ eda hab cu'ig pi sa'i ma:c nañ pi wud abs wecij o'odham.

But yet I don't really know that because I was just a young person [in old times].

An b i ha'ap hegai ñ-kekelbad pi hekid mas am iñ-beik am o ñ-a:gi, bac amjed hihim.

Besides my oldtimers never took me and told me, where we came from.

"Pegi, t-dada, has i masma i dada"—pi am hekid abs a'i kaij.

"Well, we came, how we came"—they never said that.

Ñ am s am hiwa, he'es am kakke hiwa, ñe:, k am ka: hiwa, mac ab dada Wegi Akimelt ab, k ab e-ce:mo'o.

And yet of course, I evesdropped a little, look, and I heard some, that we arrived [anciently] at the Red [Colorado] River [after conquering the Hohokam] and came to a dead end.

Kus ed am hema we:maj g O'odham (matp Jios atp wud a pionga), si geg hegai su:dagi coikudkaj,

And there was someone with the people (he might have been God's worker), he hit the water with his cane,

C ab o ta:p, am gai am iawa, hegam matp ab gawud hihim, matp he'ekia wud i c ab gai am iawa.

And it [water] split, there they poured across, those who went in a bunch, as many as there were who poured across.

I hu aigo dada.

They came on this side.

•

•

Kus ha'i an vi'i gn hu ha'ap, mas g a'alga am suan k an vi:. T am on nam g su:dagi hahava e:p.

Of course some stayed over there, since their babies cried [for some reason] and they [a bunch] stayed. The water met [the passage closed] then again.

Ñe:, k hab a:g mas ud hegam Yu:m, c Kuapá c Naksel, Kawí:ya e:p, mat am amjed am dada hegam, k an ab ki: amai Wegi Akimel babso.

Look, and they are called to be the Yumas, and Cocopa and Mojave, also the Cahuilla, that's why they live there along the Red River.

Ñe:, i:dam ab hiwa hihim c ab hihim s hiwa dada atp hebai hasko.

Look, these [Pimas] of course went ahead and went ahead and of course they arrived somewhere [nearer to here].

Hab hiwa a:g mas as S-ko:ko'igk am dada. Mui ñiok hiwa, hekihu ha'icu a:ga, am hiwa son ab amjed heg S-ko:ko'igk.

It must have been Many-snakes [Snaketown] where they arrived. There is a lot of talk, ancient times stories, that comes from Many-snakes.

Eda am med g Keli Akimel. Am i oidc g ha'i hegam O'odham, k an i ciciwiapa mmiabidj hegai akimel.

That's where the Old-man [Gila] River was flowing. Some of those Pimas followed it [up- and downstream from Snaketown].

Kutp eda ha'i wud s-wo:po'idkam, e:pai. Ab i ñeidahim g jewed i ha'ap, k am ab ce: mas i ehe med g Onk Akimel.

Yet some were [long distance] runners, too. They looked over the land in this direction [north from the Gila], and they found that there also runs [on that side] the Salt River.

Kutp he'ekiac an i e-a'agid, k an an kawudkadk ab hihim k ihu aigo dada, i:ya Onk Akimelt ab.

Then several of them talked to each other, and they banded together and went and came to this side [across the dry land from the Gila], here to the Salt River.

E-ju: k an ci:ciwiapa anai, akimel miabij. A'ahidag ab an ciciwiapa anai, ki:kahim anai.

They did it and settled there, near the river. For years they settled there, they used to live there.

E-wua c am e'esa g bawi, huñ, miliñ. We:s e-we:mad c am e-we:m cikpan. E-we:m am kua hegai, matp hascu an i e'esad.

They did and planted the tepary-beans, corn, mellon. They all helped each other and worked together. They ate sharing whatever they planted.

Kupt hab e-ju: k am ha-ju:ks, mui taskaj ju:, k am ha-vi'in no pi eda abs an med hegai akimel. Pi im hu hebai sa e-ku:pa, c abs am med.

Then it happened that it rained [hard] on them, many days of rain, and it flooded them because the river just ran. There was no dam anywhere [as now], and it just ran.

Si ge'eda g akimel k am ha-vi'in, t am ab i ce'ecs, in ab ciciwipa i:na u:g.

The river was huge and it flooded them, then they climbed, they settled higher up this way.

Hab hiwa a:g, mats an ciciwipa i:na, mo idañ g Sasanto mi:s ki: am ke:k, in ab i da:m.

So they say, that they settled here, where now the Catholic church stands, just above there [north of the church].

A kutp ama woho atp e-ju:, nañ pi am s-cegito mañ eda wud a wecij k an wa'aki da:m ki:kahim, ge'eho. I:ya, mañ i ki:

And it must be true, because I remember when I was young and lived on top of ancient ruins, long ago. Here, where I

idañ, wud a s ge wapaki eda heki hu.
Go:k am ha-vi'is idañ hiwa wapaki, im hu
ha'ap kuiwa ñ-ki: amjed.

•

Hab hiwa cu'ig, pi ha su:dagig i:na. Hegai
Milgán ha'icu e'esa k am i:ya kawudka,
am hudav i:dam O'odham, mats hab e-
wodwa ge'ecu waikka.

Am hihim, ha-pionc i:dam O'odham c ab
ha-we:m i waikadahi, k ab wodwa. Am
ha-ma: g su:dadagi, e:p.

Waikpa da:p hegai su:dagi. Im hu ha'ap
hema med, in hu Sonó:la wui, b o a'aga
amai, gm hu si weco.

In i ha'ap, a:cim, i:ya bekc a:cim mac am
s-edaof ki:. Hegam an bekc, hema e:p
hegai su:dagi, mo in hu da:m ki:, e:p.

Mat hekid a sa huhug g su:dagi, kuc i:ya
wo si ha-oidk o hu:.

live now, there used to be nothing but
mounds. Two of them remain of the
mounds, off to the west from my house.

•

Then it was, there was no water here [on
the high ground with mounds]. The
whites planted something [on their land]
and they they gathered here, they
bothered [talked to and questioned]
these Pimas, that they would [all] lay
down big canals.

It went on, the Pimas worked for them
and ditched with them, and they laid it.
That gave them water again.

Three ways split the water. Off there one
[canal] ran, there to "Sonora," as it is
called there, off below [nearest to the
river].

Over here, us, here we have it who live at
the middle [canal]. And those also have
water [the third canal], who live there
above [north].

Whenever the water would stop [in the
Salt River Valley], well we here will be
the last to stop [getting water, according
to law].

The community stopped its farming between the 1940s and 60s, but
not from lack of water. Rather, as Paul sees it, the reason was that people
could not pay for the water from a new irrigation system that was built for
them. Before the new system, until the late 1930s, everyone irrigated from
ditches dug, cleaned, and regulated by the community. Three such ditches
served the different parts of the community. The new system was easier to
use and less prone to evaporation thanks to its buried concrete pipes, but
with the new system came higher water bills. In the 1920s and 30s a fam-
ily could purchase sufficient water for ten acres, the usual irrigated allot-
ment (thirty acre-feet, the volume of water that will cover ten acres to a
depth of three feet), for about $20 per year paid in small sums after each ir-
rigation. By 1939 the annual fee for equal water was $132, preferably paid

in a lump sum.[6] With the price increase, irrigated farming did not cease at Salt River, but the Indians changed from farmers to lessors. They leased to whites who were willing and able to pay the higher rate.

There was more behind the shift from farming to leasing than the high cost of water. In one phrase, the "more" was the modernization of Pima attitudes about farming, from about 1900 before leasing had occurred to anyone at Salt River to 1960 when leasing was the way of agricultural life. We don't know all of the pieces of this history, so the following is a sketch. Much documentary study and remembering would be needed to clarify the story.

As Paul says, a great flood around 1900 (probably 1892—there was a great flood of record that year) caused the people to move from their original houses and farming sites on the river flood plain to higher terrace land to the north. As Paul also tells, the terrace land had formerly been lived on and farmed by the prehistoric Hohokam. There were ruined canals and mounds on this land. Thus, the terrace wasn't new to Indian farming, just new to farming by Paul's immediate ancestors.

Now, around the time that the Pimas moved onto the terrace, the U.S. government decided to secure to each man, woman, and child of the Salt River community (Maricopas as well as Pimas) a ten-acre plot of irrigable, soon to be irrigated, land (the Hohokam canals would be brought back to life), and twenty acres of detached unirrigated land for pasture or grazing or what-have-you. With this plan the government would raise Pima farm life to turn-of-the-century American standards. The land to be plotted and irrigated was mostly on the terrace to which the people had begun to relocate. Thus the government's and the community's thinking coincided.

The coincidence crystalized in the extension of the metropolitan (then mere town) street grid into the Salt River Reservation territory. The year of the crystalization, or actually scripturalization, was 1909. The document

---

[6] The water vendor was the Salt River Project, a regional entity subsidized by the federal government. It started operation in the teens of the century. For the thirty years before it, from 1880 to 1900, there was little to Phoenix, Mesa, Tempe, and Scottsdale; and the Salt River Indians lived clustered by the river. They did not pay for their water. They spread northward onto the present road grid and began paying for water by 1910; and as stated above, they spread still farther and paid still more following the water system's improvement in the late 30s. The 1996 price for thirty acre-feet of Salt River Project water to Salt River Indian users is about $150, half of the price charged for water to adjacent non-Indian land. (White lessors of Salt River Community land also benefit from this reduced, Indian, water fee).

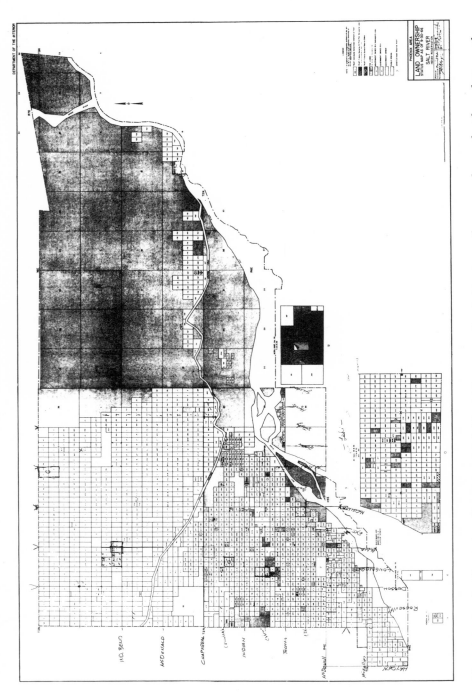

The original and still existing allotments at Salt River. The reservation is fourteen miles across the north side and nine miles along the west. Unalloted lands are shaded.

that shows it, reproduced as Map 1, is a copy of a map that Paul's brother, who worked for the government as a draftsman, made for him.

The map shows numbered allotments of small (irrigated) and large (unirrigiated) parcels. The numbers, 1–974, correspond to the official Salt River Pima and Maricopa Indian Reservation roll of the fall of 1909. Paul was not yet born, so he is not an original allottee (he inherited his land), but his wife was a three-month-old baby at the time, so she was an allottee (number 715).

The allotment was part of the general U.S. government policy to set up American Indians as independent farmers on their own private pieces of land. The plan is frequently criticized for having led to, and encouraged and forced, the sale of Indian lands to whites. This did not happen at Salt River. No allotted land has been sold to a white.[7] What did happen was somewhat similar, however, namely a modernization that resulted in the Salt River people leasing most of their land to whites.

Why did this happen? For one thing, just as the allotments were never sold to outsiders, neither were they sold, bartered, or given to insiders. In other words, no internal land market or land exchange ever developed. The original plots on the 1909 map are still *the* plots at Salt River as far as ownership is concerned. Of course the original allotees are almost all deceased, and the plots are now owned by their heirs: a 10% interest in plot number so-and-so, 25% in plot this-and-that, etc.

As of 1996 there were thousands of share holders of record in the original 974 allotments (the tribe keeps the current number secret), and waiting behind the thousands are thousands more individuals who, on the death of a present owner, will inherit some part of the present holder's fraction. The Pima ownership has multiplied and fractioned to the point where almost no one can work his or her land. At the same time farming in the region has become increasingly mechanized and therefore large scale. Horse-powered farming, which was new to the Pimas in 1910, gave way to tractor farming beginning in the 1930s and disappeared absolutely by the 1960s. Rural life changed, from lamplit and water-faucetless up to the 1920s or 60s (depending on place—reservations lagged) to electrified and bathroomed from the 30s to 70s. Pima houses changed from single-room round houses made of brush and roofed with dirt to mud walled rectangular houses with one or two rooms to cement-block walled, lumber-under-plywood-under-roofing-paper roofed, several room houses. The changes demanded increasing money. Every new

---

[7] Nor was any so-called surplus land, former Salt River tribal land left over after the allotment process, sold to a white.

Lloyd Paul in the vineyard at Phoenix Indian School.

Lloyd Paul's family, photographed by LP, with loose cotton in a bag for market.

Lloyd Paul's son, with chickens.

Lloyd Paul and his wife planting watermelons.

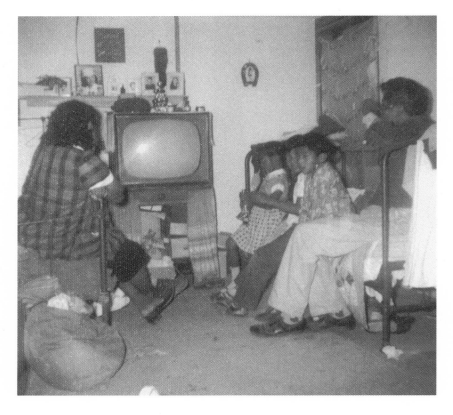

The Paul family's first television set, 1954.

thing that was added to Pima life from 1900 to 1970 was a new thing to purchase, not to make for oneself: bedspreads, panties, sugar bowls, percolators, toasters, electric fans, hairpins, cars, stereos, etc., etc.

Now, for the first twenty or thirty years of the allotments, that is, until 1930 or 1940, it was possible for Pimas to live an up-to-date modernizing, Americanizing life (in the material sense) by farming with horses on ten irrigated acres. Many did, including Paul. This was the life of rectangular mud-walled houses with no electricity or running water. One can say without stretching things that these were the good old days at Salt River. The old social dancing was thriving; the community was running its own activities; the old mythology told a full and satisfactory history of the world. The Pimas were modernizing but proud because their ten acres could pay for the little that they wanted to buy from whites, the masters and merchants of modernism.

But Paul and many like him desired the next, improved stage of modern homelife: lumber roofs, running water, electricity, cars, bedspreads, etc. This required money beyond what ten acres could provide. Also, at least in Paul's case, they wanted farming with tractors on fields of eighty or more acres. This was impossible on the basis of the orignal allotments, which by 1940 were becoming fractionated anyway.

For Paul and a few others there was an alternative to their own allotments. This was the Salt River Tribal Farm, a collective enterprise that operated on unallotted or de-allotted (reverted to tribal) land. At its peak that farm had two thousand acres. Paul was the foreman of it from 1944 to 1949, and he loved it. Later the farm fizzled, for social, not agronomical, reasons.

That failure was the last chance for active Indian farming at Salt River. The people settled into leasing, a painless existence in which the reservation superintendent, then the tribe itself, enabled white (apparently never Indian) farmers to apply tractor technology to large fields comprised of many fractioned allotments. The farmers paid the superintendent or tribe, who divided the proceeds among the land owners.

It is history's fault that the original allotments became obsolete for second-stage modern farming, and there was no way to fix the allotments for Pima use.[8] But at least all of the people kept a stake in their old scripturalized allotments.

Here is Paul on the commencement of leasing. One can see here his love of figures and motions, and also how in his opinion the increased cost of water was the principal cause of the shift into leasing:

_____

[8] Here is what could have happened, but so far as we know did not happen, at least not to any great extent. First, an internal land market could have developed, so that the

Eda hekihu, mo obs a med g su:dagi, hekid hema ama a taccwa, t am ku:kpa, c am hekaj.

Before [the construction of big dams upsteam], when the water just ran, when someone wanted it [water], he dammed [blocked] it [a flowing stream], and used it [the redirected water].

Ñe:, k am a hebai mat am ahawa kei g o'odham. mat am wud o wi:skad.

Look, and sometime then they stood up [appointed] a man, who would be the "whiz" [irrigation boss].

Heg am ahawa himcudahim hegai su:dagi, ha-ma:k g ki:kam.

He would be running the water, he would give it to the people.

Hebai hema mo taccwa g su:dagi, eda hugkam tas o hekaj, o e:p hema hemako tas o hekaj, o e:p hemako s-cuhugmam o hekaj hegai su:dagi,

Sometime someone would want the water, a half day ['s flow] he would use, or perhaps someone would use one [whole] day [-light], or else someone would use one night ['s flow],

Eda hekihu wud gi:g lial eda hugkam tas. Hegam mo om hemko tas o hekaj g su:dagi, pi:s ha-namkid; kutp am o sa hekaj g su:dagi go:ko masad, go:k pi:s o namkid.

Then at that time it [payment to whiz] was four "moneys" [or "bits," eighths of a peso] for half a day. Those who used one day of water, a peso [dollar—eight "moneys"] they paid; and if they used it twice a month, two pesos they paid.

Ñe:, k t g kownal hahawa wa: i:ya. Ab waikkad babso, hegai ge'e ge'ecu waikka, s-ju:kam waikka ep s-tadañ, waik keispa am waikkad, himc hegai waikka.

Look, then the government entered here. Along the [existing] canal, the big canal, the deep and wide canal, for three miles they made a canal, they ran a canal.

Ñe:, ko amai mo wuwhas hegam wo:pog, mo hebai at hegai waikka, walin waikka, am a'atopso ha-wo:poic hegam wapaika.

Look, and where the roads come out, where the [new] canal[s?] start[s?] [literally "have-its-ass"], the "barrel"

---

landholders of the 1930s and 40s could have transferred farm ownership during their life time. Perhaps the U.S. government discouraged this, or at least did not encourage it. Perhaps the people themselves were loath to enter into commerce over land, for fear of jealousy or other kinds of blame. As it was, people mainly made transfers by inheritance, that is, by directing the disposition of their land after their death. Sometimes they gave land to friends who were not relatives, and often they gave land to some children and refused it to others. Thus, there were selective land transfers, but not between living persons. Second, Pimas could have leased land from the superintenedent or tribe, either unalloted land or land that had been given over to leasing. Third, they could have entered the off reservation land market as private entrepreneurs or even as homesteaders (there was homesteading in this region into the 1930s and perhaps longer). We don't know how much those possibilities were considered or acted upon. They all required money or credit, which Pimas had little of and little to do with. Perhaps the options were also considered to be improper for Indians. But if so, why, and by whom? Whoever thought them improper helped push the Pimas farther into passive land leasing.

[buried cement pipe] canal[s?], there downward they ran those [new] canals.

Ñe:, t an hiwa wa: hegai su:dagi, k ab hiwa s-ap medackahim. K am hu t am i su:d g o'oiya gahu, mo om al hiacu ku:pat amjed.

Look, then surely the water entered [the new canals], and it surely ran well. Then eventually it [an open feeder canal] filled with sandy-gravel over there, below the little dam [called Evergreen].

Eda hugkam keispa hab e-ju:. Pi ap hu sa med g su:dagi, k atp am u:pam ge:s ge'ecu waikkac ed.

For half a mile it did [fill]. The water wouldn't run, it just fell back into the big canal.

T am hab hahawa cei i:dam O'odham, "Matts am o hihim k ab o waikkad." Ñe:, k t am hiwa hihim, k am cem oiyophim, go:k tas ab oiyophim. Pi has sa'i ju:.

Then the people said, "Let's go and [fix the] canal." Look, there they went and went around, two days of going around. No success.

E: s-ju:k, s-ju:k g o'oiya. Im hu ju:kahim g waikka, waikka tonk im hup u:gahim e:p. Hiwa cikpanc ha'as huami i:da.

Oh, it was deep, deep was the sandy-gravel. As the ditch deepened [from their shoveling], the mounded-bank rose [from their tossing]. It was quite a toil.

Ñe:, t am aha wa i ñei hegai kowinal da:sa, mat i dahiwa i:ya, hi: matt pi t-na:ko. Kt hab cei mats am hema bei g ma:gina k am o kegc.

Look, then the one whom the government seated saw it, he who sat here [the white superintendent], that we couldn't do it. And he said he will get a machine and do it right.

Ñe:, t am hema bei Parkert amjedk i uapa, k am s-ap ju:, k am dai. Ñe:, k am him.

Look, and he got one from Parker [Mojave Indian agency, Arizona] and brought it, and put it together, and sat it down. Look, and it went.

Abs i bibbia hegai o'oiya, c imhu e-we:gaj ñe:cud. C abs am himadk gahu ji:via gahu. Aigo ep i gei, e:p, k am ahawa atops hud, juñhim k am i na:to. Ñe:, t ab hahawa me: g su:dagi, yahawa.

It just scooped that sandy-gravel, and behind itself threw it. And it just went and arrived at the end. Back again it fell [turned], then downward it declined [down the other side of the canal], doing [scooping and throwing] and finished. Look, then the water ran, finally.

•

•

Ñe:, t am amjed hab hahawa ju:, hahawa, mat g pi:s ab i kakoblant g a:gli, k am hu hebai hab i juñim k am ba'ic ep i cesajk d hahawa waik pi:s.

Look, then afterwards [seeing the failure of the hand shovelers] it [government] did it, then, when it had cost a peso [dollar] per acre, then sometime it [government] did and raised it [price] and then it was three pesos.

Ñe:, t am aha hema bei g wi:s, k wud
milga:n. Kalit ehe ma:, e:p, an has
melhim c am ha-ma:k g su:dagi i:dam
O'odham. Ñe:, hab a:g mats g amjed a u'u
g e-lialga hegai milga:n wi:s ab amjed,
mac am ha-namkid.

Ñe:, t am ep i cesaj, e:p, gamai waik pi:s,
da:m go:ko westma:m s-uamcu i hahawa
t-kokoblant ahawa e:p, g a:gli.

Ñe:, k am o sa e'esa g westma:m a:gli, g
siant waiko westma:m gamai go:k go:k,
go:k westma:m s-uamcu heg ge:sad g
ahidag.

Ñe:, t hab i cei i:dam O'odham mas ab si
s-namkig, t am i haha'asa ha'ic.

Ha'ic am hiwa cem e-nako, eda am s-ap
hab cu:cu'ig hegam wapaikka. C ab dada
g pupualt, hema da:kad g pualt mo hebai
e-kaihyubins g wo:g, c ab amjed da'iwuñ
g su:dagi.

C am i ñei i:dam milga:n, ñe:, k am b i a:
mat of e'es g O'odham jewed. Am a
hudaof i:dam oidag eñigakam. Pi am hu
sa ha'icu ap'ecud tapialt ab, k abs hab-a
ñioki, ab am s-ho:ho'id.

Ñe:, t am s-mai, hegai milga:n mat i dai,
mas pi sa'i ap'e. Am b e-elid mat am ha'i
tua g e-lial hegam milga:n, k i da:m am b
ahawa e-ju:.

Ñe:, t hab hiwa e-ju:, hiwa, ñe:, k am i
amjed am hahawa i himc g tapial, ka
hahwa li:ndad g e-jejewedga, i:dam
O'odham. Wecij o'odham am hiwa o'oho,
c hab-a hegam kekel abs am o kots. T am

Look, then it [government] got a "whiz"
[irrigation boss], and he was white
[named Shumway]. A cart [car] it also
got for him, too, and he ran around and
gave water to the Indians. Look, they
intended that from that [running] he
would get his money as the white whiz,
that we would pay for him.

Look, then it [water price] rose again,
[to the sum of] past-it [ten] three [= thir-
teen] pesos, on-top [plus] two-times ten
[=twenty] yellows [pennies] they
charged us then, per acre.

Look, and if they planted ten acres, a
hundred, three-times ten, past-it [ten]
two, on-top two tens yellows [=$132.20]
they spent per year.

Look, then the Indians started to say that
it was very expensive, and some started
to quit [farming].

Some of them tried to stay in, since the
canals were so good, and there had been
doors [gates, standpipes] set, seated gates
wherever the [car] roads crossed, and
from there sprang the water.

And the whites saw it, look, and they
thought they would plant the Indian
land. They talked business to the field
owners. There was nothing fixed on
paper, but they talked, they [owners]
liked it [idea of leasing].

Look, and he found out, the white who
was seated here [reservation farming
administrator, named George Hall], that
it wasn't right. He thought they [whites]
should put some of their own money [as
a bond], then after that they can do it
[plant].

Look, then it happened, of course, look,
and from then they passed the papers
around, and then they leased their lands,
these Indians. Young people would write
their names, but the old ones just made a

o hema wo ñeidad, c g hekaj am wuḍ o
wohokamk hegam mat am koṭs.

Ñe:, t i wepom i muidahi, i:dam milga:n
e:sdam i:ya. Mañ hab kaij mo waikpa e-
tapañc hegai su:dagi, k an ha-ma:khim.
Abṣ hab-a am hebai hab i e-ju:, pi sa'i
ge'ec ha-we:hejed i:dam milga:n. Kutp
has masma b e-juñ, pi iñ sa'i ma:c, mas
hekid hab i i-ju:, mat g Salt River Valley
Water Users' Association am ep ha-ma: g
go:k westma:m, mi:l agli tad g su:dagi.

cross. Someone had to watch [witness]
for them, and that would make it valid
for those who made a cross.

Look, it seems like they increased, the
white planters here. As I said [in the
previous text], the [original, old timers'
system of] water split three ways, and
they gave that [amount of water] to
them. But sometime it happened that this
wasn't a lot [enough] for these whites
[lessees]. Then it happened, I don't know
[all about it], that the Salt River Valley
Water Users' Association also gave them
[lessees, via the tribe] two tens, thousand
[20,000] acre feet of water [as a normal,
historical free entitlement].

Ga hu waspipc, gahu, Bartlett kupat ab,
ñe:, k am hekaj hahawa e:p hegai. T abṣ
hab-a hab e-wua mat hekid am o sa hugio
hegai go:ko, westma:m agli tad, ab hiwa
melcud g su:dagi. C abṣ hab-a hahawa ep
kokoblanc g kowinal haha, e:p.

Off there it [water] is contained, off
there, at Bartlett Dam, look, and therefore
then there is also that [additionally
needed water]. But it happens that
whenever they finish the two tens,
thousand acre feet, then they run that
[additional] water, but they [some
government] has to pay for it, too.

Kupt idañ has e-wua, o has e si ge e-wua,
no omtp s am ba hia e-wua. Idañ am hiwa
ep wo o-nako i:dam o'odham, mats am o
bei hegai su:dagi. Kupt has masma am o
melcudad. hahawa, Ñe:, b o cu'ig, ant
hiwa hugkam hab o cei.

Now they're [tribe] doing something, or
there's some idea, which they may try to
do. Now these Indians may try again to
take back the [management of the] water.
Somehow they'll run it, supposedly.
Look, here it is, the end of what I say.

SOCIAL DANCING

The Ant songs belong to a category called social dancing songs, that is,
songs used to celebrate something (holidays, harvests, birthdays), not
songs to change things, which is the use of other types of songs (to diag-
nose sickness, to cure sickness, to foretell the rain, to learn where deer
are). These songs are accompanied either by scraping a notched stick
onto another, which is held pressed onto a basket resonator, or by hand-
held rattles. The dancing is in a long, circling line, or concentric lines, of
men, women, and children mixed as they please. The dancers hold hands
and "stomp" (cu:dk, a sprightly stomp) counterclockwise. Each song is

Salt River Indian Band, with Lloyd Paul on sousaphone.

Lloyd Paul

danced for several minutes. Thirty to fifty songs will fill a night, with intermissions at intervals for resting and socializing.

A seated singing leader picks and starts each song. The dancers join in loudly or softly depending on how well they know the songs. This is the normal way to learn them, by singing while dancing. It is rare now for dances to last all night and even rare to have shortened night dances, which end at one in the morning. Brief afternoon performances are now the rule. In these, the dancers tend to be specially costumed children. Salt River adult dancing meanwhile has become like that of the rest of Phoenix—American and Mexican style—in bars, at proms and weddings, etc.

Like its farming, Salt River's stomp dancing stopped slowly from 1940 to 1980. By the time the Ant songs were taped in the early 70s, only a few people knew enough songs of a given type to sing them for a full night. (Ant, Swallow, Nighthawk, Dragonfly, and a bird called *U:n Mu'uhig*[9] were the main Salt River song series in the good old days).

THE BAND

According to Paul, singers dying without understudies caused the dancing to stop. An additional factor, he says, was "the law," that is, the tribal police who cracked down on a rowdiness that was always expected and sometimes occurred at dances. With the good singers gone, the practice barely tolerated, and other forms of entertainment beckoning, Pima adult stomp dancing died. People took up dancing to American and Mexican musics, especially to an adopted Mexican form of dancing called "chicken scratch."

But before discussing that, I want to note a splendid form of something like dancing that flourished briefly at Salt River and on several other reservations. This form was the military style marching band. The Salt River band played at John Kennedy's presidential inauguration and at large and small Indian and non-Indian festivities through Arizona and into New Mexico, from the 1950s to the 70s. The band had about forty members, (five rows, seven or eight across), mostly Salt River people, men and women, young and old. Besides Pimas and Maricopas, there were Papagos, Apaches, some Mexicans, and a Chinese. It was one of

---

[9] I had thought this might be *Uam U'uhig*, "Yellow Bird," the goldfinch, according to Saxton and Saxton, 1969:167. But Paul says that the word is *U:n Mu'uhig*, not the same thing, and that the whole string is the name of that bird and nothing else. The string isn't analyzable into meaningful words.

several reservation-based bands that formed in those decades. The others were from the Quechans at Yuma, the Mojaves at Parker, the Hopis, and Navajos (who camped separately and cooked their own sheep), and, in New Mexico, the Zunis. (Gila River did not have a band, nor did the Apaches). They played at each others' reservation celebrations and at ceremonials in cities and towns near one or another home reservation: Gallup, Flagstaff, Winslow, Mesa, Phoenix, Casa Grande, Tucson. This was the beginning of those towns' public acknowledgement of Indians, that is, of Indians' progress. A very American and yet Indian band marching down main street symbolized progress.

The bands' members had begun marching and playing together in off-reservation schools. After graduation, it seemed natural to them to form bands at home and, in effect, to build an intertribal marching band society—and all the better to have many of the marches through neighboring towns. The society members knew each other and could host each other during visits, and even fill in if needed in each other's bands. In addition to the shared school experience, cars and trucks made this society possible. Motor vehicles became commonly owned in the 1950s. With them came easy long-distance travel. Thus, cars carried the bands that trumpeted the arrival of the first generation of modern Arizona Indians.

Paul was eleven years out of high school when the band formed, with him as tuba player and pillar. For him and his peers, this was a stimulating new addition to social dancing. The old way had "singing" (ñe'e) and "stomp-dancing" (cu:dk), while the new one had "playing" (kuhu, "hoot, toot, play-a-wind-instrument") and "marching" (e-himcud, "to-parade," literally "to-make-oneself-go"). One would think that the band marching could also be called "stomping," but it wasn't, presumably because the feeling was different.[10]

The important points of comparison in the dancing versus the marching are of origin (native versus white), of mood (romantic versus military), of time (nighttime versus daytime), and of location (on village soil versus town streets). I will return to the dancing side later. The points of contrast on the singing versus playing, or tooting, are subtler and more literary, and they include problems in translation. 'Singing' and 'playing'[11] are similar in that they both make sounds with the breath, but

------

[10]   I imagine that marching could be called *Milgan cu:dk* or *mumsiko ha-cu:dk*, "American [white] stomping" and "musicians' stomping," respectively, but this would be taken as a joke.

[11]   With single quotes I mean to hold the English word to the sense of its equivalent in Pima. Thus 'playing' is equated with and made to stand for the meaning of Pima *kuhu*.

'singing' has *words* and 'playing' does not. Pima is strict on this: birds do not 'sing' (*ñe'e*), they *kuhu* ('hoot/toot/coo'[12]). Also, peoples' whistling and humming are not called 'singing,' presumably at least in part because they do not articulate words.[13]

That is the linguistic background for the self-evident point that band 'playing' lacks the poetry of 'singing'. Not so obvious but also entailed in the above is that the Pimas had no songs that were not poetry. And I will now repeat that they also had no poetry, at least no versified, lyric poetry, that was not sung.[14] Thus, versified, lyric poetry and song were identical, the same thing; and the songs that we will study represent *the* lyric poetry of the old time Pimas.

The bands supplemented the old social dancing. Indeed, from the 1950s to the 70s it was common at holidays to have band parades in the day and traditional social dancing at night. And a third ingredient was often added, couples dancing "chicken scratch" (two step and polka) to Mexican style instrumental music. With few exceptions, the Mexican tunes were only 'played' and not 'sung'; they lacked words, or if they had them in Mexican use, they lacked them among the Pima.

Traditional social dancing stopped in the 1970s, and so did the bands. Meanwhile the Mexican style playing/dancing, which began before the bands, persists.[15] These dances are held at Catholic churches, of which Salt River got its first around 1920. But for as long as there were Mexicans nearby, since well before 1920, such dances were also held at bars and private houses, and they continue at such places today. Thus Salt River Mexican style dancing occurs at bars (always off the reservation) and at houses as well as at churches. And since the 1950s there has been the full diversity of non-Mexican urban American nightlife to tempt Salt River people.

It is nightlife of free choice, driven to in cars. I do not suppose that the sole reason why the social dancing *and* the marching band stopped, and why the Mexican dancing persists, is "the law;" for the law patrols

---

[12] Pimas had flutes which they called 'cooers/hooters/tooters' (*kuikud*—from *kuhu*).

[13] There is a distinct word for 'whistle,' *gikuj*, although Saxton, Saxton, and Enos give the 'hoot' related word *ku:gkim* as an alternative (1983:110). Various words are given as equivalent to "hum": 'low singing,' *jupij ñe'e* (this would be a humming that *does* articulate words); 'hum/rumble,' *doahim*; and 'drone/buzz/hum,' *weweg* (1983:88).

[14] I would not withhold the word "poetry" from the prose myths that are discussed in the next section, but that is a poetry of oral prose about origins, not verse about visions.

[15] That playing/dancing may have begun soon after the first Spanish contact, which for the ancestral Salt River people, then along the Gila, would have been around 1700. The Mexican style playing/dancing was certainly established among Pimas by 1900.

Mexican dances as well as Native ones, and the law *escorted* the marching bands. I won't guess the reasons for this double disappearance, but will excuse myself by noting a general lack of published tellings by Indians of their experience at home and at play from the 1960s to the 90s. There is a good deal of fiction and prose and verse on these times, and there are autobiographies from writers of Paul's generation about earlier years. But to see what is missing from the record one need only to think of the testimonies elicited in the 1960s by Oscar Lewis from Mexicans, Puerto Ricans, and Cubans. There is nothing like those from Indians in the U.S.[16]

SOCIAL DANCE MYTHS

By "myth" I mean "a story about ancient times, that people retain, that they take on faith, and that is largely or entirely immune from proof or disproof." We must distinguish this from another possible definition of myth, "a story about any time, past, present, or future, that people retain, that was freshly created by someone, that is taken as fiction." Chapter three demonstrates that a social dance fulfills some and fails to fulfill

---

[16]   Lewis specialized in personal testimonies on contemporary, more or less everyday, events. He had a gift for drawing such sometimes scandalous-seeming testimony from people. Other more impersonal histories would be welcome and safer. But all histories are and by definition must be based on documents (personal testimony is not document until it is saved), and it is not too much to ask that historians of contemporary Indian events should include Indian-made documents: speeches, council resolutions (that is, "laws"), works of fiction—but not dream songs since the singers do not profess to "make" those songs, but rather to get them in dreams. To make the relevant Indian-made documents into histories, one simply needs to construct a theory of that past that would explain the documents' content. This history may be large or small, sophisticated or naive, positivist or spiritualist, authored by Indians or whites. All that is simple about it is that the history stands apart from the documents that it seeks to explain.

Fiction, like personal testimony, becomes a document. Thus fiction is not history itself, although it may be grist for history. But to me, more interesting than fictional documents are those that are meant to tell the true events and experiences of existing people. (One can say that such documents are histories as well, being based on some form of document-like evidence. I agree and assent that there are histories of histories ad infinitum.)

Now, in Pima opinion the Ant and Oriole songs are true statements made by spirit persons. They are documents, but not humanly made. Furthermore they are not histories by my definition because they do not try to explain other documents, at least they do not express that intention openly. One can say that the *singers* of these spirit documents implicity use one text to explain another, and in fact I try to show how this is so. And since the singers do this with allegedly true documents, one can say that a social dance singer is a kind of mad, ever dissatisfied anthologizer of true past documents.

Finally, if the histories of Indians at home and at play are few, what are the published contemporary histories about? Indians at school, at hospitals, at work, in prisons, etc.: Indians in institutions that whites designed for them.

other aspects of both definitions. The individual songs are myths in the first sense, except that they are extremely short and are not necessarily ancient. Full sings are freshly created like myths by the second definition, and because their sequences are continually revised, they are ephemeral, not permanent stories.

The points I want to discuss now are that the Pimas have an organized body of myths by the first definition, that this body is a literature distinct from social dancing songs or sings, and that those myths touch on the origins of social dancing. To see how those points are true, most especially the last point, involves a review of the myths on the dancing. And before I start I must warn of an additional complication: although the myths discussed here are mostly told in prose, they also include songs which are distinguished from the songs used in social dancing.[17]

The Pimas organized their myths about ancientness into one majestic chronicle. They may be unusual among North American native peoples in this respect. This topic is discussed, and a full Pima mythology is given and commented upon, in *The Short, Swift Time of Gods on Earth* by

---

[17] On this problem see especially the section "Myths and Songs" in chapter three, but the topic is also treated briefly below. Here I will say that the mythology does not state or narrate the origin of songs, but it does state the origin of dreams; and it also makes a passing comment on the obtaining of dream songs. No origin of songs is given simply because the gods sang intermittently from the beginning of time. Song, then, was part of the original order of things: gods talked "normally" (in prose or what I call plain, quiet speech) and they sang.

Presumably, however, there was a first *human* singing. As I understand the mythology, that first singing would likely have been in imitation of the songs that the gods sang among humans. Indeed, that the gods' ancient songs are still remembered implies that the humans of that time heard the texts and retained them. Presumably, there should also have been a first human *dreaming* of songs, not a wakeful learning as above, but a learning of quite the same sort—hearing and retaining—while asleep or in some other unusual spiritual or psychic state. As the following passage shows, the onset of human dreaming is described, but, by chance I suppose, the desciption omits the acquisition of songs:

Everybody [of the ancient human community] was asleep, and he [the god who made these people] sang two more songs:

> I just now made the world
> And in that world I have gotten everybody to sleep
> And the breath of man in that darkness
> went out with more understanding.

> I have just made the mountains
> And in among those mountains
> I have put my people to sleep

Bahr, Smith, Allison, and Hayden (1994). The following summary and remarks pertain to that mythology, which was taken down from Juan Smith in the Gila River (not Salt) reservation in 1935. It is the longest and most thoroughly analyzed Pima mythology to be published to date.

The mythology has thirty-six stories in temporal order. Just two of them, widely separated (the sixth and the nineteenth), deal with social dancing. The temporally earlier one prefigures dancing, while the later one tells the origin of a kind of dance and links that dance to the origin of jealousy over adultery. Since the earlier myth also treats something like adultery, namely a woman's movement from man to man, we can say that marital inconstancy dominates the mythic treatment of social dancing. We will find that topic in the Ant and Oriole songs, too, but it will not be as important and is not handled as moralistically as in the mythology.

Here is the first myth. The text lacks the mention of social dancing, as if such dancing did not yet exist, but it prefigures the custom with characters who are Bird-people. A young woman named 'Throat-black' (Ba'i-cuklim), a black-throated desert sparrow or a Harris's sparrow (both have black throats and exist locally), leaves a series of husbands. She enters her first marriage through an arrangement made by the groom's mother. After staying with him for half a night, she leaves and travels in the dark to a village where she marries on her own accord. The first husband is not named. The second, also unnamed, is the son of a man, or part-man, named Cadigum. The narrator Smith said that this is the name of a rare, unfamiliar bird, but the teller of a different story attached the name to a

---

And the understanding of those people has gone out
And dwells there
[translations by W. Allison, original Pima text unknown].

So a man slept and dreamed that he would make fine cloth. Not all of those people were going to make cloth. Another slept and dreamed that he would be a good hunter. A woman slept and dreamed she was going to make a fine straw mat..." (Bahr, et al., 1994:82–83).

Here, from a much later point in the mythology, is the passing comment on the obtaining of dream songs:

... [a] medicine man went to work for them [the ancestral Pima-Papagos during the conquest of the Hohokam]. He had the power of the bluebird, Huh wut jutt nam kum [He:wcud Namkam, 'Bluejay Meeter'].

[W. Allison, the Pima translator of the mythology then said] Namkum [namkam, 'meeter'] means that a person sleeps at night, and if he is very interested in something, such as birds and animals, and if the bird or animal knows that, then it comes to him in his dream and shows him how to act like the bird or animal. That's how medicine people get their power, by learning from different things [creatures] that they are interested in, in their dreams. That's what namkum means (Bahr, et al., 1994:251).

plant (see Bahr et al., 1994:99n1, 309n8).[18] This husband is soon abandoned for Bluebird-man who is then left for Butterfly-man. Then, after a period with a foreign Indian tribe, the woman goes to Cadigum, the father of her second husband. The story ends with her and her former father-in-law enjoying disgrace.

The woman corresponds to a female character type called *ce:paowi* in social dancing songs. I translate the word as "whore," but "prostitute" or "naughty woman" are more polite alternatives. It is not clear if the Pima word was actually used in telling the prose myth of Throat-black.[19] If it was used, the myth, which is the first in the mythology to have such a woman, is an origin story of the ce:paowi or whore. If it was not used, this may be because the heroine is a *bird*-woman and all whores are human.[20]

There are no dances in the myth, but the husbands approximate dancing. In the Ant and Oriole songs whores travel between dances as Throat-black travels between husbands, dizzily and theatrically. The whores' goals are to hear singers, not to acquire mates. It is *almost* the same with Throat-black in this myth. None of her husbands sings a song whose text is remembered, but the sound of the distant singing of one of them, Cadigum (her second father-in-law, then her fifth husband), causes *her* to sing the following song while pondering whether to go to him:[21]

---

[18] See chapter three on the hazy physiological representation of "myth persons," a trait of both song and prose myth that is not unique to the Pimas, but seems general to Native America. Close textual study may show whether characters are presented as unambiguously human, unambiguously animal, or "mixed." The textual norm seems to be as follows: if a character is referred to by a species name (plant, animal, celestial, etc.), the character is a hazy combination of human and inhuman. If called by something other than a natural species name (e.g., if called "Green Woman," or "Drink-it-all-up"), the character is human. On this theory there are no fully animal, or "natural," characters in myth texts. I suspect that the theory is true. The "true" natural species had not yet diverged from anthropomorphs, or better, from hazy anthropozoos.

[19] The text was given in Pima over several evenings. It was translated into English as part of the telling. The Pima was not written down, but the translator's English was taken down nearly verbatim. The translator was a Presbyterian deacon.

[20] I can imagine the narrator insisting on this distinction, but I can also imagine him saying "Throat-black" in order to keep the matter ambiguous.

[21] A song like this in a myth is not danced to. It is taken as part of the story, but also as a verbatim quotation of the ancient character. It is not a recent revelation, as are social dancing songs.

One virtue of this particular mythology by Juan Smith is the abundance of songs in it. The Smith text has three or four times as many songs as its nearest Pima or Papago rival. Unfortunately the Pima texts are not given, so one cannot check the translations. See chapter three for a discussion of the difference between songs used in telling myths and those used in social dancing.

I came here
I came here
And you sing unbelievable words
And I'm shaking myself (p.121).

It is classic ce:paowism to quiver while resisting a man's singing and then to give in.

The other myth seems to refer to a time after some kind of social dancing was established, although there is no earlier story in the mythlogy that says, "This was the first dancing." The dancing episode comes at the end of one of several stories on the Pimas' conquest of the Hohokam, a topic which occupies the final part of the mythology. The Hohokam person at issue in this story, named Buzzard, saves his life by singing new songs, Buzzard songs, for a social dance—in exchange for his life, he gives the Pimas his songs.

The dance he sings for is performed in straight lines rather than circles like most social dances, which fact connects it to ceremonies traditionally used to celebrate girls' puberty and war.[22] At the turn of the century when Pimas were still largely without white influence the girls' puberty ceremonies were the grandest of all Pima social dances. The atmosphere at the girls' ceremony was similar to the more common and longer lasting round dances. But while round dances could be used to celebrate many kinds of things, the straight dances concentrated on two: puberty and war (of which war ceremonies were largely a thing of the past).

As I stated above, the myth gives the origin of marital jealousy:

Buzzard sang for four days and four nights. This was a great joy for the Wooshkam [Pimas]. They did not give him food or drink for eight days, four days of arguing and four days of dancing. He sang and danced all that time without any rest. This was to suffer for what he had done.

The people dancing with Buzzard took turns to eat and rest. At that ... month ... the squawberries were plentiful for food. It happened that a young woman went to her home to eat berries. When she finished, she got up and returned to the dance. Her husband asked her if she was going to dance again, and she said that she was.

Her husband thought that maybe she didn't do right at the dance but might be going with another man. This thought came from the breath

---

[22] Other versions of the mythology state that a another character's girl-chasing at such dances causes his execution. See Bahr, et al., 1994:203–33. The occasion for the dance is the scalping of Buzzard. Besides singing, he dances with his own scalp. The use of straight dances for war ceremonies is consistent with this episode, and of course bareheaded Buzzard is a good scalp victim—except that he lives.

that Buzzard had made on the rattle handle, which caused jealousy. So the husband said bad things about his wife. The language was so bad that it must not be repeated (Bahr et al., 1994:226–27).

That the mythology dates from 1935, when the Pimas were three generations into Christian missionization, may explain the moralism. It seems that Smith, a Gila rather than a Salt River man, was as ready as the preachers to denigrate social dancing. Not quite, though: he didn't preach dancing's irredeemable wickedness, but only said that social dancing was the occasion for the first sexual jealousy, that Buzzard's breath was the actual cause. This would not condemn all dancing. Such was Smith's hairsplitting defense of the institution in the decade when Stepp was a young man and Paul was a boy.

CHAPTER TWO

The Texts

This chapter begins with the sing in free translation. The rest of it explains how the various translations were arrived at. The subheads in the sing refer to its thematic parts, explained in chapter four, "The Sing Interpreted." I supplied these names and the song numbers; they were not announced in the sing.

Sun, West to Flower Field

1. Songs start,
   Manic sounding singing.
   Night follow,
   Manic sounding singing.

2. Dead Field Mountain stands.
   Women inside run out,
   Earth flowers crowned and
   Toward me run.
   Here run up to,
   My head, toss onto.

3. Greasy Mountain,
   Greasy Mountain stands.
   There inside
   Green flowers
   Cover me.
   There inside
   Manic is.

4. Westward the world flowers,
   Westward the world flowers,
   And I run through.

Everywhere flowers,
The here below
Lying world manic flowers.

Man, West to Water

5. Iron Mountain
   Not inviting sounds.
   Wind runs and
   Hits on me:
   Everywhere hoots.

6. Away I run,
   Away westward run.
   Woman Bringer Mountain stands:
   Run on top and something know.

7. Broad Mountain stands,
   And I run to it.
   There a man comes out,
   Songs he tells me.
   What can I do and know?
   There before me,
   Erected songs.
   And I take them,
   Use to serenade.

8. Broad Mountain stands.
   There below, waters primed to spurt.
   And I below there go,
   On stick's end cling:
   Stick glitters,
   Then enter.

Death

9. Bitter Wind,
   Here run up and
   Away far
   Take me.

Poorly treat me,
My heart separated dies.

10. Does your singing speak?
I'm doing but dead
And wander here.
Long Mountain
There manically calls.
Behind I circle,
Suddenly dizziness
Makes lines back and forth.

Dizziness

11. Far land upon go,
Away, rainbow comes out.
I jump out below,
What will I do and run there?

12. Long Red stands,
Long Red stands.
Its base, cloud comes out.
All kinds of trees stand,
Everywhere flowers and,
Suddenly butterflies pour:
Great handsome fluttering.

13. Gray killdeer bird,
Away, world's edge runs:
So songlike hooting,
Land striding,
Wings spreading.

14. Gray fly,
Squawberry flowers make wine and,
Here bring it.
I drink with and, drunk,
Pitiably speak,
Songs tell.

15. Flatly run and run and run,
    World cover and run.
    And I go on and run and run,
    World upon,
    Back and forth dodging.

16. Eastern inner rumbling,
    Eastern inner rumbling,
    And I run there to see.
    Night there rumbles,
    Far, loudly,
    There inside rumbles.

17. Many birds fly,
    Many birds fly.
    At spread sky's front flying,
    Nicely cooing, primed to run.

18. Dizzy woman,
    Off and toward me runs.
    Takes my heart,
    Straight westward runs.
    Oh, I don't know,
    Night chasing.

19. Oh-oh, my husband,
    Oh-oh, my husband,
    Here I leave-you
    And go.
    What will I do
    To know?
    Darkness emerges
    And goes.
    Oh-oh, my husband,
    And I leave you
    And go.

Halfway, Sun Again

20. Sun sets,
    And we there run.
    Below the east are songs,
    Manic telling.
    Oh-oh, younger brother,
    Songs of your telling.

Water

21. Shining Water lies,
    Shining Water lies.
    Within mudhen wanders,
    Come and look:
    Handsome floating!

22. Marsh Water lies,
    And I around it circle.
    Within, very green moss
    Zig-zag away spreads.
    And I so like it,
    One take and
    Head wrap with:
    Around me circles.

Death

23. Oh-oh, my younger brother,
    Oh-oh, my-younger brother,
    Here I leave you
    And far go.
    Wind in me ex-
    plodes and leaps out.
    Here I leave you,
    Eastward running.

24. I arrive here,
    Oh-oh, I arrive here.
    What to do?
    I don't know.

I'm Ghost Woman
And arrive here.
Oh-oh, oh-oh,
What to do?
I don't know.

25. Oh-oh, my singing partner,
Oh-oh, my singing partner,
Nowhere I see you.
Far off land,
Running to it,
Nowhere I see-you.

26. Gray helper,
Here to our song run up and
Nicely sounding dance.
Swishingly dance,
Nicely sounding away go.

27. I'm sick,
I'm sick,
Land below wandering.
In it my flower,
Already dead.
Oh-oh, oh-oh,
I'm sick,
East toward
I run.

Dizziness

28. My heart dizzies,
Dizzily I wander.
Oh-oh, my heart,
Unbear-
ably feels.
Running to,
Unbear-
ably feels.

Glory

 29. You start the songs,
   And you start the songs.
   Suddenly whore woman
   Suddenly runs up,
   Everything saying.
   And you, of Ant
   Songs, many unwrap.
   All around me,
   People akimbo.

 30. Away off the wind runs and
   Away off far takes me.
   To the Cane Land
   Surface takes me,
   Where wind runs hooting,
   Where songs are really known.

 31. Do you hear me?
   Do you hear me?
   All earth sounding,
   On top, circles stomped.
   On top, eagle down puffs,
   Cloud enter.

THE TAPES

Fr. O'Brien had recordings of two Ant song sings, one with thirty-one songs and the other with twenty-eight. A total of thirty-seven different songs were sung. Of those, twenty-one were sung in both performances. Nine were unique to the thirty-one song session and six were unique to the other. The thirty-one item sing is the subject of this study.

 The tapes are sixty-minute cassettes, recorded on both sides, about forty-five minutes of singing per tape. There is no ordinary speech on the tapes. Written on each casette is simply, "Ant songs, A. Stepp and Claire Seota," with no date or any indication of which side of a given tape was sung first. The songs seem to have been recorded without interruption: the only "clicks" from starting or stopping the recorder are at the ends of the sides. In addition to the singers' voices, one can hear a box being tapped by a stick (probably by Stepp) in rhythm with the singing,[23] a dog bark once, a door slam, a baby cry, and a car driving up. Apparently it was a performance at a house, either inside one with the door open or outside one in the yard.

When I began to write the songs from the tapes, before meeting Lloyd Paul but after meeting Earl Ray, I thought that the sing studied here began with what I now think is the fifteenth song in the performance, whose first line is "Flatly run and run and run." I thought this because that song is the first on a side, and the references to flat running and then to covering the earth struck me as "anty." It did not take long to decide that this song is probably the fifteenth, midway through the sing, a decision prompted by an insight into the first four songs of the sing as I now conceive it.

THE TEXTS SUNG, SPOKEN, AND TRANSLATED

This section gives metered, but not melodic, transcriptions of the songs as sung; and renditions of the songs as they can be spoken in Pima; and literal translations of the spoken renditions. The previous, free translations are based on these literal ones. The rationale for the entire process has been stated in various earlier papers, one of which, with a small group of different songs, is included in the appendix of this book ("Three Papago Airplane Songs"). There one can find a fuller discussion of technicalities than will be given here.

Three orienting remarks are in order here. First, the vowels of Pima are pronounced like those of written Spanish, except the Pima "e." The Pima "e" is pronounced as in English "cool," but with the lips straight rather than rounded. (Neither Spanish nor English has this precise sound, but it is very frequent in Pima words). A bold face "s" (**s**) in my writing is pronounced "sh," and a bolded "d" (**d**) is pronounced as a "d" with the tongue folded back onto the roof of the mouth. "C" is pronounced "ch," "ñ" as in Spanish, and bolded "n" (**n**), which only occurs in songs, is pronounced as the "ng" in "sing."

Second, the evenly spaced dots that frame each full song transcript,

---

[23] This form of accompaniment, a kind of drumming, had largely replaced the rattling and scraping mentioned earlier. In my opinion, it mocks powwow drumming. Thus, one Gila River singing group of the 1970s was called the "Box Tops," a play on "Flat Tops," which is a play on "Crew Cuts," the name of a white American popular singing group of the fifties. The whole chain of names was a dig at the feathered singers of Powwow Indians. (Powwows and feathers were considered un-Pima.)

above and below, like a ceiling and floor, represent the beats that pulse
steadily through the song. The duration of sung syllables is strictly regu-
lated by those beats. Each syllable lasts either a half, a whole, one and a
half, or two beats. Ordinary speech is not so strictly regulated. It has two
vowel lengths instead of four, and no mental metronome ticks behind the
flow of ordinary speech.

A single word of ordinary speech can be sung in one configuration in
one song and another in another. Here, for example, are two ways to sing
the ordinary language phrase "*toton ñeñei*," which means "ant songs":

```
toto        ñi ñe       ñe   hi
 .     .    .    .    .     .    .

to     to ho    ñi ñe     he ñei
 .     .     .      .      .     .
```

As can be seen, some syllables start on beats and some start halfway be-
tween them (placed above and between the dots). Note, too, that the first
example of the phrase has more syllables than the second; and the first
example has syllables of a half, a whole, and two beats' duration while
the second has syllables of a half and one and a half beats.

Whichever way a word is configured in a song, that configuration is
permanent. One is not free to sing a given song's phrase "ant songs" (or
whatever) in one way one time, and then to switch to a different config-
uration for the next singing of that song. Indeed, the greatest difficulty in
learning Pima songs is to get each song's total configuation exactly right.
If one varies or stumbles, one has not learned the song.

Third, the placement of song lines on a page is determined by what I
call the song's "key metered zone." Some rule of placement is necessary
for writing, which of course was not a concern of the old singers. Rather
than simply flush the lines to the left, which I think is too uninformative,
I have opted for a rule which tells us something about meter in this art,
namely a rule based on key zones. These zones are recurrent short seg-
ments of text, with from two to four beats, that have nearly identical
rhythmic and sound values.

Thus, no matter what else is going on in a song, these segments will
echo each other intermittently throughout. Theoretically—in my line
writing theory, that is—there is just one of these rhymed, echoing seg-
ments per line. And since the segments are short, they never comprise a
whole line: there are varying amounts of unrhymed material before and

after them. In a given song, the zone may occur near the beginning of one line and near the end of the next.

I place the lines on a page by skewering them, so to speak, on their key metered zones. The zone is written as a column and is marked with colons placed on the relevant beats above and below the transcript (the unzoned beats are marked simply with dots). Since there are varying numbers of beats and syllables to the left and right of the zone, the song appears as a shishkabob, or better, a mountain with balconies.

There is no perfect, objective method to identify the key zones in a song. They are intuitively and somewhat arbitrarily arrived at. They are more evident and regular in some songs than others. For all of the arbitrariness, however, the theory of zones points to three important and true properties of Pima song: that meter in this art consists of both sound and rhythm, that meter only organizes portions of lines, and that the metered portions can come almost anywhere in a given line—and the theory provides a method for placing songs on a page.

1.

```
 .      .      .      :      :      :      .      .      .      .      .      .      .      .
Ñe          ñei  wo   so   na   cu    ,
       wa        mo        wo   kai   da          mo  ñe        da   .
cu          kake yoi       ne   kai   ji    ,
       wa        mo        wo   kai   da          hame ñe       da   .
 .      .      .      :      :      :      .      .      .      .      .      .      .
```

```
Ñeñei  o  soncud,
Songs make-to-start,

Wa:m   o  kaidam ñe'et.
Manic sounding sing.

Cuhugam   oidka'i,
Darkness following,

Wa:m   o  kaidam am ñe'et.
Manic sounding sing.
```

2.

```
.     .     .     .     .     .     .     :     :     .     .     .     .     .     .     .
            oi    na    pa    de    no    o     wa    ne    na    ne    ke          ke    .
ke    de    ge    yu    u     hu    vi    ñei   yo    pa    ke    na    ne    wo          oi    me    da    ,
            je          we    na    yo          si    ge    gi    gi    kwa   ce
                        I     yañe  we          he    wi    wa    wo          po    .
                        ya    to    woi         hi    wo          ,
                        oi    a     ñi    mo    mo    da    me    su    sule  ga    .
.     .     .     .     .     .     .     :     :     .     .     .     .     .     .     .
```

Oidbad   duag   an   ke:k.
Dead-field mountain there stands.

Eda   g u'uwi ñeiyopak   wo:po,
Just-then women   jump-out-and run,

Jewed hiosig gigikwac
Earth flower crowned-and

I:ya ñ-wui wo:po.
Here to-me run.

I: at o wo'i,
Here   arrive-running,

Oiya ñ-mo'o da:m sulig.
Then my-head upon toss.

3.

```
.     .     .     .     .     .     .     :     :     :     .     .     .     .     .     .
      mwa         to          ñi    do          an    ,
      mwa         to          ñi    do          wa          no    ke          ke    .
            ga    mo          wa    ye          da    ,
ge    si    ce    ce    no          hoge  yo    si    ga    ,
                              ciñe  ma    sa    pa    .
      a     mi    wa    ye          da    ,
      ci    wa    ha          mo    cu    i     ga    .
.     .     .     .     .     .     .     :     :     :     .     .     .     .     .     .
```

Muhadag Duag,
Greasy Mountain,

Muhadag Duag   an o ke:k.
Greasy Mountain there stands.

Gam hu wa e**d**a,
There   in-it,

Ge si cehedag hiosig-
Very green   flowers-

kaj ñ-ma'i**s**pa.
With me-cover.

Am hi wa e**d**a,
There   in-it,

Wa:m o cu'ig.
Manic is.

4.

.	.	.	.	.	.	:	:	:	.	.	.	.
hu	du	ñi	ta	hagyo		je	we	ne	syo	sim	,	
hu	du	ñi	ta	hagyo		je	we	ne	syo	o	sim	,
		ku	ñe	ge	yoi	ne	ka	mo	hi	meta	.	
				ha		we	si	ko	yo	o	sim	,
				he		**n**a	te	we	co			
ka	ci	me	je	we	ne	wa	mo	wa	syo	o	sim	.
.	.	.	.	.	.	:	:	:	.	.	.	.

Hu**d**uñig tagyo   jewe**d** s-hiosig,
West   direction land flowers,

Hu**d**uñig tagyo   jewe**d** s-hiosig,
West   direction land flowers,

Kuñ g oidk   am him.
And-I follow-and go.

We:sko   s-hiosim,
Everywhere flowers,

Heg t-weco
The us-below

Ka:cim jewed wa:m   s-hiosim.
Lying land manically flowers.

5.

```
.    .    .    .    :    :    :    :    :    .    .    .    .    .
                   wai  nomi do        wa   ne   ,
pi   ya   bo   ta  ñi   wimo kai  ñe   ta   .
               ye   we   lane me   ne   ke
               ña   bai  co   ne   ne   se   .
               ke   dene we   si   ko   la   ku   ku   ke   .
.    .    .    .    :    :    :    :    :    .    .    .    .    .
```

Wainom Duag,
Iron   Mountain,

Pi ab o ta-ji:wim o kaidag.
Not invitingly   it-sounds.

Hewel an medk
Wind   there-runs-and

Añ-ba'ic   ge:gew.
Against-me hits:

G-eda wesko   kuhu.
In-it everywhere hoots.

6.

```
.    .    .    .    .    .    .    .    .    :    :    :    :    :    .    .
                              ku   ñi   ga   mo   me   de   he   ne   ,
          game hu        du   ñi   we        wi   wo   me   de   he   ne   .
yu        hu   we   wa   ku   ne   to   no   wa   no   ke        ke   ,
da   he   ma   ne   me   li   wa   ke   yai  ai   cu   si   ma   ma   ce   .
.    .    .    .    .    .    .    .    .    :    :    :    :    :    .    .
```

Kuñ   gam hu me**d**
d,
And-I away   run,

Gam hu huduñig wui   wo me**d**.
Away   west   toward run.

Uwi   U'ɑkud Duag   ke:k,
Woman Bringer Mountain stands:

Da:m   meliwak   haicu   s-ma:mc.
On-top run-up-and something know.

7.

.	.	.	.	.	.	:	:	.	.	.	.	.
		ko	me	na	ke	no	nowa		ne ke	ke	,	
		ku	ñi	se	ge	we	hewi		wo me	ne	da	.
ke	de	ge	yo	ta	mo	wu	**s**añe	,				
		ñe	ñei	wo	ña	**n**ida	.					
		sa	ne	ñi	ju	hai	si	ma	ma	ce	.	
		wa	**s**u	ñi	bai	cu	ni					
			ñe	heñei	wo cu	cwa	him	.				
		ku	ñi	**s**a	ma	be	me	he	,			
		he	ga	ñi	ñei	cuda	.					
.	.	.	.	.	.	:	:	.	.	.	.	

Komadk Duag   ke:k,
Broad Mountain stands,

Kuñs g wui   wo me**d**.
And-I toward-it run.

G e**d**a   g o'odham wu:**s**añ,
Just-then man   comes-out,

Ñeñei wo ñ-a:gid.
Songs he-tells-me.

Sa:ñ hi ñ-ju:hai s-ma:c?
What-can I-do-and know?

Washu ñ-ba'ic
Away me-in-front

Ñeñei o cu:cia.
Songs stands-them-up.

Kuñ   sam   behe,
And-I there take-them,

Hekaj   ñe'icud.
With-which cause-to-sing.

8.

```
.    .    .    .    .    .    .    .    :    :    :    .    .    .    .    .
                    ko  me  na  ke  no  nowa ne ke  ke   ,
sami we     co      su  da  gi      ñei yo pa  ki  mo  cui      ga   .
                    ku  ñi  we  co  ñi  mai no ke
     yu   hu u   si ku   hu ga  bo  ñu  li  na   .
                    yu  hu  u   si  ñe  ño ki  me
                    ke      da  mo  wa  ha pa  ki  me   .
.    .    .    .    .    .    .    .    :    :    :    .    .    .    .    .
```

Komadk Duag   ke:k,
Broad Mountain stands,

Sam   weco   su:dagi ñeiyopakim   o cu'ig.
There below-it waters   ready-to-jump-out are.

Kuñ   wa weco añ himk
And-I below-there go-and

U:s   ku:g ab ñ-ulin.
Stick end at I-cling.

U:s   nenaok
Stick glitters

Keda   am   wapke.
And-just-then there enter.

9.

```
 .    .   :   :   :   .   .   .    .    .    .    .    .
     si  we  ñe  ye  we  he  li  ,
 wa      to  wa  me  li  wa  ke  ,
 ga      mu  we  me  me  ko
         wa  ñi  bei     cu  ni  me  .
 soi     ga  ñi  wa     a  to  ,
 ñi  moi da  ne  he        je  la  mu      mu  ki  me  .
 .    .   :   :   :   .   .   .    .    .    .    .    .
```

Siw   Hewel,
Bitter Wind,

I at o wa   meliwak,
Here-it-will run-up-and,

Gam hu me:ko
Away   far

Wañ-beicug.
Me-take.

Soig   añ-wuad,
Poorly it-does-to-me,

Ñ-i:bdag hejel   mu:k.
My-heart by-itself dies.

10.

```
 .    .    .    .    .    .    .    .    :    :    :    .    .
 na  me  to  si  ñe  he  da  mo  kai ñe  da  .
 he     ñe  kyo si  mu  ki  mai ñi  wa      ta
                    ci  ya  hoi yoi me  da  .
                    ce      ce  to  no  wa  ne
     he  no  si  wa  mo  ne  ya  ne  da  ta  .
         we      ga  ñe  bi  ñi  me  ,
         ke      da  ge  no  na  gi  ge
         ya      hai we  wao     pa  .
 .    .    .    .    .    .    .    :    :    :    .    .
```

Namt o si s-ñe'edam kaij?
Do-you so singingly speak?

Heki hu si mu:kim ñ-wua
Already so dyingly I-act

c   i:ya oimme**d**.
And here wander.

Cew Duag
Long Mountain

Heg   o si wa:m o a:gta.
That-one is so manic telling.

We:gaj añ bijim,
Behind-it I circle,

K e**d**a g   no**d**agig
Just-then dizziness

A'ai   wa wawpa.
Back-and-forth stretches.

11.

.	.	.	.	.	.	:	:	:	:	.	.	.	.	.	.
ga	me	ko	je	we	ne	ku	ñene	da	mano	hi	me	da	,		
	wa	**s**añi	bai	cu**n**e	kyo	hone	**s**e	nano	wu	**s**a	ñe			me	.
		ku	ñe		ka	we		camo	nai	wo	ñi		me	,	
		sa	noñi	wa		kimo	me		ne	da		.			
.	.	.	.	.	.	:	:	:	:	.	.	.	.	.	.

Ge me:k jewe**d**, kuñ g da:m   him,
Far   land, and-I upon-it go,

Wa**s**u ñ-ba'ic,   kiohod **s**-eda   o wu:**s**añ.
Away before-me, rainbow just-then comes-out.

Kuñ g weco   da'iwuñ,
And-I below-it jump-out,

Xa: o ñ-wuak   im hu med?
What will-I-do-and there run?

12.

.	.	.	.	:	:	:	:	.	.	.	.	.	.
ce	he	wai	si	we	ni	ho	mi	ke		ke	,		
ce	he	wai	si	we	ni	ho	mi	ke		ke	.		
so	**s**o	na	me	ce	wa	ha	gi	wu		**s**a	.		
we		sai	cu	yu	u	hu	si	cu		cya	,		
we		si	ko	yo	o	ho	si	me		ke	,		
		ta	ki	yo	ki	ma	li	ñei	yo	pa	,		
	ge	sa	po	ma	ma	si	mo	yane	ge	wa	hi	me	.
.	.	.	.	:	:	:	:	.	.	.	.	.	.

Cew S-wegiom ke:k,
Long Red   stands,

Cew S-wegiom ke:k.
Long Red   stands.

Son am ce:wagi wu:**s**.
Base-at cloud   comes-out.

We:s ha'icu   u:'us cu:cia,
All kinds-of trees stand,

We:sko   hiosimk,
Everywhere flowery-and,

T g hohokimal   ñeiyopa,
Then butterflies jump-out:

Ge   s-ap o mamsim a:ngew.
Great nice appearing fluttering.

13.

```
:   :   :   :   :   .   .   .   .   .   .   .   .   .   .   .   .   .   .   .
ko  ko  ma  ne  ci  wi  cu  ce  yu      hu      win ,
ga  ha  nu  wa  je  we  ne  hu  ni  da  ne  me  ne      da  .
sa  wa  si  ñe  he  da  mo  kai da  mo  ku  hu  ta ,
je  we  de  kei naki ,
ya  ha  a   ne  ce  wai me  .
:   :   :   :   :   .   .   .   .   .   .   .   .   .   .   .   .   .   .   .
```

Komagi ciwicuc u'uhig,
Gray   killdeer bird,

Gan hu wa jewed hogid an med.
Away   land edge-at runs.

Sa: wa s-ñe'edam kaidam kuhu,
Very   songlike   sounding hoots

Jewed keihi,
Land strides,

A'an cewaj.
Wing lengthens.

14.

```
.   .   .   .   .   .   .   .   :   :   :   :   .   .   .   .   .
            ko  ko  ma  gi  mu  mu  wa  li ,
            kwa he  wu  li yo      si  ne na  wai to  o   ke ,
                        wo      wi  wa ya  ha  pa  .
ku  ñi  se  e   ke  we      ma  ce i       yo  ke na  wa  mo ,
                        so  ni  no kai     je ,
                        ñe      ñei wo ya  ne  te  .
.   .   .   .   .   .   .   .   :   :   :   :   .   .   .   .   .
```

Komagi muwali,
Gray   fly,

Kwawul   hiosig nawaitk,
Squawberry flowers make-wine-with-and,

I:ya wui uapa.
Here bring-it.

Kuñs g we:maj i:yok nawam,
And-I with-him drink-it-all-and get-drunk,

So'ig kaij,
Pitiably speak,

Ñeñei a:g.
Songs tell.

15.

·	·	·	·	·	:	:	:	:	·	·	·	·	·	·	·
	ko	ma	li	ke	me	de	ne	ci	me	ne	de	ci	me	ne	de	,
	je		we	ne	ce	ce	mo	ko	me	ne	da	.			
kuñi	yoi		na	ci	me	me	da	ci	me	ne	da	,			
	je		we	ne	da		mai	,							
	ya		hai	wo	ke	ki	wo	ki	me	.					

·	·	·	·	·	:	:	:	:.	·	·	·	·	·	·	·

Komalk me**d**c me**d**c me**d**,
flatly run-and run-and run,

jewe**d** ce:mo'oc me**d**.
land permeate-and run.

kuñ oidc me**d**c me**d**,
and-I follow-and run-and run,

jewe**d** da:m,
land upon,

a'ai kekiwuphim.
back-and-forth stop-and-start.

16.

				:	:	:							
si	ya	li	**n**e	me	na	wo	be	to	ñi	me	,			
si	ya	li	**n**e	me	na	wo	be	to	ho	ñi	me	ta	,	
ku	ñine	we	wei	me	na	da	mo	ñei	da	.				
		cu	kañi	me	da	be	to	ñi	·	me	,			
				me		ko	si	kai	da	,				
			mo	me	da	**s**o	be	to	ñi	me	.			

Si'alig am   e**d**a wo betoñ,
East   there inside rumbles,

Si'alig am   e**d**a wo betoñ,
East   there inside rumbles,

Kuñ   g wui   me**d**, am ñeid.
And-I toward-it run, see-it.

Cuhugkam am   e**d**a   betoñ,
Darkness there inside rumbles,

Me:ko, si kaidam,
Far,   loudly,

Am   e**d**a   **s**o betoñ.
There inside rumbles.

17

					:	:	:	:	:			
			mu	mui	yu	hi**n**e	ñe	ñe	him	,		
			mu	mui	yu	hi**n**e	ñe	ñe	him	.		
da	mai	ka	cime	ba	ma	**s**o	hoke	ñe	ñe	hi	me	,
sa	po	kai	name	ku	kui	hi	ike	wo	poi	me	.	

Mu'i u'uhig ñe:ñ,
Many birds fly,

Mu'i u'uhig ñe:ñ.
Many birds fly.

Da:m ka:cim ba**s**o   ñe:ñ,
Sky cover in-front fly,

S-ap o kaidam   kukhuk   wo:po'im.
Nicely sounding they-coo-and prepare-to-run.

18.

no	na	gi	i	gi	yu		hu	wi	,				
	wa		ha	wa	ñi	wu		wui	wo	me	ne	da	.
					ñi	moi	da	a **ne** be	me	he	,		
			hune	ñi**n**o	wu	wui	wawe	nage me	ne	da	.		
					wa		ha	ñi	pi	ma	ma	cim	,
	cu		hu	ka	**ni**	yoi	ne	ka	mo	me	e	ne	da	.

No**d**agi uwi,
Dizzy woman,

Ga wa ñ-wui me**d**.
There to-me runs.

Ñ-i:bdag am bei,
My-heart she-takes,

Hu**d**uñig wui   wawañ   me**d**.
West   toward in-a-line   runs.

Wañ pi ma:c,
Oh-I don't-know,

Cuhugam oidk   am me**d**.
Darkness follow-and run.

19.

```
.     .     .     . .   :     :     :     :     .
                  hai  yañe  ku          na    ,
                  hai  yañe  ku          na    ,
                  ya   ñame  na    ne    to
                  hoke hi    me    ta    .
                  sa   piñe  ju          hai   ,
                  kece ma    me    ce    .
ge    si    cu    hu   nane  wu          sa    ,
                  kai  ñi    me    ta    .
                  hai  yañe  ku          na    ,
                  ku   ñene  na    ñi    ta
                  ka   hi    me    ta    .
.     .     .     .     :     :     :     :     .
```

Haiya, ñ-kun,
Oh-oh, my-husband,

Haiya, ñ-kun,
Oh-oh, my-husband,

Añ   m-dagito
Here-I leave-you

K him.
And-go.

Sa: phi ñ-ju:hai,
What-will I-do,

Kc   ma:c?
And know?

Ge si cuhukam wu:s,
Darkness   comes-out,

K him.
And goes.

Haiya, ñ-kun,
Oh-oh, my-husband,

Kuñ   m-dagito
And-I leave-you

K him.
And-go.

20.

.	:	:	:	:	.	.	.	.	.	.	.	.	.
	ta		sai	wa	yu	nu	ñim	,					
	ku		ce		ge	ye		da		hame	wo	po	.
	si	hi	ya		li	we		co	o	ge	ñe	we	ne
si	wa		mo		ge	ya	**ne**	da	.				
	hai		ya		ñe	si		kol	,				
	ñe		ñei	ha	me	na	**ni**	da	.				
.	:	:	:	:	.	.	.	.	.	.	.	.	.

Ta**s** hu**d**uñim,
Sun sets,

Kuc   g e**d**a am wo:po.
And-we in-it run.

Si'al weco g ñeñei[24]
East   below songs

Si wa:m hab a:g.
Manic   tell.

Haiya, ñ-sikol,
Oh-oh, my-younger-sibling,

---

[24] This word could be *jewed*, 'land', rather than *ñeñei*, 'songs', as translated here. We couldn't decide. Also unclear is the last word of the next line. We take it to be *a:g*, 'tell,' but we are not completely sure. Note that 'tell' as a verb goes well with 'songs' as as an object; but 'land' might also go with that verb, only as subject rather than object: "The land tells something" versus Something tells songs." We opt for the latter.

Ñeñei am a:gid.[25]
Songs you-tell.

21.

```
·    ·    ·    ·    :    :    :    :    ·    ·    ·    ·    ·    ·
                    tone dome su  dani ka        ce    ,
                    tone dome su  dani ka        ce    .
                    ke   deni wa  cu   pi  kine yoi me da    ,
                    mya  keko ñei da   ,
sa  po  ma   ma   si   hine wi i noki me        .
·    ·    ·    ·    :    :    :    :    ·    ·    ·    ·    ·    ·
```

Tondam Su:dagi ka:c,
Shining Water   lies,

Tondam Su:dagi ka:c.
Shining Water   lies.

G eda g wacpigdam oimmed,
In-it mudhen   wanders,

Miak   o ñeid:
Come-and look:

S-ap o ma:sim wi:nog!
Nice-looking it-floats!

22.

```
·    ·    ·    :    :    :    ·    ·    ·    ·
     wa   muli su  dani ka        ce    ,
     ke   ñone we  gace miñe mine ta    .
ke   no   si   ce  doni ma   ma   to   ne    ,
     gan  hu   ñu  ñuli wa   o    pa   ne    .
wa   ñe   si   yo       hoi       i    ,
he   ma   ko   be  me   he   heke
          ñi   ñi  kwa  ci
     a    moñe we  gaci miñe mine ta.
·    ·    ·    :    :    :    ·    ·    ·    ·
```

_____

[25] As with the above line, the noun and the verb here are both tentative. And assuming that the roots are correct, it is not ertain whether one should picture the brother being sung to (as grammatical object), or the brother singing (as grammatical subject).

Wamul **s**u:dagi ka:c,
Marsh water   lies,

Kuñ   g we:gaj bijim.
And-I around-it circle.

G e**d**a si   cehedagi mamto**d**,
In-it very green   moss,

Gan hu jujul   wawpan.
Away   zig-zagged spreads.

Wañ   si ho:hoid,
And-I so like-it,

Hemako behek
One take-and

Gigikwac:
Headwrap-it:

Am o ñ-we:gaj bijim.
Around-me   it-circles.

23.

	.	:	:	:	.	.	.	.	.	.	.
	hai	ya	ñe	si	ko	li	,				
	hai	ya	ñe	si	ko	li	,				
	ya	ña	me	da	ñi	to					
ka	me	me	ko	wa	me	ne	da	.			
	ye	we	li i	ñe	na	ko					
	bo	ñe	ko	nai	wo	ñim	.				
	ña	ñe	me	da	**n**i	to	,				
	si	ya	li	we	wi	wo	me	ne	da	.	
	.	:	:	:	.	.	.	.	.	.	.

Haiya, ñ-sikol,
Oh-oh, my-younger-sibling,

Haiya, ñ-sikol,
Oh-oh, my-younger-sibling,

Añ   m-dagito
Here-I leave-you

K me:k   me**d**.
And far go.

Hewel am ñ-e**d**a ko-
Wind in-me   ex-

ponk   da'iwuñ.
plodes-and jumps-out.

Añ   m-dagito,
Here-I leave-you,

Si'al wui   wo me**d**.
East   toward run.

24.

.	.	:	:	:	.	.	.
		ya	ñine	ñi	ñi	wya	,
		hai	yawa	ñi	ñi	wya	.
		sa	pi**n**e	ju	hai		
		piñe	ma	ma	ce	.	
da	ñi	ko	koi	yu	u	huwe	
		ci	yabe	ñi	ñi	wya	.
		hai	ya	hai	ya	,	
		sa	pi**n**e	ju	hai		
		piñe	ma	ma	ce	.	
.	.	:	:	:	.	.	.

Wañ   ji:wia,
I-here arrive,

Haiya, wañ   ji:wia.
Oh-oh, I-here arrive.

Sa: phig e-ju:hai
Whatever to-do

Pi ñ-ma:c.
I-don't-know.

Dañ Kok'oi Uwi
I'm Ghost Woman

C i:ya   ji:wia.
And-here arrive.

Haiya, haiya,
Oh-oh, oh-oh,

Sa: phig e-ju:hai
Whatever to-do

Pi ñ-ma:c.
I-don't-know.

25.

.	.	.	:	:	:	.	.	.
hai	ya	ñi	ma	ke	ñi	,		
hai	ya	ñi	ma	ke	ñi	,		
pya	ñi	ñi	ye	bai	mo	ñei	da	.
ga	mu	wa a	me	me	ko	je	ñewe	,
			we	wi	wo	me	nede	,
pya	ñi	ñi	ye	bai	mo	ñei	i da	.
.	.	.	:	:	:	.	.	.

Haiya, ñ-ma:kig,
Oh-oh, my-singing-partner,

Haiya, ñ-ma:kig,
Oh-oh, my-singing-partner,

Pi añ   hebai   am m-ñeid.
I-can't anyplace see-you.

```
Gam hu wa me:k jewed,
Away    far    land,

Wui wo    med,
Toward-it run,

Pi añ   hebai    am m-ñeid.
I-can't anyplace see-you.
```

26.

```
.     .     .     .     :     :     :     .     .     .     .     .     .
ko    ko    ma    gi    we    me    ga    le    ,
i     i     ya    te    ñe    i     ye    te    me    li    wa    ko
            sa    po    kai   name  kei         hi    .
                        siwo  ñimo  kei         hi    ,
            sa    po    kai   name  ga    no    wa    hi    me    ta    .
.     .     .     .     :     :     :     .     .     .     .     .     .
```

```
Komagi we:mgal,
Gray    partner,26

I:ya t-ñe'i      at meliwa ko
Here at-our-song arrives-running-and

S-ap   o kaidam keihi.
Nicely sounding dances.

Siwñim     o keihi,
Swishingly dances,

S-ap   o kaidam gamhu wa him.
Nicely sounding away  goes.
```

---

26 This is the standard epithet, or descriptive naming phrase, for Coyote.

27.

```
 .      .      :      :      :      .      .      .      .      .
              ya    ñine  mu    mu    ki    me    ,
              ya    ñine  mu    mu    ki    me    ,
Je    wede  we    coni  yoi   me    da    .
       e    da    he    ño          si    ne    ,
       he   kya   la    mu    mu    ku    .
              hai   haiyahai            ya    ,
              ya    ñine  mu    mu    ki              me    .
              si    yale  we          wi    ,
              ya    ñine  me    ne    da    .
 .      .      :      :      :      .      .      .      .      .
```

Wañ mumkim.
I'm sick.

Wañ mumkim,
I'm sick,

Jewed weco oimmed.
Land below wandering.

Eda   ñ-hiosig,
Just-there my-flower,

Hekihu   al mumku.
Already dead.

Haiya, haiya,
Oh-oh, oh-oh,

Wañ mumkim.
I'm sick.

Si'al wui,
East toward,

Wañ med.
I   run.

28.

```
.    .    .    .    :    :    :    .    .    .    .    .    .    .
                    ñi   moi  da   gi   no   da   ,
                    no   da   a    gi   mu   wo   yoi  me   da   .
hai       ya        ñi   moi  da   ne   ,
          pyo       wa   te   na   ko
ka   mo   ta   a    ha   ne   ka   .
          we        wi   wo   me   ne   da   ,
          pyo       wa   te   na   ko
ka   mo   ta   a    ta   ne   ka   .
.    .    .    .    :    :    :    .    .    .    .    .    .    .
```

Ñ-i:bdag no**d**a,
My-heart dizzies,

Nodagim iñ-oimme**d**.
Dizzily I-wander.

Haiya, ñ-i:bdag,
Oh-oh, my-heart,

Pi   o wa ta-nako-
Not bear-

kam   o ta:hadag.
ably feels.

Wui[27]   wo me**d**,
Toward-it run,

Pi   o wa ta-nako-
Not bear-

kam   o ta:hadag.
ably feels.

---

[27] We are not certain of this "*Wui*," which means 'toward.' The song seems to say "*wui*," but it doesn't say towards *what*, that is, doesn't give a destination or point of reference, as "*wui*" expressions usually do. Thus, the hero seems to be running towards no place.

29.

```
.       .    :    :    .    .    .    .     .    .
ku   pene ñe  ñei  so   so   na   cu   na    ,
ku   pene ñe  ñei  so   so   na   cu   na  . .
ke   da   na  ce   pa   wi   yu u hu   wi
ka   da   mo  me   lehi wa
ke   da   na  na   ko   ñe   ñe   kim  .
ku   pene to  noñe ñe   ñei
co   si   mu u mui  ma   to   ka   .
a    no   ñe  we   we   ga   ñi   ,
yo   da   me  ya   hai  pa   me   ne   wa   .
.       .    :    :    .    .    .    .     .    .
```

Kup   g ñeñei **so**onacud.
And-you songs   make-start.

Kup   g ñeñei **so**onacud,
And-you songs   make-start.

K e**d**a   g ce:paowi uwi
Just-then whore   woman

K e**d**a   am meliwa
Just-then runs-up

K e**d**a   nanko   ñiok.
Just-then variously talks.

Kup   g Toton ñei-
And-you Ant   song-

cud   si   mui matok.
makings very many unwrap.

An   o ñ-we:gaj,
There around-me,

O'odham a'ai   **s**a mugwa.
People back-and-forth waver.

30.

:   :   :   :   :   .   .   .   .

gamu   we   hewe   li mene   ke
gamu   we   meme   ko gamo   ñi bei   cu ki   me   .
gewe   si   wa   pe ka   me   jewe   ne
dama   ne   ñua   pa hi   me   .
kena   ge   yewe   li mene   ku   ku ki   me   ,
kena   ge   ñeñei   si mama   ci me   .

:   :   :   :   :   .   .   .   .

Gam hu hewel me**d**k
Away   wind   runs-and

Gam hu me:ko gam o ñ-beicug.
Away   far   away   takes-me.

Ge we s-wapkam jewe**d**
The   cane   land

Da:m o ñ-uapa.
Upon takes-me.

K e**d**a   g hewel me**d**, kuhu,
Just-then wind   runs, hooting,

K e**d**a,   g ñeñei si   ma:c.
Just-then, songs   very know.

31.

.   :   :   .   .   .   .

  nape   ñe kai   ha   mo   ,
hana pe   i ñe kai   ha   mo,
  jewe   ne wesi   ko kai   ya   je   ,
  damai   ne   siko   li hime   ke cu   nai kim   ,
  damai   ne   baha   ge wi   higi ye   we   te   .
  hega   ji   jewe   ni wa   a ka him   .

.   :   .   .   .   .

Nap   ñ-kaiham?
Do-you hear-me?

Nap   ñ-kaiham?
Do-you hear-me?

Jewed we:sko   kaidag,
Land everyplace sounds,

Da:m, sikol   himk   cu:dk.
On-it, circular go-and dance.

Da:m, g ba'ag wi:g   hewet,
On-it, eagle   down-feather breezing,

Hekaj[28] g cewagi wa:k.
Then   cloud   enters.

---

[28] We are not sure of this word or the final verb. This word, if "*hekaj*," normally
means "therefore," "because," or "by means of." The translation as "then" is intentionally
weaker: weak knowledge on our part, weak translation. We are not sure if the verb actu-
ally is "*wa:k*", but, if so, "enter" is the corrct translation. We cannot visualize *what* the
cloud enters, however. Thus, we don't have a clear picture of the action of this song-poem.

CHAPTER THREE

Myth and Sing: Principles of the Art

Like most Pima songs, these are named for and somehow identified with non-humans. Thus there are many kinds of bird songs, for example, Oriole, Swallow, Blackbird, Owl, and Hummingbird; and there are many named for animals, for example, Deer, Rattlesnake, Rabbit, Cow, and Dog. Only a few types are named for humans, however, and these few name gods or spirits, not live mortals: God,[29] Devil,[30] and Whore.[31]

In Pima theory, those names designate the songs' authors. All of the authors are spiritual or divine, or, as I say, "mythic." They are spirits, persons who come to people and accompany them in dreams, spirits because they are *met* spiritually. They live in the shadows and crannies of today's world, especially in the natural, wilderness world; and many if not all are said to have preceded the Pimas in this world.

I call them mythic partly because of that ancientness, but not all of them are ancient, at least they are not attested to in the Pimas' stories about the ancient past. Nor do the songs have much to do with the events narrated in that mythology. What makes the spirits mythic is that they speak from an existence that is different from today's peoples' ordinary existence, and they are believed. (To me, myths are stories that are believed; unbelieved stories are fiction.)

The Ants and the other song sources are not today's animals, etc., but are hazily ambiguous beings between today's animals and humanity. Psychologically they are like humans, but they are physically indistinct. When I once directly asked Paul what he thought the "Ant-people"

---

[29] *Jios*, from Spanish *dios*, the Christian God.

[30] *Jiawul*, from the Spanish *diablo*, the Christian devil.

[31] Besides appearing in many sets from other divine, spiritual, or mythic souces, whores are sources in their own right of songs used for curing. See Bahr, Gregorio, Lopez, and Alvarez, 1974, for the traditional system of curing that includes Whore sickness.

looked like,[32] he said, "like people but with big heads." He was more forthcoming in this remark than are the songs, which only use the word "ant" once (in song 29) and can hardly be said to dwell on antness. The "I's" of the songs, who must be taken as the persons who first enunciated them, are silent about their own physical appearance, but are quite free in telling about their interests and moods, which seem human.

Those "I's," I take it, are Ant-persons—not humans, not ants, but mythic, although contemporary, Ant-persons. This rule for reading the "I's" as indistinct, spiritual myth persons is fundamental to all that follows here. That the "I's" are indistinct is of course a property of the texts. The lack of distinction is obvious in the renditions in chapter two. That the "I's" stand for myth-persons, specifically Ant-persons, is, however, interpretation, as is the further claim that the "I's" have additional overtones of "the human dreamer" and "the human dancer." I adopt this interpretation because Pima singers, after finishing an Ant song, for example, regularly say, "Thus said the ant."[33] I have heard this attribution again and again from singers of Swallow, Oriole, Mouse, and all kinds of songs, and I assume that Stepp and Seota did the same (Paul agrees). The singers say this, but they never explain what they mean by it, that is, how the "I's" of the songs partake in antness.

Not having seen an Ant-person, I cannot help. The best I can do is give reasons why the Pima information on them is scarce. The reasoning is complex but the basic facts are easy to state: Ant-persons do not sing about what they look like, nor do the Pimas who dream of them tell what they look like, nor do the myths of the Pima. And there is a distinction between Pima song and myth and between the combinatorial forms of each, the sing and the mythology.

The songs are translated in the present tense, which is consistent with the Pima texts.[34] The texts are understood to be similar to tape recordings, to be exact reproductions of what a dreamer heard an Ant-person say

---

[32] The question was asked in English except for the phrase "*Toton hemajkam*," "Ant people."

[33] "B o hia kaij g toton."

[34] Pima has two tenses, future and "non-future," or "present-and-past" (Zepeda, 1983:10, 19, 59–64, 71–72). The songs are generally in the present-and-past tense. One might say that these could equally be translated as past or as present, but there is an additional factor that tips the balance towards a present tense translation: the language puts its verbs through inflections for "aspect" as well as for tense. There are two aspects, perfective indicating "completed" actions and imperfective indicating "incompleted" or "ongoing" actions. The song poems are generally in the present-or-past imperfective, which combination warrants a translation of "present" rather than "past."

(sing). The next section considers the structure of the typical song in some detail. Here it is enough to say that songs are brief declarations of what an intensely awake "I" sees, hears, touches, or feels. No narcissus, the "I" doesn't tell how he or she looks. Nor does the dreamer.[35]

Now, if the dreams are real, as I believe they are, some dreamer sometime must have seen what an Ant-person looked like, and could have told how an entire dream with that person looked, sounded, and felt. I have not heard of such a telling, but we should not rule out their possible existence. Still, there are reasons why singers would not say whether they actually dreamed a song or merely learned it from another Pima singer. To speak of dreaming the song would be too boastful, while to say that it was learned from another Pima would be too meek. Thus, silence is golden; and that silence rules out dream stories.

Here is an instructive statement on the subject from Paul:

Ñ-ce:cki	My Dream
Bañ hiwa ñ-wua hebaicuc, k am ha'icu ce:ck,	Sometimes it happens to me, and something dreams [up to me],
O hebai s am am s-ap kokso, pi ha'icu wo sa'i ce:ck.	Or sometimes [I] sleep well [through the night], [and] nothing dreams.
Ab o hebai mu'i ha'icu wo ce:ckad. Ha'i am taso wu:pa, o hebaicuc ha'i ep pi sa'i hekid.	Sometimes many things dream [to me]. Some come out clearly, or sometimes some of them never are [clear].
Hab añ-wua c am a sa a: hegai ñ-ce:ck, mañ hascu'i ñeid, kutp pi am hab o sa'i e-ju:, ñe:, k am hu hebai mat am b o o-ju:. O ep g ñioki am ep wo sa ka:, o ep wo ñeidad, e:p. Nt at ab o ñ-a:, "Ñe:, ba:ñ hu ñeid i:da, do: ob phen hab kaij?"	It happens to me and I might tell my dream, whatever I saw, then it [what I dreamed] won't happen [in life], look, and yet sometime it will happen [after all]. Or also I might hear talking [in life], or else might see something [dreamed earlier], too. I'll say to myself, "Look, where did I see this, who then could have said that?"

---

[35] I hold that the primary meaning of "I" must be "Ant-person," not "Pima dreamer." Some songs have a "you" as well as an "I," and I read this "you" primarily as "dreamer." My reading of the "I" is based on the tendency for singers to say, "Thus said the Ant," after singing an Ant song; and also on the fact that Pimas *say* that Ants and other spirit persons take dreamers on journeys.

But the "I" could be the dreamer. Then whatever the "I" says is what the dreamer experienced. For example, if the "I" says "I'm flying," we would understand that the dreamer had that experience, quite like any of us who dream of ourselves flying. To me, this is an overtone reading, as is the interpretion of "I" as an attender at a dance.

Ñe:, nt o ñ-oidahi, ñe:, t o om i wu:s, mañs abs ce:ckahim.

Look, I'll keep following it [thinking about it], look, it [memory] will come out, that I dreamed it [before it happened].

Abs hab-a i:da hemako ce:ck, mant go:ko wa i da:m añ ce:ck, mañ am ha-ñeid g hemajkam, mat ki im e-hemapa im hu ta'i, ge sikol jeg amai.

But [here is] this one dream, which I dreamed twice, that I saw the people, where they had gathered, off in the east [corner of the reservation] where there's a round clearing.

Am e-hemapa hegam, kus hascu aihic k am s-o'odhamag? An ha-we:gaj g sa'i hiwa, e:p.

They gathered there, yet what [event] came up so many people would be there? Around them were bushes [it was desert], too.

Oiyupoc, hihidot g koksiñel. Ñe: ñ am ho-ñeids am i himhi, i himhi k am ha-oidc oimmelim.

They moved around and the cooks cooked [as for a feast]. Look, I saw them and started to stroll, strolled and moved among them.

Pi hedai am hu sa ha-ñiok ñ-wui, pi hedai am hu sa has kaij, Abs hab hiva sa'i ñ-ñeñei, cam o ñ-hehe'edka.

No one talked to me, no one said anything. But they glanced at me, and smiled to me.

Ñe:, nt am i ke:khim, ke:khim, gm hu cem al o wu:s, am haha ep ha-ka: mo om ha'i ñe'e.

Look, I stood for a while, [and] stood [somewhere else], [and] almost came out from the edge of them, then heard some singing.

There are at least three implications to reading the "I" primarily as "myth person." First, of course, the reading distinguishes the text of a song from the first person narrative of a dream. The song is only the "sound track" of particular portions of a dream, namely the portions in which the transporters sing. Second, the reading lets the "I" have experiences that are not necessarily those of the dreamer. In fact, all of the "psychology" of a song is that of the spirit-person "I," not of the dreamer. Now, the psychology of some human dreamers is largely visual and kinesthetic (as if the dreamer were watching a movie through his or her own eyes). Possibly this is so with much Pima dream experience, too. But what Pima *song* dreamers retain and tell from their experience is not the scenes and their feelings, but the songs that their transporters sang. The emphasis is on language, and the language is that of another. Third, whenever the "I" addresses a "you" in a song, it is as if the "you's" future is being prophesied. Among whites and other people no doubt, possibly including Pimas in their "normal" dreams (those without songs), the *entire* dream may be prophetic; but on my reading only the second person ("you") addressees receive prophecies, and not all of them.

If this tripartite interpretation of "I's" (and corollary for "you's") is untrue, my interpretation of sings as complicated, nuanced wholes falls apart: null hypothesis. But the commentaries on the sings try to prove that there is something beyond nullity, namely trinity, the central illusion.

Ñe:, ñ am i ke:k c ha-kaihyamim hegam mo om dada, c am taso dada. C abs hab-a hegam mo ob ñ-wui dada, ñ-wui ñe:ña, pi sa'i taso g ha-wupuisa, c abs hab-a—pi mams.

Look, I stood and listened to those who sat there, and they sat clearly. But those who sat toward me, facing me, their faces weren't clear, they—didn't show.

Ñe:, ñ am i ke:s c am ha-kaihamim, k am hema a'aga g ñe'i mañ am s-ma:c, mant hab masma mai ab amjed i:dam kekel.

Look, I stood there and listened to them, and one of them sang a song which I knew, which I had learned from the [living] old timers.

Pi abs a'i kaidag mañ has masma s-ma:c, kus hascu ñ-a:gid? "Pi antp hi g sa ap a:ga hig," mant abs i ñ-a:.

It didn't sound the way I knew it, and what's that mean? "Maybe I wasn't singing it right," I just thought.

Ñe:, ant am u:pam ep i himhi, e:p, am ha-ñeid hegam mo om ki ap e-nakok hegam, an has oiyupo c am nakok. T am him k am hu wu:s mant hebai amjed i hi:, hahawa abs ep ha-ñeid mo om dada g u'us kaklid.

Look, I started back again, too, [and] again saw the ones who were fixing things, moving and fixing things [food]. Then [I] went on and finally came out where I started, then again saw where the wood carts [wagons] were sitting.

Dada g kaklid amai, ha'i s am i dada kaklid ed. Ñe:, an abs am si i ñia amai. Am wo'o c am oidahim. "Kutp hems hab a cu'ig hasko, mo om uliñig, i:da, mat am t-ba'ic hihi. Hab masma am ki:dag, hab-a e:p mac hab masma ki:kahim," bant abs i ñ-a:.

Arrived at the carts there, [and] some [people] were sitting in the carts. Look, I woke up there. I lay there [back in bed] and thought [literally "followed"] it. "Maybe it is this way somewhere, where they stay [literally "hang-to, hang-out"], this [kind of people] who have gone ahead of us [died]. Thus they have a life, but it's like we were living," I thought to myself.

Paul's statement comes about as close as a Pima statement will to telling a dream in which a new song is learned. It is a dream in which an old song was almost corrected, or improved. Had he remembered exactly what the spirits sang (he says he doesn't, although the above statement is silent on that), he would have corrected the song, which of course is still less than learning a new one. The latter surely did happen to people and should happen and may be happening, but no one tells about it.

If dreamers could tell song-learning dreams but don't, and Ant-persons could sing their own self portraits but don't, what about the mythology, that is, the stock of stories of events which happened long ago, which, like our sung strings, also cannot be traced back to particular sources? Do Pima myths describe Ant-persons? Paul and I have not heard any myth about ants or Ant-persons, let alone a myth with the combination of places and events in this sing.

Could songs or sings *be* myths, verse myths, about Ant-persons? They are like Pima prose myths in some ways but are different in others, and it is important to state how. First, individual songs are like myths in the negative sense that, by and large, no one can or will vouch for the events that they describe. A dream song without a dreamer's report is the same as any story of uncertain source. People say, "We heard this, but we don't know who first told it." A dream song *sing*, of course, being a unique combination, could not possibly be considered an established story.

Second, both individual songs and prose myths do tell stories. The brief declaration in each song is a story. Or better said, it is a short flash of events which could become part of a story; a declaration that one would like to know more about, which "more" would make the flash into a story.

A song corresponds to an episode in a myth, and accordingly the musical counterpart to a myth is a full sing. Now there are three points to make on the sing-myth relationship, two large and one small. The first, large point is that myths generally, and certainly Pima myths, have fixed plots, that is, fixed sequences of episodes, while the songs of a sing are not fixed in sequence. Fixity of sequence, however, does not guarantee a sense of narrative wholeness—a feeling of balance or closure—nor does variable sequence preclude such a sense. Thus, a totally fixed sequence can be mere gibberish, and a fleeting combination, a dealt hand of cards, can convey wholeness, albeit for one time only. In reality, however, people do not bother to remember gibberish, so every prose myth that lasts has some wholeness to it. And it is the narrative wholeness of sings also that we are interested in. We are not interested in ephemeral strings that do not make sense, but in how certain strings do make sense.

The next, small point is a reminder that the mythology discussed above is a whole of a higher order than a single myth. The mythology is a fixed progression of myths, an oral book whose separate myths are equivalent to chapters. There is no comparable level in pure song, no grand series or cycle that stands above and incorporates separate sings.

The final and large point is that one should not think of the events described in sings as ancient, that is, as referring to the same time period that is covered in prose myths. Indeed, since the songs come from recent dreams, they could refer to ancient events only if the dreamer could go backward in time. To be sure, at least one song seems to do this (Oriole 2), and another seems to visit the future (Ant 29). And the Yuman (Maricopa, Yuma, Mojave, and other) neighbors of the Pima have long, fixed sequence "song myths" that are entirely set in the revisited ancient past.[36]

Now, one knows that a song is a revisit to ancientness just because there are independent prose myths that attest to the events that are visited. All that is new in such a song is the intruding observing presence of the dreamer and spirit guide. That newness is thrilling, it is a kind of historian's dream, but as I understand the situation among the Pimas and Yumans, it does not change the past. (See the appendix for a fuller discussion of this issue.)

By and large the Pimas' dreamed spirit guides do not take them back to ancientness. Primarily, the guide wants to show to the dreamer geography, but a geography that workaday Pimas rarely visit. What the guide wants to tell at these places is mainly feelings about the fleetingness of things. Pima mythology tells ancient history, while Pima sings have a different tendency.

SONG STRUCTURE AND FILMICNESS

Recalling that the song language texts are written with their key metered zones set into columns, note that these zones are phenomena of sound, not of content or meaning. Another technical property of Pima-Papago song is one that pertains to content, that is, to the number and focus and topics of the sentences of the typical song. A song-poem-story (or quasi story) has a minimum of three sentences (grammatically complete statements, with subject and verb), a beginning sentence, a middle one, and one at the end. A few songs consist of no more than that, but most have a sentence or two more. Sometimes the sentences are simple, consisting of a single clause with one subject and one verb. Sometimes they are complex, with more than one verb or more than one clause. There are additional complications owing to a tendency to *omit* the nouns that would substantiate the grammatical subjects of sentences and to *supply* nouns that substantiate grammatical objects and the locations of actions. This is

---

[36] The Yuman song-myths approximate the "dreamer's eye" narratives wished for above. They consist of a fixed series of songs interspersed with prose narrative. That prose tells how things looked to the dreamer (as distinct from the spirit guide) and tells events of the spirit journey between the points where the guide sang the songs.

In addition to these song myths, the Yumans have myths like those of the Pima. The difference between a "song myth" of the Yuman sort and the "mythology myths" found with both peoples is "song myths" are narratives of dreamed visits to the events described in "mythology myths." The songs of the myth are attributed to the spirit guide, not to the characters of the ancient events. Those events are observed by the dreamer and spirit as if through a pane of glass. As I understand it, the observers do not touch actual ancient characters or enter in any way into the ancient events.

the linguistic correlate, actually cause, of the haziness of Ant persons, discussed above. In songs, it is easy to see the scene of a poem-story, but it is difficult to see precisely who is there.

The three canonical sentences correspond to the three named parts of a Pima-Papago song, the "beginning" (*son*), the "turn" (*nod*), and the "end" (*ku:g*). The Pima words do not stipulate how much text falls into these divisions. Pima-Papagos do not have an explicit notion of sentences as units of language. They have no terms for subjects, predicates, nouns, verbs, or the wholes (phrases, clauses, and sentences) that those things comprise. Thus, the "beginning," "middle," and "end" are points rather than segments.[37]

The following table divides the 31 songs into such segments. Ellipses after a sentence indicate that although the segment is finished, there is some more song, more poem, prior to the onset of the next segment; ellipses indicate that there is more to a song than the minimum three sentences. Only four (3, 5, 17 and 25) of the thirty-one songs are without ellipses. Six have two sets of them and the rest have one. In general the omitted segments are short sentences. Thus most songs just slightly exceed the three sentence minumum.

It is important that the three or four sentences tend to be pictorial and different; each makes a different word picture. The pictures may be parts of one larger scene, but the visual focus of each sentence is different. Thus, the grammatical subjects and verbs are different in each sentence of nineteen songs, while twelve have common subjects or verbs across two sentences (a picayune criterion for nondifference). I call this tendency for difference the "filmic" quality of Pima-Papago song, meaning that these songs use the same techniques that have dominated films from the 1920s to today: abrupt shifts of visual field from far off to close up, from character to character, and thing to thing. Since the songs are so short, the shifts of focus across the sentences give an illusion of motion even if the pictures produced by the sentences are themselves static. But they are not static. The great majority of verbs describe things in motion: "unwrap," "toss," "spread," "tell," "puff," "explode," and, in almost every song, "run."

In sum, where the Yumans have "song myths" that tell the circumstances of the acquisition of songs, the Pimas and Papagos have sings that omit those circumstances. The Yuma song myths are fixed stories, as they would have to be if the visionary journey were definite and real, but the Pima-Papago song sets are reshuffled for each sing. And both peoples have fixed, mostly prose myths about ancient times. These matters are discussed further, and a Yuman song myth quoted, in the appendix of this book.

[37] They surely do talk of whole songs as "stretching lineally" (*sel wawañ*). It is just that they don't carry that mode of speaking into the subdivisions of songs.

The columns tabulated below yield the following composite profile:

> *Beginning*: There *was* something (a mountain standing, songs starting, etc.)
> *Middle*: Something else (I or a he, she, or it) *travels* or acts at a distance (runs, sees, hears, etc.)
> *End*: And I *do* something.

There are many exceptions to the profile which, being generic, also lacks the mystery and beauty in individual songs and in sequence.

ANT SONG SEGMENTS

Beginning	*Middle ("Turning")*	*End*
	Manic sounding [i,t,y,etc.] sing. . . .	
1. Songs [it,they,you,we,I?] make-to-start,[38]		Manic sounding [i,t,y,etc.] sing.
2. Dead-field Mountain there stands.	Just-then, women jump-out- and run, . . .	Then my-head upon, [women] toss.
3. Greasy Mountain, /Greasy Mountain there stands.	There in-it /Very green flowers-/With [i,t,y,etc?] me-cover.	There in-it, /Manic [mountain? my condition?] is.
4. West direction land flowers, /West direction land flowers,	And-I follow-and go. . . .	The us-below /Lying land manically flowers.
5. Iron Mountain, /Not invitingly it-sounds.	Wind there-runs-and / Against-me hits:	In-it everywhere [I? wind?] hoot[s].
6. And-I away run,	Away west toward [I] run. . . .	On top [I] run-up-and something know.

---

[38] I judge this line and the next to be separate sentences. They are not proper sentences according to the principal published Pima-Papago grammar (Zepeda, 1983:8) because they lack "[subject complex] auxiliaries," which are short, abstract words that signal the person (first, second, or third) and number of the subects of sentences. In theory all sentences should have auxiliaries. A sentence may lack a stated substantive subject, but the auxiliary makes it proper.

Pima-Papago song "sentences" commonly lack both an auxiliary and a substantive subject. This seems intentional, the intention apparently to keep the hearer or reader wondering.

I consider these two subjectless lines to be separate sentences because the second line introduces new substantive material, namely two adverbs, that corresponds to something (a noun that is a direct object) in the first line: the lines are separate, sentence-like poetic utterances.

7. Broad Mountain stands,	And-I toward-it run. . . .	And-I there take-them [songs], /With-which cause-to-sing.
8. Broad Mountain stands,	There below-it waters ready-to-jump-out are. . . .	And-just-then there [water? I? tree?] enter[s].
9. Bitter Wind,[39]	Here-it [wind]-will run-up-and, . . .	My-heart by-itself dies.
10. Do-you so singingly speak? . . .	Long Mountain /That-one [mountain] is so manic telling. . . .	Just-then dizziness /Back-and-forth stretches.
11. Far land, and-I upon-it go,	Away before-me, rainbow just-then comes-out. . . .	What will-I-do-and there run?
12. Long Red stands, /Long red stands.	Base-at cloud comes-out. . . .	[There is] Great nice appearing [butterfly] fluttering.
13. Gray killdeer bird, / Away, land edge-at runs. . . .	Land [killdeer] strides,	Wing [killdeer] lengthens.[40]
14. Gray fly, /Squawberry flowers make-wine-with-and, . . .	And-I with-him drink-it-all-and get-drunk, . . .	Songs [I] tell.[41]
15. Flatly run-and run-and run, . . .	And-I follow-and run-and run,	Land upon, /Back-and-forth [I] stop-and-start.
16. East there inside rumbles,/East there inside rumbles,	And-I toward-it run, see-it. . . .	Far, loudly, /There [darkness] inside rumbles.
17. Many birds fly, /Many birds fly.	Sky cover in-front fly,	Nicely sounding they-coo-and prepare-to-run.
18. Dizzy woman,[42]	There to-me runs. . . .	Darkness [I] follow-and run.
19. Oh-oh, my-husband, / Oh-oh, my husband, / Here-I leave-you /And-go. . . .	Darkness comes-out, / And-goes.	Oh-oh, my-husband, /And-I leave-you /And-go.

[39] The rest of this incomplete sentence is in the next column, that is, in the "turning" part of the song. This is the only song in the set where the "beginning" and "turning" share the same sentence.

[40] As in song 1, the subjects are unstated, the lines lack a subject complex auxiliary, and the rationale for treating the lines as separate sentences is the use of different materials (nouns here, but not sentence subjects) before the verbs.

[41] Another subjectless, auxiliaryless sentence. This time the implied subject is pretty clearly "I." The dots after the "turning" stand for the parallel short line, "Pitiably [I] speak." Thus we have the same phenomenon as in songs 1 and 13, but this time one of the sentence-like utterances goes untabulated, not being a "start," "turning," or "end."

[42] An incomplete sentence, the predicate is in the "turning."

20. Sun sets, ...	East below songs /Manic [i,t,y,etc.] tell.	Oh-oh, my-younger-sibling, / Songs you-tell.
21. Shining Water lies, / Shining Water lies.	In-it mudhen wanders, ...	Nice-looking it [mudhen]-floats.
22. Marsh Water lies, ...	In-it very green moss, /Away zig-zagged spreads. ...	Around-me it [moss]-circles.
23. Oh-oh, my-younger-sibling, /Oh-oh, my-younger-sibling, /Here-I leave-you /And far go.	Wind in-me ex-/plodes-and jumps-out. ...	East toward [I] run.
24. I-here arrive, /Oh-oh, I-here arrive. ...	I'm Ghost Woman/ And-here arrive.	Oh-oh, oh-oh, /Whatever to-do /I-don't-know.
25. Oh-oh, my-singing-partner, /Oh-oh, my-singing-partner, /I-can't anyplace see-you.	Away far land,/ Toward-it [I] run.	I-can't anyplace see-you.
26. Gray partner, /Here at-our-song arrives-running-and	Nicely sounding [helper] dances. ...	Nicely sounding [helper] away goes.
27. I'm sick, /I'm sick, ...	Oh-oh, oh-oh, /I'm sick.	East toward, /I run.
28. My-heart dizzies, ...	Oh-oh, my-heart, /Not bear-/ably feels. ...	Not bear-/ably [my heart] feels.
29. And-you songs make-start, /And-you songs make-to-start. ...	And-you Ant song-/makings very many unwrap.	There around-me, /People back-and-forth waver.
30. Away wind runs-and. ...	The cane land /Upon [wind] takes-me. ...	Just-then, songs [I] very know.
31. Do-you hear-me? /Do-you hear-me? ...	On-it [land], [i,t,y,etc.] circular go-and dance. ...	Then [into?] cloud [I? wind? feather?] enter[s].

EPHEMERALITY

In discussing sings and prose myths earlier, I said that sings do not have a fixed sequence.[43] Now, this is true of the Ant songs and of several other kinds of social dancing sets that I have written about: Swallow (1986),

[43] The earlier discussion did not define the "prose," which to me is "dicourse formed in the meter, diction, and intonation of ordinary speech." Of course all traditional Pima prose was oral. There was no written prose art. To me, the two important features of Pima and all other solely oral proses are that they are quiet and intimate, that is, used in private, contemplative communications (this feature distinguishes oral prose from song, chant, oratory, preaching, etc.); and that prose pieces, although deliberative (spoken with practiced care), are not so fully memorized as to be precisely repeatable on a later occasion.

Heaven (1987), Airplane (1994 and the appendix of this book), and Oriole (Bahr and Joseph, 1994 and part two of this book).[44] On the other hand, curing (as opposed to social dancing) songs, which come in smaller sets, tend to fixity in sequence (examples are given in Bahr and Haefer, 1978 and Bahr, Giff, and Havila, 1979); and the songs used as quotations in prose myths are sequentially fixed by the plot of the myth.

It is well to think of social dance song sequences as postcards sent from someone on an impassioned journey. On receiving the card one speculates about the mood of the sender, about all that was happening at the moment of the message (the card can't say much), about what could have changed since the last message, and what the next step in the journey might be.

The songs heard at social dances differ from postcards because there is no actual traveling correspondent. In place of a person who sends postcards from "out there," there is a singer "right here." The latter's songs have all been sung before. They are not original. They are, however, unique in their combination which gives the performance a kind of originality which, added to the filmic quality of the individual messages, yields a second principle or rule of social dance poetry (the first, stated in the previous section, is that the "I's" of the texts should be read as "myth persons"), and that is the *vivid ephemerality of story.*

It is a rare Pima-Papago social dance sing that has a prose myth behind it[45] because, as we noted, most singers vary their songs' selection and sequence each time they sing. Thus, the sequence of the postcard-

---

(Writing of course makes such repetition possible, and I would say that it is the main purpose of writing). I call this second feature the paraphrasing nature of prose. Each performance of a piece of oral prose is a paraphrase of the last performance of that work.

[44] The singer of the Oriole set, Vincent Joseph, acquired the songs in several lessons of varied song sequence (I was there). Joseph arranged them in a fixed order—temporarily fixed at least. As he acquired more songs on his own, he inserted them in the previously fixed sequence. Had he sung them for more years and acquired many more of them, I assume that he would have begun to treat them as Stepp seems to have done, with long favored runs that would be retained basically intact, with pairs or trios that would stay together but whose internal sequence could change, and with individual songs that would move rather freely. This shift into variability occurs when a singer knows more songs than he can sing in one sitting. Joseph learned about fifty-six songs without making the shift, but other singers might reach that point sooner (of course some singers might like to vary their sequences as an end in itself—for example, a person who knows twenty-five songs, and usually sings all of them, but changes their order each time).

[45] The Heaven songs have the biblical myth of Jesus and Mary behind them. This does not guarantee that the songs are sung in the same sequence, only that the singer and audience would know that the Bible gives *a* sequential version to events identical with or similar to those described in the songs. In fact, as I heard the songs sung they did not come in a fixed sequence. I assembled all those that I heard into *a* sequence that corresponds

like songs of a given sing has not been put together in quite the same way
before and will not be so again. It is today's, tonight's, ephemeral myth.

This myth is not a story but an organized, selected medley. And the is-
sue here is the organization of the medley, in other words, the principles
that guide the selection of songs. In the Ant sing, and in general, I say
that two principles are at work. One principle requires certain contents
for the beginning and end of a sing. The other is neutral with regard to
any particular content, but requires that later songs "answer back" to dis-
contiguous earlier ones. These organizing principles do not produce sto-
ries. Although the first might do so since it requires references to time,
direction, and activity, it is silent on actors (consistent with having in-
distinct mythic persons); and indeed the actors in the sequences, includ-
ing the "I's," are varied and artful, but the art is not that of a continual
story. The second principle is anti-story by nature. To answer back, to
hark back over the heads of several intervening songs, is the opposite of
moving ahead. True, narratives can have flashbacks, but with social
dancing sequences we have flashbacks without continuity of character:
talkbacks, a chorus of crickets.

These principles employed by the singer organize a sing. They do not,
of course, illuminate or explain everything of interest in every song. Far
from it, they act upon songs that the singer already has. They take the
songs as givens, they feed on them, they provide the singer with abstract
guidelines for organizing a medley. Since no two medleys are the same—
or better said, since the medleys are not fixed—the principles surely do
not fully determine the nature or content of a sing.

Was Stepp conscious of these principles? I believe Stepp was con-
scious of the first principle, although I never saw him. I have never heard
any singer spell out the principle as it is stated below. The second is so in-
exact that I doubt that Stepp or any singer would be conscious of it. They
would feel it when they know they have made a happy selection, but they
would not consciously employ it while deciding what song to sing next.[46]

---

to the biblical record on the one hand and to Pima conceptions on the starting and ending
of sings on the other. I doubt that I heard all of the songs that the singer (Blaine Pablo) knew.

I hold that social dance sings rarely have definite "real" private visionary journeys be-
hind them. The changing of sequences militates against definiteness, and so does the
singers' practice of exchanging songs with each other. Thus, Stepp's Ant song 5 is the same
as Vincent Joseph's Oriole song 16. At some time in the past someone, not necessarily
Stepp or Joseph, took an Ant song for an Oriole or vice versa.

[46] I wish to note a kinship in spirit between Stepp's sequences and what M. L. Rosen-
thal and Sally Gall (1983) found to be the heart (they call it the "genius") of modern
American and English poetry from Emily Dickinson to Walt Whitman to T. S. Eliot to

We have just two tapes of Stepp performances. Nine songs in the sequence presented here are not in the other singing (numbers 1, 15, 16, 18, 19, 20, 23, 24, 27). The other singing has six unique songs. Of the twenty-one songs common to both, there are some changes in sequence. The run from 2 to 8 is common to both (our song 1 is missing in the other sing); and the pairs 9 and 10 as well as 12 and 13 stay together, but their orders are inverted. The remaining ten, common to both, are scattered differently through what I take to be the last half of each sing.[47] I will not discuss the other performance in full, but will refer to parts of it while interpreting "our" sing, in the next chapter.

Ezra Pound, William Carlos Williams, and others more contemporary. I did not know of their study until well into this one, and I cannot summarize or judge it. But I will tell how their general ideas relate to my ideas about Stepp.

    The principal idea is that the modern sequential poets make balances among islands, or "lyric centers," of intense emotional expression. Those balances are "organic," that is, unannounced or, as they put it, undeclaimed. Thus, poets lay in and balance their islands without talking about them. Readers encounter them and critics explain them. The islands state emotions or what I will call "moods," the subjectivities and sensibilities of restless "I's." The poetic work is a kind of expressionism, a representation of emotions and moods.

    I am not sure whether Rosenthal and Gall would accept this summary of their theory; or perhaps they would accept the summary but hold that there is more to the theory than that. I am content with this much of a statement, however, because it makes a bond between Stepp and his school and the modernists. I hope the summary will seem true of Stepp. As we read Stepp in translation and discuss him in English my concern is to be certain that we are actually discussing Stepp. Thus I will take pains to establish that his poetry is as I say it is: that the ambiguities (multiple plausible meanings) that I cite were intended, and in general that what I say about the translations is true of the originals.

    [47] The full sequence of the other singing, according to the song numberings used here, is: 2, 3, 4, 5, 6, 7, 8, 10, 9, 11, 13, 12, 14, 31, 26, 21, 22, 28, 30, 32, 33, 25, 17, 29, 34, 35, 36. 37. Songs 32 to 37 are unique to that sing. Songs 2–12 are on one side of the tape, 14–37 are on the other. Stepp might conceivably have sung the second block first. I can not completely exlude that his ordering in "our" sing was actually songs 15–31 (as I number them), then 1–14.

CHAPTER FOUR

The Sing Interpreted

A PRINCIPLE ON STARTING AND STOPPING, SONGS 1–4

No matter their use, whether for social dancing, curing, rain divination, or whatever, Pima-Papago sings can be counted on to make some reference in the first two or three or more songs to someone's act of starting to sing, to the sun's descent in the west, to the coming of darkness, or to someone's journey westward. At the end of a dance the singer will select songs with the reverse of these references, the stopping of singing, sunrise, light, or eastward travel. The first three of those pairs of topics correspond to events that take place at an actual Pima dance, for the dances traditionally start at sundown and end at dawn. The last pair of actions, the west or east journey, can not actually take place at a dance, for the dancers do not journey anywhere, but merely circle around a fixed point. Not all of the actions are mentioned in each singing, either at the beginning or the end. One or more of them are, however, the only guaranteed references in a performance. They are touchstones.

Stepp took great liberties with those touchstones. The rules can not be inferred from his tapes. Other singers are more conservative, but I doubt that any keep with precisely the same beginning or end for long. They will all have various ways to satisfy the formal requirements and verious ways to defy them.

Stepp started quite normally. His first song could describe a darkening Pima village and his next seven amount to a westward journey. The nature of that journey and two words in the first song require comment. The song is:

> 1. Songs start,
>   Manic sounding singing.
>   Night follow,
>   Manic sounding singing.

The two words of interest are "follow" and "manic". Both raise problems of translation, "follow" on ambiguity and "manic" on perjorative nuance. Concerning "follow," I try on principle to make translations that are no more and no less ambiguous than the original Pima. Thus, although one might like a more precise verb in the line "Night follow," and might dismiss the line as poetically hopeless, I ask that it be taken as part of a poem in a poetry with an unfamilar tolerance for ambiguity, or, let us say, a tolerance for some unfamiliar particular ambiguities.

The ambiguity about "follow" is whether someone is moving so as to follow the night's blackness as it advances in the sky or on the ground, or someone is merely "passing" the night, as we say in English, at one place. In either case, one would like to know who the person could be. The Pima word in question is "*oidka'i*." I think that the word literally means "to-follow-something-and," and so it literally implies the first meaning. But when paired with "night" in ordinary speech, the word does not keep the literal meaning. Then it means, idiomatically, "to-pass", "to-stay-throughout."[48] This being a song, I do not preclude the literal, now magical, meaning. But as we will see, the next songs in the sequence imply the idiomatic sense (a different run of sequels might favor the literal).

The translation problem with "manic" is whether it is permissible to render Pima into pejorative or stigmatizing words. I believe that it is, if one explains how the original Pima is pejorative. That explanation then

---

[48] I analyze "*oidka'i*," into the root *oid-* and the suffix *-ka'i*. *Oid* is a transtive verb, "to follow some object." *-Ka'i* means "and then"; it is a conjuction. (According to Saxton, Saxton, and Enos, 1983 p. 30, this element adds the meaning of "and go"—not "go and," but "and go" to the verb that it is attached to. I like their interpretion but opt for the more conservative translation, with a mere "and.") The whole means "follow-and" (or, according to Saxton, Saxton, and Enos, "follow-and-go").

There is another important form with *oid-*, namely *oidk*. According to Madeleine Mathiot in her undated but recent dictionary, this word is a postposition (an adjective or adverb positioned after the noun or verb that it modifies). It means "during" (temporally) or "along" (spatially). I accept that analysis and accept it as equally applicable to *oidka'i*: both words can be postpositions meaning "during" or "along." But I hold that both can also be the verb "to-follow-and." Thus, the phrases *cuhug oidka'i* and *cuhug oidk* can be interpreted either as clauses comprised of a noun and a verb ("Night [somebody] follows"), or as phrases comprised of a noun and a modifying postpositional adjective ("Night during"). I use the former translation, but the other would also be legitimate. The other, however, I consider to be a weakened version of the former. To me, *oidka'i* and *oidk* primarily mean "follow-and," and only secondarily and meekly mean "during."

One other Ant song has the phrase in question, namely song 18. There it is in the form of *oidk*, and there I translate it freely with the verb "chase." I do so because the phrase is combined with *med*, "to run." My interpretation is that the "I" chases the night, or rather the black nightness.

becomes a special translational sense for the English word. In a way this problem is the opposite of that with translational ambiguities. Translation into an ambiguity makes a passage seem to say too little by English standards, while translation into a pejorative (of which there are really only two in these songs, "manic" and "whore") makes a passage seem to say too much by *Pima* standards.

Wa:m, an adverb, means that someone is doing something "excessively," "too elatedly," "too overbearingly." In Pima, *wa:m* does not designate a permanent state. People can be *wa:m* and return to normal with no ill effects. For this reason "manic" might be too strong a translation for "*wa:m*." I use it with that reservation, but with the certainty that "*wa:m*" like "manic" is no compliment.

Thus, song 1 is motionally ambiguous (staying in one place versus moving) and psychologically slightly pejorative. The song could equally describe a village congregation that will stay the night or a person following the early night's darkness within earshot of someone's (not necessarily a human's) songs. The three sequel songs, however, resolve the motional issue. Briefly, 2 and 3 give an implicitly west traveling "I" (one must know the local geography to affirm this), and 4 puts the "I" in the sky like the sun. Here is 4:

> Westward the land flowers,
> Westward the land flowers,
> And I run through.
> Everywhere flowers,
> The here below
> Lying world manic flowers.

Now, if song 1 *could* have a village setting and song 4 definitely has a traveling, world surveying "I", how do the two songs in between link a village to world travel? They do so quite simply. Their "I's" stop at mountains called Dead-field and Greasy. These are the first two mountains downstream, which is westward, from Stepp's village on the Salt River. Dead-field, called "A Mountain" by whites, is two miles downstream from the village.[49] Greasy, a larger mountain four miles below Dead-field, imposes a south boundary or barrier on Phoenix. It is called "South Mountain" by whites.

One can see the whole sequence as solar. The sun passes Salt River

---

[49] The name "Dead-field" is apparently in reference to ruins of Hohokam fields. Now the property of Tempe, Ariz., the mountain shelters the football stadium of Arizona State University.

Village and remarks on a dance starting there, then passes Dead-field and Greasy, and then looks down from above upon a world that is flowery for as far as it can see, perhaps to Los Angeles. I doubt that Stepp would have accepted this interpretation, and not just because of envisioning Los Angeles. True, the nineteenth-century Pimas knew about California, which they called *Mondlai*, after the Spanish Monterey. Monterey, not Los Angeles, was California to them. But the greater reason for his rejecting the interpretation is that in principle the "I" cannot be the sun, but must be an Ant-person. At most it could be an Ant-person who acts like the sun.

But I think that Stepp would have accepted the following: first, a reading of the Salt River community as the location of song 1 gives the first four songs a nearly perfect sunlike westward itinerary;[50] second, the aerial view of song 4 implies the sun; third, the first songs in a singing generally mention the sun's westward descent (Oriole 2 is a good example); and fourth, a reading of "I, the Sun" would supply that missing element to this singing. Therefore, although he would deny that the "I" is the sun, he should assent that it *sounds* like it is.[51]

SONGS 5–8, THE TRAVELING MAN

The next four[52] songs do away with the solar "I." The directional path is no longer westward. Instead, there is a northern deviation and then a return to the west path. Also, the perspective is no longer aerial. Now the "I" is earthbound and seems to be a man.

Of course the "I" of the first four songs also has earthly experiences, especially in songs 2 and 3. We will consider those experiences and those of the current "I's" after dealing with the geography of 5–8. As was just noted, the mountains named in songs 5–8 do not lie in a westward line with those in 2 and 3. Broad Mountain, called Estrella by Whites, the next prominence west of Greasy, is on that line and is the subject of 7 and

[50] Actually the sing's itinerary is southwestward, not due west. But in the *winter* the sun as seen from Paul's house sets at the west end of Greasy Mountain.

[51] Returning to the literal interpretation of "follow," if one actually followed the tips of the shadows of fixed objects caused by a sunset, one would travel east and not west. They stretch eastward at sunset and shrink eastward at sunrise. But suppose that "night" refers to the dark sky instead of to earth surface shadows. That darkness advances westward both at sunset and dawn. No matter. As I read it, this sequence refers to the bright, west-moving sun and not to shadows.

[52] Pima singers tend, by no means rigorously, to group things in fours. Thus, when one suspects a bit of art through a sequence, as with the above solar sequence, and when the sequence is fourfold, the fourness is a clue that the art may be there.

8.[53] But song 5's Iron Mountain is north of Greasy at the north fringe of Phoenix according to Paul.[54] And not having heard of Woman Bringer Mountain, we can't place it; but assuredly it is not on the main westward line.

By 7 and 8, the songs have proceeded a mere twenty miles west of Stepp's community. In the remaining twenty-three songs only one more place is surely identified—another mountain, called Long Red (Camelback to whites), ten miles north of Greasy. It figures in song 12, which is to say that all of the surely identifiable places are mountains, are confined to the first half of the sing, and are in sight from Stepp's village.

But there are also unidentified places. Woman Bringer Mountain, mentioned above, and Long Mountain in song 10; two "waters" (could be ponds) called Marsh and Shining in 21 and 22; a "land" called Cane in 30; and some additional more vaguely specified land places: far land in 11 and 25, world's edge in 13, earth in 31, eastern inner [land] in 16, below the east [land] in 20, and land below [=underworld] in 27. "Land," "world," and "earth" are all translations of the same word, *jewed*, which can also mean "soil" or "plain" (as opposed to mountain or hill). We have, then, a geography of mountain, water, and plain. A complete survey of possible settings for sung actions would include "sky" (*da:m ka:cim*, literally "above lying"), "ocean" (*ka:cim su:dagi*, "lying water"), and "river" (*akimel*, literally "wash [water-channel] running"), although no songs in this set mention them.[55]

More permanent than the waters and more bounded than the lands, the mountains lend themselves to geographical pinpointing. From any

---

[53] The Gila River flows through the gap between Greasy and Broad. The Gila and Salt Rivers join at the north tip of Broad (the orientation of which is north-south in contrast to Greasy, which lies east-to-west.)

[54] It is just to the north of Camelback Mountain, according to him. Vincent Joseph, who sang this as an Oriole song, locates the mountain farther north, between the Verde River and the present town of Payson. We should defer to Paul because the mountain he calls "Iron" is visible from his house. To Joseph in the next valley to the south, the mountain was remote and invisible.

[55] The old Pimas and Papagos did not seem to view their rivers as wholes—did not conceive of them as single entities or individuals from source to outlet. Consistent with that, the Pimas' great river, the Gila, is simply called "river." It does not have an individualized name. Paul, however, calls it "Old-man River," *Keli Akimel*. Pima-Papagos have individual names for the American-named Verde (Spanish for "green"), Colorado (Sp. for "red") and Salt Rivers. They call them the "Green" (*Cehedagi*), "Red" (*Wegi*), and "Salt" (*On*) Rivers, respectively. There are songs about the first two, but I have never heard a song name the Salt. Neither has Paul. Of course since the Gila has no individualized name, there are no songs about it. Nor, I must say, are there many songs that simply say "river" (or "River"). The River People, as the Pimas are called (*Akimel O'odham*), are more mountain and land singers than river singers.

point with a broad vista in the Pima-Papago region one can see a good twenty-five discontinuous mountains silhouetted like islands or ships, some in front of others. They do not form long ranges but have flat land around and between them. A large mountain is ten miles long, a small one a mile (lesser than mountains are "hills," *kakwulk*). They are stony and steep, and only the largest are topped with trees. Until the whites, no one lived on the tops or steep sides.

All of the mountains in these songs and most mountains in the Pima-Papago record are named for how they appear, that is, for color, shape, or material.[56] A small minority of the names are explained in myths. Thus, the Greasy in 3 is named for grease that dripped from a cremated god's heart.[57] Another mountain, not present in our songs, is "Rock Raw," named for a the bloody smell on the rocks at the base of a cliff where an eagle ate humans that he had captured. Mountains do not bear the names of Pima persons or gods.

It is difficult to know whether a song means *a* red mountain or *the* Red Mountain, that is, whether a phrase is a fleeting description or a proper name. Every Pima-Papago community probably has a locally named Red Mountain nearby. The naming is descriptive, not monumental. Monumentalism does enter, however, in the *sequence* of names, as we have seen in songs 1–8. There is just one sequence in the Pima-Papago world that starts with a village and then proceeds westward past Deadfield and Greasy to Broad. The village can only be Salt River (called *Su:dk*, "Full," in Pima), and the sequence is monumental, that is, a unique combination, a signature, for Salt River.[58]

If the first eight songs are a puzzle whose solution is Salt River, what

---

[56] I count Dead-field as an appearance name, the appearance of something at the base of the mountain.

[57] The myth is acknowledged by Pima-Papagos to be Maricopa. Their name "Greasy" is in deference to the Maricopas' sense of the ancient past. (The Maricopas use their own quite unrelated word for "Greasy" to name the mountain). From a Yuma and Mojave myth comes the various tribes' names for the mountain by Tucson that whites call "Mount Lemon." The tribes call it "Frog," because a Frog person who killed the god retired to this place. To name a mountain after a mythic Frog person would be un-Pima in my opinion, unless the mountain looked like a frog. See Spier, 1933:345–52 and Russell, 1908:215–17 for the Maricopa and Pima versions of this story.

[58] A possible definition of "monument," is "a venerable uniqueness." Note that many American towns have monuments in the form of statues of mythic or historic heroes. If the hero is local, this is a monument to the town. If the hero is national, the monument is to the nation and was accepted as such by the town. It is not the town that is venerated, but the nation. Singular national monuments such as the U.S. Park Service administers are like our sing's mountain sequence in that they enshrine something unique, but the nation claims them rather than the local community.

do they tell us about the identity of the "I's"? I have said that the hint of the sun in 1–4 gives way to a human hero in the present group, 5–8. The "I" is probably a male in the present group, but this is not always the case in the sing as a whole. The present group is interestingly male, but the fact that some later songs are not affirms that the "I's" are not a unity. The great majority of I's are not identified as to gender. None is explicitly male, but in two songs (19 and 24) the I's are expressly female. Of the people encountered (I exclude the animals or animal-persons), the gender of two is not stated (songs 24 and 25). Four are male (7, 19, 20, and 23)[59] and three are female (2, 18, and 29).

I think that most Pimas would imagine the characters with unspecified genders as male, in other words, male is the assumed or "unmarked" gender of dream song characters. We will now apply that assumption to songs 2 and 3. In 2 the "I" has its head pelted with the flowers worn as crowns by women who live in Dead-field mountain, a great narrative tumbling of concrete images for such a short song. The flowers, "earth flowers," are famous among Pimas as an aphrodisiac. People say that men hide them on their persons, especially at dances, so that women will find the men to be irresistible. Paul and I have not heard of women using the plant for any reason, nor have we heard of men using it to attract men, either in dream songs or in reported real experience. And while we are certain that men actually use earth flowers, we do not know if all earth flowers are the same botanical thing. No such flower has ever been given to whites for identification, and Pimas are secretive with each other about their specimens.

As Paul tells it, earth flowers do not raise women's desire for men, but rather make men homosexual. He knows of the other aspect as well, but chooses to emphasize this side effect, so to speak:

I think the sing begins with this mountain sequence rather than songs 15–31 for two reasons. First, the same sequence, minus song 1, occurs in Stepp's other sing. It is the single long sequence held in common between the two performances. And I believe that the sequence was retained because it monumentalizes Salt River; it was retained for identity giving or patriotic reasons. It also fulfills the sing opening conventions. Admittedly it does so better in our sing than in the other one because the other lacks song 1 on songs starting. It is possible that Stepp actually sang that song the other time, but it wasn't recorded. Even if not, 2–8 give a convention-satisfying westward journey. The final reason why I think the sings started with these songs is that Vincent Joseph started his Oriole songs with a westward tending mountain sequence that monumentalizes the home village of the man from whom he learned the songs. That Joseph did so does not prove that Stepp did, but it shows a Pima precedent for doing so. Still, I imagine that it is possible that a case *could* be made for the inversion of the two blocks.

[59] Two of these are actually not male. The "brothers" of 20 and 23 are literally "younger-*siblings*." The Pima-Papago word (*sikol*) does not discriminate for gender. I translated the word as "brother" because "sibling" seems too stuffy.

Hema jijiwa i:ya mo om s-ma:cim mas hascu d hegai jewed hiosig. Am ñ-kakke matp hab masma wuwhañ mo g maliwa:na.

Ñe:, ñ hab kaid mo pi hab sa'i masma, mo obs ab hohodait ab amjed e-na:tok, wa'osigt amjed e-na:tok.

Hema ke:k g duag, amai ku:pa we:gaj, g O'odham b a'aga "S-weg."

Kutp hems heg ab hab cu'ig, nañ pi am ha-kakke hegam mat am hihhim, ñ am a kakke mat i i dada, "Mas hebai oiyupahim?"

Am b ep kaij mats jewed hiosig behiyo. Ñ am a kakke mas has masma u'u hegai jewed hiosig.

Am ñ-a:gid mas g wainom ku:gaj o hukbiñ hegai matp ag dada, hab ab cu'ig g ab hegai hohodai. Am ba:phim, to:la viw kostalc ed o uapa.

Ñe:, k am je:ñ, Hekid am o s-je:jnam hegai, k am o uac, k am o i a wuwhas go:k hegam e-wui'i. Sa al ba'ic i ge'eda mam g o'oiya, am o ce:hu am e-uac ed, k am o je:j.

Ñe:, k am o ge s-ap u:w, ñe:, k abs hab-a g kekel ep pi sa'i ho'ihid hegai, nats pi has atp cu'ig. Has atp e-wua, ha-uwikwad hegai, mat hema am o je:ñid.

Atp hiwa hab e-wua ha'ic i:dam, sam cekcid am hu e-wo:lsig ed, hekaj am s-ap u:w. S hab-a i:dañ pi hedai sa'i hekaj hegai jewed hiosig. Am wud a gawul ha'icu am o hahawa ep hekaj, hegai malihua:na. Atp hascu e:p mo om hekaj bebbe g s-ta:hadkam ab amjed, atp hascu'i e:p.

Someone [Bahr] comes here who wants to know what is the earth flower. He asks if it comes out [grows] like marijuana. [I don't think I asked that.]

Look, I've heard that it's not like that, it's made in the rocks, in the dampness [on rocks] it's made.

There is a mountain standing, there behind the [Granite Reef] dam, the Pimas call it "Red."

Maybe it's there, because I asked those who went [for earth flowers], I asked those who arrived here [after going], "Where [were you] going around?"

They said they had gone to get earth flowers. Then I asked how they got the earth flowers.

They told me that with the knife tip they picked it as it sat there, as it was fastened to the rocks. They bagged it, in a bull tobacco [Bull Durham] bag they brought it.

Look, and they smoked it. Whenever they want to smoke it, they roll a cigarette [with tobacco], and take out two [pieces] from their getting [bagged earth flowers]. They [the pieces] are a little bigger than sand, they crumble them in their cigarette, and they smoke.

Look, and it smells nice, look, but the old timers didn't like it, because it is some way [bad]. It did something, it made them sissies [homosexuals], if someone smoked it.

Of course some of them [also] did, [that] they would keep it in their pocket, thus they smelled good [and might attract women]. But now nobody uses earth flowers. There is something else to use now, that marijuana. And there is something else [other drugs] to use to get pleasure from, or whatever else [besides pleasure].

Paul and I think song 2 tells a masculine dream, not a waking-world use of earth flowers. In reality men prey on women, but this song says the opposite. It would be a fortunate man in real life who had women pursue him with earth flowers. And since the song's women live at the first mountain from the Salt River community, the song is an advertisement for that village.

Song 3 repeats "flowers" and has song 1's word "manic" at the end. In my opinion, song 2 with its tumbling improbabilities is a paradigm of Pima dream manicness; the word itself is unnecessary. Song 3 then is a simplified variant of 2: it has no women, it has "green" flowers instead of the notorious earth ones[60], and the "I" is buried inside rather than pelted outside a mountain. Or one could say that the pelting is consummated in song 3 by tunnel-flowered manic envelopment, that is, by green sex.

> 2. Dead Field Mountain stands.
> Women inside run out,
> Earth flower crowned and
> Toward me run.
> Here run up to,
> My head, toss onto.

> 3. Greasy Mountain,
> Greasy Mountain stands.
> There inside,
> Green flowers
> Cover me.
> There inside
> Manic is.

Considering the actions in songs 5–8, that is, the songs that contain the departure from and return to the westward path, I will not comment on song 5, at Iron Mountain, save to say that it replaces the sex of the above pair with something like terror. The "I" who was welcomed with flower pelting and flower burial is now repelled by hooting, hostile winds. But 6 warrants notice as an example of how little substance a song can actually convey. The text concerns Woman Bringer Mountain, which, as stated before, neither Paul nor I have heard of. Nor can one

---

[60] The "green flower" of this song almost rhymes with the "earth flower" of song 2. "Green" is *cehedag* in spoken Pima, "earth" is *jewed*. The sung versions, however are not particularly close (although they could have been; the words are more similarly rendered in other songs): *ce ce no hoge* vs. *je we ne*; five syllables over five beats vs. three over four.

count the song among those with a woman in the scene; it only says that once there was a woman there. Here then is a text with an indefiniteness to rival song 2's effusiveness:

> And I away run,
> Away westward run.
> Woman Bringer Mountain stands:
> Run on top and something know.

The text avers to definite knowledge, and one hopes that the next song—the next postcard so to speak—will fulfill the implied promise by giving the knowledge. In fact the next *two* songs, both from Broad Mountain, back on the westward road, anchor the entire remainder of the sing. The place is an appropriate anchor. The mountain stands at the west end of today's Pima territorial sovereignty. The Salt River reservation does not reach it (their land ends before Dead-field), but the Gila River reservations does and, as stated in chapter one, the Salt River people came from there. The Salt and Gila Rivers join at Broad Mountain, which forms then the west backdrop of the modern Pima-owned world.

The two Broad Mountain songs affect the rest of the sing. Song 7 is about a lone man (I suppose) who receives songs in an almost tangible form from a lone man (explicit) who lives at the mountain. The text goes nicely with song 2 in that it replaces the women of that song with a man and raucus flowers in 2 with something suitable for use in public: songs. It is an answering back, an example of the principle enunciated earlier. Song 8 on the other hand is unprecedented and seems unfathomable. Its "I" nearly drowns, on one reading of the text, from water spurting from the mountain.

After song 8, the sing falls into two unequal portions. The songs from 9 to 28 form longish loose cycles about moods, cycles that confirm that drowning is indeed the problem in song 8. Then there are three final songs which return in their way to the issues raised in the Broad Mountain pair. These issues are the relationship of spirits to humans (in songs 29 and 30, raised in song 7); the originality of songs (in song 30, raised in 7); and apocalypse (in 31, raised, in effect, in 8). Song 31 has the same difficult last word, "enter," as 8. Thus, the sing will end resoundingly and philosophically.

> 7. Broad Mountain stands,
>   And I run to it.
>   There a man jumps out,
>   Songs he tells me.

What can I do and know?
There before me
Erected songs.
And I take them,
Use to serenade.

8. Broad Mountain stands.
There below, waters primed to spurt.
And I below there go,
On stick's end cling:
Stick glitters,
Then enter.

On hearing the songs, the "I" of text 7 cannot get or grasp them—the
Pima metaphor is the same as the English. The man from the mountain is
considerate. After first "telling" the songs,[61] he "stands" them in front of
the traveler so that the latter can "take" them to serenade with, presum-
ably back at home.

There is no thing that is Ant-like in this episode. The word used for
the man at the mountain is the normal word for "man," *o'odham*. Simi-
larly, the women at Dead-field were called by the normal "woman" word,
uwi.[62] They are not ants in any obvious way, but neither are they com-
pletely normal people since they live in mountains, have precious pos-
sessions (earth flowers), and toil not. Let us call them spirits.[63]

Now, the "I," our Ant-person, is also a spirit, one who came to a Pima in
a dream and, as I understand it, took the dreamer to these places. The Ant-
person sang the songs either in remembering, or at the time of, the events
that the songs describe. Whichever, the song is like the "thought balloons"
of characters in comic books. But rather than think the thoughts silently,
the "I" tells them in a song to the dreamer. The latter silently listens.

Thus there are three spirit persons in song 7, the man-spirit, the Ant-
spirit, and the dreamer. We really cannot say, or *see*, from the song what

---

[61] That is, singing them, vocalizing them. "Tell" (*a:g*) is the normal way to refer to the
performance of a song, no doubt because the songs have intelligible words. Band players
do not "tell" their songs, they 'hoot/toot/coo' (*kuhu*) them.

[62] *O'odham*, "man," also means "Pima-Papago-person." The way to say "Pima
woman" in Pima is *O'odham uwi*. In that case, the "*O'odham*" means "Pima-Papago," not
"man."

[63] As noted in the introduction, there is no unambiguous way to say "spirit" in Pima-
Papago. "Heart" (*i:bdag*) implies spirit (or equally soul) when it is used in reference to a
live Pima. Here however the reference is to a stranger, a mythic person who lives in a
mountain, has precious things, and may be immortal—a spirit as far as English semantics
and usage are concerned.

they look like—I imagine them all as blurred Pima-like men. What is clear is that in song 7 there are two acts of giving. The spirit-man gives many songs to the Ant-person, who gives one song, about the first giving, to the dreamer. Thus we can distinguish between repeated and original songs. The dreamer has surely repeated the one song that the Ant-person sang out; and the Ant-person expects to repeat the spirit-man's many songs. It is not clear whether the spirit-man originated *his* songs on the spot, nor whether the dreamer, being present at the event, will be able to remember and repeat those same many songs. Perhaps they evaded the dreamer's learning.

These same classes of actors are relevant to every song. First, although some songs do not have a spoken "I," they are still someone's words, namely an Ant-person's. The "I" may not be the *same* Ant-person throughout—it may be the Ant-person as sun, as traveling man, etc. But there is always some "I," explicitly or implicitly, an Ant-person. Second, although only a few songs have a spoken "you" (we have not discussed one yet), there is always an implicit addressee, a dreaming Pima. This dreamer goes wherever the Ant-person goes, like a silent flea. Third, although only a few songs have the Ant-person meet a human spirit, all songs have that person meet *something*, often an animal, but sometimes a cloud, wind, or mere stick. Human spirits as in song 7 are a special but important case of this encountered thing.

Song 8 introduces the spiritual matter of death.[64] When all is said and done, song and death will stand as the dominant themes of the sing. Song 8 does not *say* death, it merely implies death in its ambiguous last line. The succeeding songs in the middle part, songs 9–28, will say death.

Paul and I think that we understand the words of this song's last line, "Then enter," but we don't know who enters what: the "I" into the stick (the same word could be translated as "tree"), or into the water, or the stick into the water (presumably with the "I" still clinging), or the water into the earth. The middle two could be deadly (I assume that to enter water is to risk drowning), the first and last would merely be picturesque.[65]

Song 8 doesn't resolve the ambiguity or establish a death, but the next one does—from wind, however, not water:

---

[64] It seems that spirits can die. If all "I"s are spirits, as I suppose, then some spirits die; or at least they say that they are dead. There are many examples below.

[65] Pimas do not dread swimming or wading above all things; their culture does not make them markedly or unusually hydrophobic. Like whites, they merely allow that unwanted entries into floods may result in drowning. That is the hint that I find in this song. There is a drowning song in the Oriole sing (number 30) and the mythology has a flood myth (Bahr et al., 1994:67–74).

9. Bitter wind,
       Here run up and
       Away far
       Take me.
       Poorly treat me,
       My heart separated dies.

THE LAST THREE SONGS

Before proceeding, I want to discuss the end of the sing, the last three
songs. They are

29. You start the songs,
        And you start the songs.
        Suddenly whore woman
        Suddenly runs up,
        Everything saying.
        And you, of Ant
        Songs, many unwrap.
        All around me,
        People akimbo.

30. Away off the wind runs and
        Away off far takes me.
        To the Cane Land
        Surface takes me,
        Where wind runs hooting,
        Where songs are really known.

31. Do you hear me?
        Do you hear me?
        All earth sounding,
        On top, circles stomped.
        On top, eagle down puffs,
        Cloud enter.

In song 29 Stepp shows his originality in sequencing by putting a text
about starting at what I take to be the end of the sing.[66] Interestingly, this

---

[66] If the two sides of the tape had been performed in the reverse of the order that I
suppose, this song would come in the middle of the sing. The performance would have
started with the present song 15 and proceeded through "moods" (see below) until

is the only song that explicitly mentions ants—not Ant-persons, how-ever, but Ant songs.[67] Finally, the drama in this story is the arrival of whores who, if the translation "akimbo" is correct,[68] cause a great agita-tion.

These observations make sense if we interpret the place as Salt River village, the "you" as the Pima dreamer, the people and whore (perhaps) as Pimas, and the "I," as usual, as an Ant-person. The village, people, whore, and Ant-person are seen in a dream in which the dreamer also sees himself, that is, his future self, himself after mastering the Ant songs and being ready to use them. "You will start, a whore will come," the Ant-person prophesies.

In favor of this interpretation is that the sing starts with a scene of songs being sung—not started, but being sung—at Salt River. Now here at the end there is a statement about starting. This seems perverse except that we are now at the start of *Ant* songs. No type of song is named in song 1. Thus song 29 seems to say, "You have heard twenty-eight Ant songs, now good luck as a singer." To me the inclusion of the whore nei-ther adds to nor detracts from this interpretation, save for the minor fact that Dead-field is the first mountain below Salt River and in song 2 its women act like whores.

Considering the "you" of song 29, I said earlier that there are three classes of things in any song: a dreaming Pima "you," an Ant-person "I," and something, sometimes a spirit, encountered by the Ant-person. In my opinion the present song merges the "you" and the encountered thing, so that the flea-like dreaming "you" witnesses its own future self, as with Dickens's Ghost of Christmas Future in "A Christmas Carol." I would like to say that it is well known that Pimas dream of their own fu-ture selves, but I cannot say that. I can say that they are a luck-conscious,

---

reaching this text and its companions (30 and 31). Then would come the series 1–14, the westward and some others. While I can see a reason for placing this song at the end, I can-not see a point for having it in the middle. Moreover, I cannot see the mood sequence from 15 to 29 as a good first half for a sing, and neither can I see that sequence as more than a categorial medley on moods, mostly morbid ones.

[67] There are just two songs whose "I's" make me think of Ants. These are songs 8 and 15, 8 for its image of something (small, one supposes) sticking to a twig in a flood (one sees ants fleeing water in that fashion), and 15 for its expressions, "flatly run" (*komal med*) and "earth cover" (*jewed ce:mo'o*). To me these suggest ants spreading over the world. They do so if one *thinks* that the song has to do with ants. Paul is skeptical about this in-terpretation. Still, I hold that there must be something antish to Ant songs.

[68] The Pima is *a'ai mugwa. A'ai* means "back-and-forth," "to-and-fro" (Saxton, Sax-ton, and Enos, 1983:3, under "*aigo*"). *Mugwa* means "undulate" (*Ibid.*, p. 43, spelled "*mugew*" and placed under "*muda*", "tassel"; but also, I think, "to wave" or "to waver." The last translation is used for the same word in Oriole song 1.

power-conscious, dream-prone people. Thus, dreaming one's future would interest them, and here is a likely instance of it.

Is there an alternative interpretation of the identities of the "you"? The "you" might just be *some* spirit whom the Ant-person and dreamer see, analogous to the song giving spirit of text 7. This is to say that not all "you's" are Pima dreamers. This "you" would be an independent denizen of spirit land. There are surely diverse *kinds* of "you's" in the songs: "you" as a woman's husband (in song 19), as someone's brother (actually sibling, male or female, in song 23), and as a singing partner (in song 25). I don't think that all of those "you's" are a *single* dreamer.[69] Thus, if all "you's" are Pima dreamers, which is what I believe, then these thirty-one songs were dreamed by more than one Pima—which I also believe. And, bowed but not broken, I still believe that the "you" of song 29 sees a future of singing.

Song 30 shifts the scene from a village to what seems to be a wilderness place, Cane Land. A wind carries the Ant-person and dreamer to this place where songs are "really known." One can interpret this phrase to mean "accurately repeated, well learned" but I prefer the referential meaning, "accurately descriptive of what *is*." To really know in this sense is not just to repeat accurately, but to speak the truth about something.

I would say that the holy goal of all speech is to speak accurately about something, to describe. It is a goal unattainable in social dance sings, where one is never sure from one text to the next who is doing what to whom where. Cane Land in this song is a paradise where the goal is attained—on my reading of "really known." The "I," presumably an Ant-person, arrives there on hooting wind, and behind the din hears songs saying what we would wish them to, the real truth. We (Bahr and Paul) haven't heard of Cane Land. It is not an actual village.[70] We conclude it is a spirit-peoples' place.

Although song 30 lacks a "you," song 31 has one again. And now the

---

[69] If the Ant-persons and the "you's" were unitary characters, the "you" would be married to his Ant-person sister, therefore presumably not a Pima. But the Ant-persons are certainly not unitary, therefore the you-as-wife is not necessarily the same as the you-as-sibling. It is conceivable that the you-as-sibling and you-as-singing-partner are the same, which implies either that the "you" is an Ant-person, or that the Ant-person is a deceased Pima. (It is generally said that owls and Owl-persons are deceased persons, and they teach songs to Pimas. I would not exclude the possibility that a deceased person could come back as an owl.) It is not a well defined puzzle.

[70] There could be a village named "Cane." Villages are named the likes of "Burnt Seeds," "Marsh," "Cottonwoods," etc. We do not know of a village named "Cane." When speaking of actual villages in songs, one often refers to the "land" of that village: "Burnt Seeds Land," etc.

topic shifts from singing to dancing. The word "stomp" tells us that so-
cial dancing is taking place. "Stomp" (*cu:dk*) is the normal Pima word for
"to social-dance."[71] If we take the text literally, the dance ground is now
the whole world. This is a grand vision. The "you" dreamer, having been
shown his future at Salt River, and then wisked to a place of truth-telling
songs, is now present at the great final cosmic dance. "Hear me now,"
roars the Ant-person as the world rumbles with stomping, its surface
marked with a path made by humanity's circling feet.

After that glory comes a tender end with two lines which resemble
but do not duplicate the last lines of the baffling song 8:

8....	31....
Stick glitters,	On top, eagle down puffs,
Then enter.	Cloud enter.

In the sung Pima the penultimate lines of the two songs have eight and
twelve syllables respectively, and the last lines have eight and ten. These
are significant differences—the two texts are not variants of the same
metrical song. Nor are their grammatical architectures identical. Finally,
there are the *ambiguities*. The question in song 8 is whether the "I" enters
the water. In song 31 I don't think that the "I" is a participant. This song's
ambiguity is whether it is eagle down or a wind puff from the down that
enters the cloud; or whether a cloud enters the down or the puff. I be-
lieve that there is no way to know which. We are not meant to resolve the
ambiguity, but simply to be surprised by the quietness of this last, un-
solvable image, with which the song and the sing end.

The Moods

The last portion of the sing considered here, the long middle, has a song
about sunset halfway through:

> 20. Sun sets,
>   And we there run.
>   Below the east are songs,
>   Manic telling.
>   Oh-oh, younger brother,
>   Songs of your telling.

---

[71] There is no general word for "dance." Types of dances are named for the nature of
the dancers' movements "kick," "run-in-the-middle," "circle," "straight," etc. (These are
the main ones).

There is no mention of sunset either at the beginning or end of the sing. By convention this song should have been at the beginning.[72] In my opinion, the present beginning with its hint of the Ant-person as sun takes the place of an overt sunset song; and furthermore, the message of this text would clash with the happy mood set in the present beginning. This song's "I" is distracted from the east, while songs 1–4 have a steady westward movement that ends with the hero looking upon flowers still farther westward. The "east" of song 20 would be out of place there. Moreover, the expression "below the east" refers to the Pima land of the dead. Death is absent from the first four songs, is barely hinted at in the fifth (Iron Mountain), and is hinted more strongly in the eighth (Broad Mountain).

Death dominates the sing's middle part where this song fits and belongs, dividing the middle into the following two cycles:

> (Water, song 8, the first "enter"),
> Death (9, 10),
> Dizziness (11–19),
> The sunset song (20),
> Water (21,22),
> Death (23–27),
> Dizziness (28)
> (and Whore, song 29, the beginning of the final part).

This scheme raises three questions. First, how accurate is it? Second, if it is precise, why are death and dizziness paired? Last, why is dizziness more prominent before the sunset song and death more prominent after?

Regarding precision, of the seven songs classified under death, five openly or implicitly say "I'm dead." Of those, one is not obvious. This is song 23 with its "Wind in me explodes and leaps out." The statement signifies death according to Paul who adds that the song became prophetic. It was the favorite of a man he knew who died in a way that the song seemed to foretell. The man had learned the song at dances. Consciously or not, Paul implies, the man saw his future in the story.

Note that the man did not personally experience the story as I hold was the case with the "you" of song 29. Moreover, the man who liked the present song saw himself as the "I," not the "you." Here is the text:

---

[72] If the tape sides were performed in the reverse order of how I have them, this text would be the sixth of the sing, somewhat close to the beginning. One could try to make a case for the preceding songs, 15–19, as a preamble to it. To my mind the prospects for such a case are not good; a sing thus executed would not be as satisfying as the one presented here.

23. Oh-oh, my younger brother,
    Oh-oh, my younger brother,
    Here I leave you
    And far go.
    Wind in me ex-
    plodes and leaps out.
    Here I leave you,
    Eastward running.

Thus there are two kinds of song prophecy, the one that I outlined for song 29, where a dreamer is told in direct address what his or her future will be (the dreamer is "you"), and this kind where a waking person identifies with another person's story (a waking person feels like the "I"). The first requires a spiritual or divine experience, which is something that people are reluctant to report or lay claim to. Still, such experience is implicit in the "yous" of all songs, and I think it was put to use in song 29. The second kind of prophecy, that of song 23, does not involve the divine. In this case one assimilates to or identifies with what an Ant-person said, one takes the Ant-person story as an omen. Note that the two kinds of prophecy are not mutually exclusive. The first belongs to the dreamed "birth" of a song, when the human must be a "you." The second pertains to a song after it has become established in a human community, after the details of its dreamed origin have been lost (or perhaps were not publically expressed in the first place). At this time anyone can identify with any song character.[73]

Another song, 25, implies the death of the "you":

25. Oh-oh, my singing partner,
    Oh-oh, my singing partner,
    Nowhere I see you.
    Far off land,
    Running to it,
    Nowhere I see you.

To Paul and me, this is an "I" mourning an unfindable "you." (The singing partner, Pima *ma:kig*, means a person who teaches songs to one.[74])

---

[73] The "you" of song 23 could be interpreted as the person of the original Pima dreamer. If so, what was revealed was the death of the Ant-person "I."

[74] Sometimes Paul pronounces this word as *ma:kaj*, as in ñ-*ma:kaj*, "my-singing-partner-leader." I think that it is related to *ma:k*, "to give." The way that I write it, as *ma:kig*, equates it with a word that other Pimas interpret as "gift."

I don't think that Stepp intended for songs 23 and 25 to be taken as pieces of one story in which the "I" sang of its death and then, having died, mourned for the death of his or her audience. The series is a medley *on* death, not a story of *some* deaths; a miscellany, not a sequential argument. If so, it does not matter which individual song comes first and which second, it only matters which category or *classification* (about death or dizziness) comes first. Or so I think—an interim judgement. I find no significance in the sequence of these individual songs, but someone may find it.

Nor is my classification perfect. One song under the alleged death classification does not seem to be about death:

> 26. Gray helper,
>   Here to our song run up and
>   Nicely sounding dance.
>   Swishingly dance,
>   Nicely sounding away go.

I think that Stepp simply wanted to sing this song about a coyote attending a dance. He did not want it at the beginning or end, even though there are other songs there about dances. Those songs fit in a way that I have shown, and this song would not fit. He put it here where the control is lax.

The dizziness classification has a similar problem of fit. First, dizziness is to me, and I think to the Pimas, the experience of an inability to focus, to stand still, to stand straight, and to walk straight. It is the state in which one fails the screening for a sobriety test, although Pimas, like whites, also hold that dizziness may be caused by factors other than taking intoxicants.

Generally speaking, "dizzy" is incompatible with the earlier discussed "manic." Dizzy people cannot concentrate, manic people concentrate excessively. Thus, the characters in these songs who are called dizzy are not manic, and vice versa. Specifically, people over-bent on singing or on learning songs are manic, and those over-bent on dancing or going with the flow are dizzy.

So I propose: of the ten songs classified as dizzy (nine before the sunset song), only two have the word "dizzy" (songs 18 and 27), although one more (song 14) has the equivalent word "drunk"[75] and others have the idea. "Dizzy" does occur in one song outside the designated se-

---

[75] All drunks are dizzy but not all dizzies are drunk.

quences, the death song 10. This is agreeable because the dizzy sequence
begins with the next song. There are no instances of "manic" in the dizzy
sequences or anywhere in the middle part of the sing, and none of
"dizzy" in the beginning and end parts.

The case for a precise or bounded set of dizzy songs depends on the
prevalence of the word or idea in the nine pre-sunset songs (11 to 19), for
after the sunset the dizziness slot is filled by a single song, 28, with the
word. Song 14 with its "drunk" and 18 with its "dizzy" are secure, and 12,
15, and 19 have the idea: 12 because fluttering butterflies represent dizzi-
ness (people say this), 15 on the strength of "back and forth dodging,"
and song 19 because the whore who abandons her husband asks in the
dark "What will I do and know."[76] That makes a weak five out of nine.

Straining for one of two more passages suggestive of dizziness will
not help. The source of the interference is a different theme that is lodged
in the alleged dizzy sequence. This theme is landscape—nature pictures.
Dizziness is a state of mind, and yet one notes that a good many songs are
not psychological portraits. Rather they tell what a delighted "I" sees, and
the sight is a lovely bit of nature, a tableau with no dizziness. Thus,
within this block of nine songs I designated as "dizzy" there are

> 13. Gray killdeer bird,
>   Away world's edge run:
>   So songlike hooting,
>   Land striding,
>   Wings spreading.

> 17. Many birds fly,
>   Many birds fly.
>   At spread sky's front flying,
>   Nicely cooing, primed to run.

And outside the block there is

> 21. Shining Water lies,
>   Shining Water lies.
>   Within mudhen wanders,
>   Come and look:
>   Handsome floating!

---

[76] The song seeker in text 7 asked the same question, and yet I claim that people bent
on song learning are manic, not dizzy. But the seeker in 7 asked the question while *unable*
to learn the songs, before the spirit man stood them up for him.

Now, broadly speaking, all the songs in this study are about nature. Thus Salt River village is identified by its configuration of mountains, not by its human-made skyline. The Pimas lived nested in nature. But the above songs are about nothing *but* nature. They either lack an "I" or, in a minority of songs, the "I" directs attention to the natural scene. Usually the "I" intrudes in the scene, and the intruder usually speaks of human, therefore social, things: how to learn songs to use at a dance, what to think about death, how to speak truly. This is probably because the songs are addressed to a human "you" whose home is a village, that is, whose home is society.

On balance, it is remarkable how much of this ostensive nature poetry, this poetry set in natural landscapes, is about social relations. Like the city people who take nature walks primarily to meet other humans, or Throat-black the whore who crossed nature primarily to take up with new husbands, the "I's" of the songs are not "true" hermits, that is, they are not completely, contentedly absorbed in their natural surroundings. They long for villagers if not villages. Why else, we may ask, would they sing their hearts out to dreaming humans?

My second question was, why are death and dizziness paired? In other words, why those two moods? My answer is the one that Claude Levi-Strauss gave to the question of *how* the mind builds things when its ambition is high and its materials are few. He named the practice *bricolage*, which roughly speaking means "recycling," "continual reassembly" (1966:16–36). Stepp had a finite number of Ant songs, perhaps forty, perhaps a hundred.[77] He probably sang about thirty in each performance; he recycled. As I will argue, in recycling he found one song, 8, to serve both as the end of one part and the beginning of the next.

Of the three parts of the sing we are studying, only the first, interpreted as monumentalism, was sung in virtually the same way in both of Stepp's recorded performances. The other parts, middle and end, are variables. Now, the explanation of the moods of this sing is that the fixed monumental part ends with a song that implies but does not openly state "death." The song's immediate sequels make explicit that implication. Thus the first part calls for the passage into the death mood, not in its essential subject matter of westward monumentalism but by the accident

---

[77] He sang thirty-seven different ones in two sings. Vincent Joseph sang fifty-six in his third recording of Oriole songs, and those were all that he had command of at that time. His teacher, Blaine Pablo, sang a total of sixty-eight Oriole songs for recording, never all of them on the same occasion. Paul Manuel, a Swallow singer, knew hundreds of that kind of song (Bahr, 1986).

that the last song of the fixed part hints "death." (In favor of this expla-
nation, I note that the other Stepp sing has the same pair of death songs
after the Broad Mountain text. Their order is reversed, but the pair is
there. It is as if Stepp "knew" that song 8 had a dual purpose, for west
journeying and for death.)

The dizziness sequences in this sing are true to their namesake. They
drift. In reality this classification is a catchall. I call the long run of obvi-
ously non-death songs of the middle part "dizzy" simply because those
songs express that idea more frequently than any other.

Now, there would be less warrant for that classification if the middle
part were not divided by the sunset song into the two relatively well de-
fined death sequences.[78] The other Stepp sing is not so divided. Because
it lacks the middle sunset song and the long subsequent death sequence,
then by the logic followed here, one should call the entire middle of that
sing "dizzy." But that would be a feeble analysis. I consider the block
classification "dizziness" acceptable for this sing, but not for the other.
Nor do I know what *would* be acceptable there.

To recapitulate the argument for this sing, westward monumentality,
plus the accident of the hint of death in song 8, prompts a death mood,
the clear handling of which frames a catchall group of songs dominated
by dizziness.

But why is dizziness the more prominent before the sunset and death the
more prominent after? It seems that all social dance sings have some songs
about dizziness. Such songs are a hallmark of the genre as David Kozak
(1992) and Bahr (1986) have written.[79] The death songs on the other hand
are special to this sing. Song 8 needed a brief explicit sequel on death to
make its meaning clear, but the long later sequence on death of this sing is
unique to it—Stepp's other performance lacks such a sequence. The last
question therefore is why Stepp put the hallmark dizziness early and saved
the unique death run until later? I think he did so to make a finale, to save
this most interesting category for the concluding part of the sing.

CONCLUSION

I said in the introduction that we should not think of this Ant sing or the
Oriole sing that follows as the best that the singers or this people could pro-

---

[78] Also, the two water songs, 21 and 22, between the sunset and the long run on
death, repeat the water and death association of song 8.
[79] They wrote about Swallow songs, but they were meant to apply more broadly. The
Ant songs supply breadth.

duce. We should think of them as good works that happened to be recorded.
A sufficient reason for this caution is that I lack experience in sing criticism.
Judgments of excellence require standards that require experience.

Not knowing Stepp, at first not even knowing which side of his tape
to begin with (it is better with Joseph), I don't know his sing well. The
two matters of substance in it that I am confident of are the westward
itinerary and the relation between that itinerary's last two songs and the
last three of the sing. Those were discoveries. Through them I thought I
knew Stepp.

They are the strong parts of the commentary. The section just com-
pleted is weak, that is, inattentive to every detail and forced into block
classifications. Perhaps there is more to this middle part than I have said.
With that possibility in mind, I want to state an additional thought on
the final run of death songs. As was already said, this run is unusual for
its size and subject—unusual in my experience of sings (about six
singers, a few dozen sings[80]). Song 27 seems to be particularly overt and
almost taunting on the subject:

> 27. I'm sick,
>   I'm sick,
>   Land below wandering.
>   In it my flower,
>   Already dead.
>   Oh-oh, oh-oh,
>   I'm sick,
>   East toward
>   I run.

Perhaps the "flowers" mean songs. There is precedent for this reading in
the criticism of neighboring peoples' songs (Evers and Molina, 1987;
Hill, 1992), and one finds the flower-song equation in other Pima and
Papago texts.[81] The "I" in song 27, then, could be ailing because his or
her songs are dying from lack of use.

---

[80] "Sings" as opposed to practice sessions. I attended about a hundred practice ses-
sions with the Swallow song singer Paul Manuel.

[81] For example,

> Basket-on face-down I lie and sing,
> Basket-on face-down I lie and sing.
> Swallow-with, shifting hips,
> This, my body, flowers.

This is a Swallow social dancing song. The "basket" refers to the resonator on which the
"I" scrapes a stick while singing, the same kind of accompaniment as is referred to in the

That reading would tie the death run (songs 23–27) to the last songs of the sing, and the song about Coyote dancing would not be such an orphan. Furthermore, there is a song about the extinction of singing in the Oriole performance (song 31). But while I favor this reading for the extra measure of integration that it affords and the solicitous thoughts on singing that it entails, I can't honestly say that it was Stepp's intended meaning. That he cryptically referred to his village at the start seems clear enough, and also that he was complexly skeptical about the truth of songs at the end. But I am unsure that he meant us to take song 27 as a plea, or a taunt, for the art.

Ant songs. The singing "I" flowers with the entire body, like the earth sprouting blossoms (Giff, 1980:136).

PART TWO

Oriole Songs

CHAPTER FIVE

Oriole Lessons

Every important thing that was said about the Ant songs holds for Oriole songs also. The Ant-persons are like Oriole-persons; Stepp was similar to Vincent Joseph, the singer of these songs; and the poetic and musical and dancing culture on the Gila River reservation, where the songs were recorded, was like that at Salt River. There are, however, some improvements in the documentation of this sing. Joseph was recorded three times in the early 1980s as he polished and fleshed out a large new stock of Oriole songs. More importantly, in the recording transcribed here he not only sang the songs but also stated their words in quiet ordinary language. As was noted in chapter two, on the Ant songs, some singers dislike reducing their texts to plain Pima, possibly because they are not sure what some sung phrases mean. But to Joseph a plain Pima rendition was the test of knowing a song. One does not truly know one, he thought, until each syllable can be explained as retained, transformed, or lost in a plain language "translation." I imagine that Stepp would have agreed and could have stated the Ant songs in ordinary language, but he was not asked to do so when the unknown recorder taped him. To have done so would have put him in the role of a teacher. Not all singers enjoy this, nor do all audiences request or require it. Joseph seemed to enjoy it, and not just with me. Several Pimas learned songs from him, probably better than I did.

Because he was building his repertory,[82] and perhaps because as a teacher he liked definiteness, Joseph mentally filed every Oriole song that he knew into a provisionally fixed but always revisable set of subcategories. Thus he was constantly primed to sing his entire repertory. Each of the three times he was recorded he did so. The sings were little changed in sequence, but they increased from forty-five to forty-seven to fifty-six items.

---

[82] See the next section on the assembling of his Oriole collection. In addition to those, he also knew at least twenty Blackbird, some Swallow, some other kinds of social dancing, and some myth telling and curing songs.

Vincent Joseph's traditional Christmas party for the neighborhood.

Vincent Joseph in middle age.

Stepp took a different approach in his two recorded sings. He included some items in each that he withheld from the other, and he was freer than Joseph in changing the order of the songs he retained. He was more the improvisor, and Joseph more the builder. This could have been because of his temperament, or because he had known the Ant songs longer than Joseph knew the Orioles, or because of differences in the audience. I asked Joseph to sing all of his songs, but Stepp's recorder probably did not do so.

Joseph's mental filing system is similar to the parts of Stepp's sing, which were: the beginning, comprising eight songs with a Salt-River-specific westward journey; a long and loosely organized middle part of twenty songs with two cycles of water, death, and dizziness; and a short end part on the truth of songs and apocalypse, a play on the conventional subject matter of songs ending, sunrise, and eastward journeying.

Joseph has those divisions, but they are somewhat differently fleshed out. The most important difference is that he placed a strict and not too imaginative discipline on the equivalent of Stepp's loose middle. Stepp's water, death, and dizziness give way to Joseph's birds, cataclysms, medicine men, and whores, in that order. In the Joseph sing presented here, the middle section occupies twenty-two of the total forty-seven songs, which is to say that Joseph has more songs in the equivalents of Stepp's beginning or end. The addition actually is to the beginning, where he has twenty-two songs to Stepp's eight. The additional songs give a longer westward journey than in Stepp, and one that originates at a Gila River village rather than at Stepp's Salt River village. Joseph's end part is as brief as Stepp's (three songs), and like Stepp's, it is a philosophical reflection on songs. In sum, and notwithstanding that Stepp improvised where Joseph built, there is an uncanny thematic similarity between the two sings.

On my interpretation, both singers dedicated their finest poetic efforts to relating the issues of death and song dreaming. I doubt that they knew each other and doubt that many Pima singers of the time took the same tack. This was a coincidence, then, but an appropriate one. It was a swan song for Pima singing as these men knew it. In good sequential improvisation, each expressed a fear that his art was dying.

They did so in 1972 (Stepp) and 1983 (Joseph). Their fear seemed well founded, in a qualified sense. Singing as it is described here, the singing of great varying sequences of thirty to forty songs, was not so much dying as turning into something else. The great sequences had been used for all night adult dances. In theory, the songs were made for those dances. The mythic persons meant for Pimas to dance to them.

Some songs mention dancing ("stomping") explicitly; and as we saw (and it is the same with the Orioles), all of the songs have an indirect connection, say a connection of mood, to those dance events.

By the time of the Stepp and Joseph recordings, which were recitals rather than dances, all-night dancing had given way to other nighttime activities. Social dance sings were now usually held in the day, for an hour or two. The same songs were used but in lesser number, usually from four to a dozen to twenty songs, and the dancers were specially costumed children and adolescents. This was a new kind of event. What had formerly lacked adult spectators, since every adult who came would join in the dancing, now had adults watching their children. With that change came a new attitude. Formerly the poetry satirized the slightly wicked moods of the dancers. Now the same songs were intended to evoke reverence for the things of the old Pimas: their mountains, birds, and flowers, and their children as symbolized by the costumed youth.[83]

I don't think that Stepp or Joseph sang for the new ceremonies. The new head singers are younger men who recruit and rehearse the dancers and arrange for the dancers' performance. Actually the new ceremonies have grown in the direction of the old Salt River Band, with special costumes, short daytime performances, a need for prior arrangements, and a distinction between performer and audience. All these align the new ceremonies with band marches and distinguish them from the old social dances. Stepp and Joseph, I think, let the younger generation develop this new use for the songs.

Actually, I am not aware that Ant songs have been used in the new way. I know of no current singer of them. Paul danced to them in the old way and learned many of them (as well as other kinds), but he never led a sing (selected the sequence) of them at an old or new style dance. The Oriole songs thrive better than the Ant songs, partly because Joseph taught them to others who use them in the new, but sometimes also in the the old, way.[84]

---

[83] It is a good question whether the old generation of singers responded primarily to the subjective states expressed in the songs, that is, to the verbs and adverbs of feeling; and whether the new generation responds primarily to the material things, that is, the nouns about mountains and life forms. By rights each generation should be interested in both, but there is a complicating question of the suitability of the moods of many of the texts to today's morality and emotional culture. I have not heard this discussed. If it were discussed, I imagine that people would be impressed by the emotional depth of the songs.

[84] I believe that both the Gila River and Salt River tribes have passed ordinances against all-night dances, for both chicken scratch bands and social dance events. All dances must stop at 1:00 A.M. This rule is easier to uphold at places such as churches and public "community buildings" than at private houses or in the thickets.

JOSEPH'S ASSEMBLING

Although he had heard them before, Joseph mastered and organized the songs by attending a few practice sessions at the home of a man who knew them well, and by listening to tapes made at those sessions. The man, Blaine Pablo, lived at Sacaton Flats village, about twenty-five miles east of Joseph's home at Casa Blanca village. Besides Vincent Joseph, Joseph Giff, from St. John's village twenty-five miles west of Casa Blanca, and I (Tempe, Ariz.) attended the sessions. I provided the transportation and made the tapes.

It was normal for men who liked singing to visit each other and practice songs, but the norm was actually to practice them prior to a sing, for example for Joseph or Giff to go to Pablo some days before assisting him at a dance.[85] It was not the norm to substitute listening to a tape at home for assisting at a dance, nor was it normal to practice songs with a singer from a distant village. Thus we visitors reduced the contact between teacher and learner, increased the geographical distance, and speeded the learning.[86]

Giff died about two years after these practices, Pablo about two years after that, and Joseph about four years after Pablo, all of old age. I don't believe that Giff taught the songs to anyone at St. John's. Pablo on the other hand was not the only Oriole singer in his immediate area of Sacaton Flats and Blackwater villages. In fact, a tape with about eight of the songs was issued commercially in the 1970s (Pablo was one of the singers), and the songs continue to be used there today, both in the old and new ways.

There were eight practice sessions, in which Pablo sang a total of sixty-eight Oriole songs.[87] Two or three songs were incompletely sung

---

Social dancing songs were commonly sung in alternation with chicken scratch music at half-the-night celebrations in the 1980s and 90s, but I doubt if anyone then filled a whole night with pure social dance singing. Still, there is nothing to prevent people from holding a home-based sing through the night. All-night Native American or "Peyote" church services are held at homes. These consist largely of singing, but the songs are normally not in Pima and are not social dancing songs. There is nothing to prevent Pima social dancing songs from being introduced at those services, not for dancing but for reverence, that is, in the manner of hymns. Some may already have been used in this manner. Also, nothing prevents such songs from being used for all-night reverential services without the peyote liturgy. If done without dancing, these would be like devout practice sessions. The song leader might take on a priestly function.

[85] Such practices would not necessarily imply a clear idea on the part of the lead singer of exactly what songs would be used at the dance.

[86] Of course that is what spirits do in dreams, and it seems from the songs, for example Ant song 7, that they accomplish this through a single visit.

[87] There were also two visits by me alone to Pablo, one before the fifth and one after the eighth joint practice. In my notebooks and tapes, those private visits are numbered in with the joint practices. Thus, the sixth joint practice is numbered tape seven, etc.

because he could not remember the whole (the sessions were impromptu, we would arrive without prior arrangement). Songs other than Oriole were sung, and sometimes it was unclear whether Pablo considered a certain song to be an Oriole. In fact, that identity is somewhat arbitrary. As noted earlier, Stepp's Ant song 5 was sung as an Oriole by Pablo and was accepted as such by Joseph (song 16); and Joseph took as an Oriole a song that Pablo gave as a Heaven, that is, as a song dreamed from Mary the mother of Jesus (song 24).

Of the sixty-eight-odd songs that Pablo sang (some only once, some several times), Joseph eventually, by his third singing, included forty-six. He also sang ten songs that Pablo did not. Nine of those were established in Joseph's first recording and were retained thereafter. I assume that he knew them prior to our visits with Pablo. And there are reasons why Joseph could not include all of Pablo's songs. First, I forgot to give him tapes of the last two practices, and these included several new songs. Unless he already knew them, which apparently he didn't, he would not have been able to learn them without the tapes. Second, as mentioned above, Pablo sang some songs incompletely. He came back to one in particular several times, but never managed to get it right. Joseph excluded these songs. In sum, a fifth of Joesph's Oriole songs were learned independent of the practices, and a third of those he practiced did not enter into his repertory.

He sang his current repertory for recording three times in the years 1983 to 1985. The sequences were much the same each time. He never dropped a song, but added two between the first and second sing and added nine more between the second and third.[88] The two songs new to the second sing were a pair on a birdish mother's lament to her children. Pablo had sung one of these as an Oriole song and one as a Heaven. He did not sing them together, but Joseph sensed their similarity and incorporated both into his "Bird" filing category (they are songs 24 and 25, below). Of the nine new items in the last sing, eight were from tapes of

---

[88] Numbering the songs by their sequence in the second singing (given below), here are the sequences of the first and third sing. Numbers 48–56 were sung only in the third sing; they are his additions since the second recording.

First sing:
1, 2, 3, 4, 5, 6, 7, 8, 9, 10, 11, 12, 13, 14, 15, 16, 17, 18, 19, 20, 21, 22, 33, 31, 27, 23, 26, 28, 29, 30, 32, 34, 35, 36, 40, 41, 42, 43, 44, 37, 38, 45, 46, 47.

Third sing:
1, 2, 3, 48, 49, 50, 4, 5, 6, 7, 8, 9, 10, 11, 12, 13, 14, 15, 16, 17, 18, 19, 20, 21, 22, 23, 51, 52, 27, 24, 25, 53, 54, 26, 28, 29, 55, 30, 56, 31, 32, 34, 35, 36, 33, 37, 38, 39, 40, 41, 42, 43, 44, 45, 46, 47.

Pablo sessions that included large numbers of non-Oriole songs. I imag-
ine that Joseph set those tapes aside until after his second singing. Then
he distributed them (and one more) among the forty-seven that he had
already positioned.

The order that he established was different from that of Pablo's prac-
tice sessions. I don't recall ever discussing whether the songs should "re-
ally" be ordered differently from the order in which Pablo introduced
them to us.[89] In fact, Pablo's comments were mostly about how his mind
(or "head"—*mo'o*—as he put it) was weak from age. If he meant that, and
I think he did, then Joseph could not expect firm guidance. Joseph was
obliged to organize the songs himself. As we will see, he begins the sing
with a westward journey that originates in Pablo's part of the reservation.
This was a courtesy, but it is difficult to see how he could have used those
geographically pinpointed songs otherwise.

---

[89] Here are the songs of Pablo's practice sessions, numbered according to their posi-
tion in Joseph's second sing (or, after 48, for their order of introduction in the third sing).
Not all the songs receive numbers. The letter "O" stands for an Oriole song that Joseph did
not sing, and the letter "X" stands for non-Oriole song.

Session 1. 1, 9, 4, 2, 28, 44, 46, X, X, 43.

Session 2. 3, 12, 10, 11, O, 14, 15, 17, 18, 19, 20, 31, 7, 8, 21, 22, 45.

Session 3. X, X, X, X, X, 52, 23, 51, 53, 54, 40, 48, 50, 38, X.

Session 4. O, 56, 55, 19, O, X, X, X, X, 29, 44, O, 43, O, O, O.

Session 5. Heaven songs sung without Joseph and Giff.

Session 6. 1, 2, 3, 12, 14, 11, 15, O, 14, 18, 22, 19, 20, 6, O, 9, 33, 34, 44, 43, 29, 28,
25, 37, 45, 47, X.

Session 7. O, 33, 2, 3, 12, O, 8, O, 7, O, 9, 12, 11, 10, 14, 15, O, O, O, O, X, O, 13,
46, X.

Session 8. Heaven, Cow, and Devil songs.

Session 9. O, O, O, O, 56, O, 42, O, O, 51, X, X, X.

Session 10. Oriole songs sung without Joseph and Giff.

CHAPTER SIX

The Sing Quietly

I alter the procedure that was used for the Ant songs to profit from the fact that Joseph both spoke the songs in ordinary language and sang them. In this chapter the Oriole texts are given in Joseph's "quiet" register of speaking, then in the next chapter they are given "loudly" as he sang them.

Actually, Joseph alternated between those registers as he proceeded, first speaking a text quietly (as if telling it in a story, or as we whites speak most of our verse), then singing it. His language was Pima. I will do differently. The quiet versions, given in this chapter, are exclusively in English. These are translations, first of Joseph's quietly speaking each song, then of the words of a song as I understand them.

The two translations are similar but not identical, which I discuss below. First, note that my "quiet" song translations are basically of the same sort as were given for the Ant songs, and herein lies a lesson: such translations are false to the sound and the feel of the songs. The next chapter will give accoustically truer renditions in conjunction with the Pima language transcript for each song. Those "loud" translations match the syllable count, stress, rhythm, and word units of the originals. They are not beautiful, not even handsome, but they stand as "loud" proxies for what sounds beautiful in Pima.

Now, regarding Joseph's quiet tellings versus my quiet translations, first, I apologize for not giving his Pima. I omitted it to save space. Also, Joseph's quiet Pima telling of a song was not always the same as how I hear, and quietly translate, the text. Our differences are few, but because I didn't resolve them with him, it would be necessary for accuracy to give not one but two Pima ordinary ("quiet") versions for many songs, his and mine. For simplicity I give neither, but offer this explanation of why my translation of Joseph's speaking a song is sometimes different from my translation of the same song.[90]

---

[90] This is not merely because my song translations use lines and the translation of his speech is written as running prose. That is graphic style. The differences I have in mind

MYTHOLOGICAL PRELUDE

I said that Joseph has starting songs and a long westward journey, but that is not quite accurate. He has *a* starting song, then a run that I will call "mythological," then a westward journey. The mythological songs refer to ancient events or places. Here is the run as Joseph presented it, including the starting song. The numbering of the songs and the material in brackets are my own.

1. [Joseph quietly speaks what the Oriole-person sang] "Here I sit, here down feather topknot[91] sticks to me. It waves nicely with my song." And thus says this [song], this which is the first, and says,

> I'm seated,
> Crowded by people,
> Crowded by down-feather topknots,
> Everything handsomely
> Wavering with songs.

2. Look, and this tells, when the sun will rise, where it is called—uh— Casa Grande Ruin.[92] Here the sun was newly made. "Sun is newly made. Away in front of the east toss it, and it rises. Here above us it goes, and away westward it sinks." So says this song. It says,

> Make a new sun.
> Toss it east.
> It will climb,
> Will light up the ground,
> Pass over me and
> Sink in the west.

3. Look, and that which stands there [in the east beyond Casa Grande National Monument] is the Shining Great-house. "In front of the east the Shining Rainhouse stands. Who sings there? Inside a song is locked. I unlock it and see." So this one sounds,

---

are of substance, where we disagree on what a sung word means, or where one of us "hears" more quieted words in a song than the other. The different quiet hearings are available for study in my notes.

[91] The Pima word is *siwdag*, or *siwoda*, which means topknot (of birds), feathered headdress (of people), flame, and sunray. Orioles, the namesake of these songs, do not have topknots. The reference is to human or spirit people, possibly Oriole people, who crowd around wearing headdresses while the "I" settles down for a night of singing.

[92] Not according to me. See the discussion after this run. (Joseph here said "Casa Grande" in Spanish/English).

Who sings?
Away the East Shining Great-house stands.
Inside various kinds of song,
Inside locked.
I unlock them and
Then see.

4. Then is the one [song] that says, "Where will you take me? Away far is
the Witch's Making-place. Upon it take me. On the Witch's Bed the land
sparkles."

Where are you taking me?
Where are you taking me—
To the Witch making land
Trying to take me?
The Witch's bed
Where earth sparkles?

5. Then [the Oriole-person reaches] there, where Santa Rosa is,[93] where
there is the Children's Burial, as we call it, which [song] is, "Children's
Burial, Children's Burial, I just then run. There around me the ocotillo[94]
flowers enclose. And I just then run." It [ocotillo enclosure] stands there,
[at] the Children's Burial.

Children's Burial.
Children's Burial
I come upon.
Round about the ocoti-
llo flowers enclose
Where I come upon.

6. Then the "Red Rock,"[95] as it is called, which is Red Rock Hill. "There
behind it I circle. There behind it burnt bows crumbling lie, and I see it.
Then my heart hurts."

---

[93] A location discussed after this run.

[94] A cactus-like plant that grows as long, straight, green sticks from a central point on
the ground. The Children's Burial is fenced with these poles, which are ceremonially re-
newed every two or four years (the ceremony persists). The shrine poles are stipped of
their green skin, so they cannot take root and flower as this song implies. Unstripped
ocotillo poles, used as fences, do commonly take root and flower in season.

[95] Joseph first said this name in English, then in Pima. For once the two peoples agree
on a name. The place is not terribly conspicuous and one wonders who applied the name
first—presumably the Pimas.

Red Rock Hill,
Red Rock Hill
I circle behind.
There behind it
Burnt bows crumbling lie.
This I see and
My heart so hurts.

7. Look, and then it [Oriole-person] comes to Chief's Great-house where two [songs for the set] stand. It [first song] says, "Chief's Great-house stands, and inside I enter. Inside a chief's drink lies, and I drink it and get drunk. Much singing." It says,

Chief's Great-house stands.
Chief's Great-house stands
And I enter.
Inside, chief's drink lies.
I drink it and, drunk,
Many will sing.

8. There is also this one that is [about] Chief's Great-house. "Chief's Great-house, where right there Bitter Wind[96] jumps out. There it back and forth staggers, and like a rainbow, it curves across [space]. There on top of Feeler[97] it stops." Sounds this song,

Chief's Great-house
Inside Bitter Wind jumps out,
Back and forth staggering,
Rainbow-like across staggering,
Extends to Feeler Mountain.

Song 2 is suprisingly lighthearted. If this was a new sun, was it the first and only? According to the mythology there was only one sun-making, so one would suppose that this was that moment. When I say that the song is lighthearted, I mean that it makes the creation both of the sun and of the order of *days* (sunrise, westward sky travel, sunset) seem effortless. Something that would have great consequence later was just started one time, not one *day* because until then there had been no days, but one "time:" make the sun, toss it east, watch it travel and set. Also of

---

[96] A wind, or Wind-person, referred to in myth, especially in Densmore (1929, pp.35–39). This myth is from a Papago, but Pimas would have known it, too.

[97] A mountain east of Eloy, Arizona, called Newman Peak in English. Below and east of it is the Red Rock of song 6.

course and characteristic of songs, we don't know from the text who made the sun and why. We can only surmise that an Oriole-person watched it with a dreamer in tow, in what seems to be a time-travel ride back to ancientness.

Of course it is the sun*set* that qualifies this song for the start of a sing. The text is a report on the origin of sunsets. It is also the only origin song in the entire sing. The remaining texts of this run tell of returns to places where originating events had happened, but these are revisits to ancient places.

Song 3, and finally 7 and 8, are about "great-houses," my translation for the difficult Pima-Papago word *wa'aki* (*wa:paki* in the plural). Mythologically speaking, these are the massive clay-walled buildings in which Hohokam "chiefs" (*sisiwañ*) lived. Several such are mentioned in the mythology.[98] Songs 7 and 8 refer to a generic "Chief's Great-house," but Pimas today tend to use that expression to refer to two particular places, Casa Grande Ruin National Monument near Coolidge, Arizona, and a ruin not well known to whites on the Gila River reservation near the village of Casa Blanca.[99] The "Shining Great-house" in song 3, on the other hand, and contrary to Joseph, is not a ruin that waking Pimas can visit. It is the easternmost place on the earth. As I have heard it, at least, this remote and ordinarily unvisitable great-house has counterparts at the other cardinal directions: Red in the north, Green in the south, and Black in the west. There are ceremonial speeches, or "ritual orations," to this effect (for example, Underhill et al., 1979:17–35).[100]

The Witch-making place of song 4 is said in the mythology to be the great-house of a Hohokam chief named Morning Blue (see Bahr, et al., 1994:137–52 for the myth), at today's Casa Grande Ruin; and the Witch's Bed of the same song is an "earth figure" (geoglyph or intaglio) incised in the ground about fifteen miles northwest of the Ruin (see Russell, 1908:255 for a photograph).

The Children's burial of song 5 is a shrine to an ancient sacrifice of

---

[98] See Bahr et al. (1994, pp. 203–7, 285–89) for a discussion of them. Note also that Paul used the word in reference to the prehistorical Hohokam mounds near his house at Salt River. These particular mounds are not mentioned in the mythology we are following, and Paul knows no stories about the deeds of those particular Hohokam. "*Wa'aki*," then, can mean "the ruins or mounds remaining from any Hohokam people," or just "prehistoric mound."

[99] Conceivably the name Casa Blanca, "White House," did or does refer to that ruin.

[100] I didn't think to ask Joseph about this. Perhaps "Shining Great-house" really was identical to Casa Grande Ruin to him, but he seemed hesitant when he said so during the sing, as if he had an inkling that it was someplace else.

children near the Papago or Tohono O'odham village of Santa Rosa (as Joesph states), about fifty miles south-south-west of Casa Grande Ruin. Last, the Red Rock Hill of song 6 is not the site of an event told in the prose mythology (which stops with the conquest of the Hohokam), but is the place of a deadly skirmish between Pima-Papagos and Apaches. (Pablo explained this when he sang the song.) The burnt bows are those of Pima-Papagos who were killed there. The place, near a present rail-road section stop called Red Rock between the Papago (Tohono O'od-ham) and Gila River reservations, is about midway between Santa Rosa and Casa Grande Ruin. Perhaps that is why Joseph included the song here, or perhaps it was because this nineteenth-century event did not seem disconnected in time or in mood from the events of the prose mythology. I think both reasons apply.[101]

I see no rhyme or reason to the moods of this run. What the "I" does at these places is a fair sampler of what the "I's" did throughout the Ant songs: feels delight (song 2), feels sad (song 6), gets drunk (7). In my opinion, Joseph did not organize these songs with an eye to mood; he organized them for the kind (mythological) and location (south and east) of the places that they refer to. It is as if one cannot organize both by moods and by space-time. I suspect that this is true *if* as in Joseph's case one is unwilling to discard any songs. In his first eight songs Stepp did both at once. But as we saw, he discarded some space-time candidates because of their mood. Joseph didn't do this.

THE WESTWARD JOURNEY

The sites of songs 9 through 22 fall on a different geographical path from those of songs 1 through 8. Of course the places are all different, and this fact alone tells us something about the geographical references in sings: the same place is rarely mentioned twice, and when it is, the songs are contiguous (and therefore the place gets a certain emphasis). Sings do not scatter references to the same place throughout their course. Their place lists are geographically linear or circular or meandering, but they are not prone to returns. That is true in general, but Joseph's sing is

---

[101] We will see that all of the places in this group lie to the south or east of Sacaton Flats/Blackwater, while the places of songs 9 through 22 all lie to the north or west. On the proximity of nineteenth century events to the time of the Hohokam, I explained in the Pima mythology book that the era of ancient events is only about a hundred years back by Pima and most tribal peoples' reckoning (see Bahr et al., 1994:2–6). Thus, if this event actually happened in 1860 (that is just a guess), it is old enough to be ancient. I don't know if the event was registered in white-written histories—probably not.

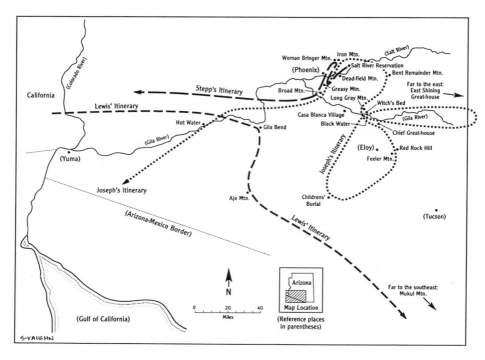

Sing Itineraries.

something of an exception. Determined to use all of the many Oriole place songs that he knew, he did something more complex geographically than Stepp. He first gives us a journey to places that figure into mythology, and then he gives a spatially non-overlapping westward journey of the same sort as Stepp, but longer (Map 1).

The westward journey begins at Blackwater, next to Pablo's Sacaton Flats. I think that the Oriole songs were a joint possession of singers at Blackwater and Sacaton Flats, and from the evidence of this sing (ordered, it will be recalled, by Joseph, a resident of neither), Blackwater is the "true" home of the songs. Thus, if we assume on the analogy of the Ant songs that Joseph's song 1 indicates Blackwater although it does not actually say so (the same as Stepp's song 1 indicates Salt River Village), then the mythological circuit starts at that place and returns to it by dint of the explicit Blackwater song, 9, which starts the westward journey (see map 2).

I am not sure of the location of the mountain features of songs 10 through 12. As I recall, Pablo pointed all of them out to us as we sat outside at his house, which is to say that they are *very* local, being the shape of a point on a hill, etc. I imagine that Joseph and Giff knew them already, being members although westerners of the same Gila River community. Thereafter, from songs 13 to 22, the mountains are larger and more widely known (for example, to me). These include two that are honored with double but contiguous mention, Bent Remainder (Superstition Mountain to whites) and Broad (Estrella) Mountain. Broad Mountain also received double mention in the Ant sing discussed here. Also common to Stepp's and Joseph's westward journeys are single song stops at Greasy and Iron Mountains.

9. Look, from here it reaches Black Water where it says this, that "Women spring out from Black Water. And they run to us, all crowned with cattail leaves they come running. Green dragon-flies see it and sit on them." Sounds this Black Water [song],

> Black Water lies.
> Just then women jump out
> And run to us,
> All crowned with cattail leaves,
> Green dragon-flies
> Acling.

10. Look, and then behind the [Gila] river is White Pinched [Mountain]. "From inside a shining wind [should be 'rainbow'] jumps," as it says. Another mountain also stands. "On top of that it [wind] stops," this song also says. It [other mountain] is called Gray Hill. There, that way [northeast from Joseph's house] it stands.

> White Pinched,
> White Pinched
> Inside a shining rainbow comes out and, spinning,
> Extends to Gray Hill.

11. So it (Oriole-person) says, and then reaches where there stands what is Zigzag Connected [Mountain]. "Zigzag mountains so connected. On top of that it [traveler] rests. There alongside, a black cloud zigzags. It [traveler] likes it and watches." Thus this sounds,

> Zigzag Connected,
> On top I pause.
> Here beside me,
> Black cloud floats zigzags,
> Pleasant for watching.

12. Then [Oriole-person comes] this way to what is called Red Bent [Mountain] where "inside a song sounds." This one [traveler] circles behind it. But it can't find a way to enter since they say that it's the devil's house. "Yet I—what can I do to enter, in there many songs to learn." It also sounds,

> Red Bent,
> Red Bent.
> Inside songs sound
> And I'm poor.
> I circle behind,
> Oh, what can I do?
> Now, enter and
> Then, many songs know.

13. Then, in this direction stands the Long Gray [Mountain]. It says, "Long Gray below sings. Companion [Coyote] towards it runs, and a reed flute he holds. He runs and runs, then dances toward me, then toots and tells songs with me." Thus says our companion,

> Long Gray beneath singing.
> Companion runs far,
> Then near,
> Then dances to me,
> Then flutes
> And tells songs to me.

14. Then afterward it reaches Bent,[102] Remainder Bent [Mountain]. It says, "[from] inside, a shining wind comes out." It's the oriole bird that takes it [Oriole-person], brings him to it [mountain]. "No one sees, no one knows." So also sounds that Bent [Mountain] song,

> Remainder Bent,
> Remainder Bent,
> From in a shining rainbow comes out.
> Oriole bird leads me there
> And I enter.
> No one sees,
> No one knows.

---

[102] A large mountain east of Apache Junction, Arizona, called Superstition Mountain in English. Pima-Papagos say that there are petrified pre-Hohokam people on its top (the next song refers to them). See Russell, 1908:211–12 for the story. (Russell translated the mountain name as "Crooked").

15. Then there is another [song] on this Bent, Remainder Bent, that "inside it a song sounds loudly." It [Oriole-person] "heard it and hurried there. It seems to be stone people, and it is they who loudly sing," since people there had turned to stone, and they speak and are stone people.

> Remainder Bent,
> Remainder Bent,
> Inside where songs excitedly sound.
> I listen and run to sing.
> It must be stone people
> Who sound so excited in singing.

16. Look, and then away there stands beyond Camel Back [Mountain], what is called Iron Mountain. "Not invitingly it sounds," it makes frightening sounds. "Wind runs there, and there is hooting inside." There really is an Iron Mountain there, as I have gone there, gone and crossed the [Verde] river, and reached Iron Mountain.

> Iron Mountain.
> Iron Mountain
> Uninvitingly sounds.
> Wind runs there,
> Then stands,
> Then hoots.

17. Look, and then next it [Oriole-person] arrives where a mountain stands, where an Apache spoke. One [Apache] was [named] Narrow Leg [tape interrupted].... "Pitifully dying." He [Thin Leg] had been treated pitifully. "They [Pimas] did it to me, and [I] die pitifully. [My] feather, [and] it's already moist." Sounds this Thin Leg song, and it says,

> Many people gather there
> While I here
> Sorrily die.
> This my feather tip,
> Already dead.

18. Thus said Narrow Leg. Then there it falls [hits ground] at Greasy [Mountain],[103] where it says that I'itoi came out from below. "Below Greasy, I'itoi comes out. He poses on a peak. Like the Morning Star he seems, and [his] flames[104] shine." Thus says this I'itoi song,

---

[103] South Mountain, the southern border of Phoenix, Arizona.

[104] The word for "flame" is the same that was used for "topknot" in song 1. See the note there about this word. Alternatively to seeing I'itoi in this song as having a flaming head, one could see him as wearing a feathered headdress.

Below Greasy, little I'itoi comes out,
Then pauses at the edge,
Like the Morning Star,
Distant flame lighting.

19. Look, and then it crosses the [Gila] river again. At Broad [Mountain] it arrives, and two [songs] stand there. It [first] says, "Broad [Mountain] stands. At its front, drizzle stretches. [Although] I go along the front, my wing is already wet."

Broad stands,
In front drizzle goes,
In front I go,
My wings already wet.

20. Then one more [song] sounds, which is also [about] Broad [Mountain]. "Broad Mountain stands," it says, "inside it speaks very windily. And I circle behind it, and peep in, and hear that it sounds rainy inside." It [Oriole-person] also says,

Broad Mountain,
Broad Mountain
Inside speaks windily.
Along behind
I slowly peep and listen.
Broad Mountain
Inside speaks rainily.

21. Look, and then there, down that way [eighty miles west from Joseph's house], [is] the Hot Spring, "Hot Spring" as you call it [in English], "Hot Water" [as said in Pima-Papago]. [The song says,] "Hot Water distantly, noisily lays. I arrive upon it and look, and above it are various colored dragon flies. Above it they hover—hovering lies." It says,

Hot Water
Far noisily lies.
Above it I arrive and watch.
Above various colors of
Dragonflies hovering.
Hovering lies.

22. Look, and then [next] ends the line [of travel songs], there where the ocean front is, which is called Spongy Water, where "above [it] many times [I, traveler] come. Behind it, peoples' running path shows."

Sounds this one,

> Spongy Water lies,
> Above I often come.
> There around it
> Peoples' running path shows.

First, some mythological references. Bent Remainder (in songs 14 and 15) and Greasy (in song 18) mountains figure in the mythology, respectively, as a place where people turned to stone while taking refuge from a flood, and as the home of a principal Pima-Papago man-god.[105] The rest of the places in these songs have no mythological significance, and that is normal. Only a handful of the hundreds of mountains in Pima-Papago country enter the prose mythology. The people have more songs than prose myths about mountains. We see an example of this in songs 2 through 8. Those are songs about places noted in the prose mythology and the places are not mountains (except Red Rock Hill; in this rocky region, a hill is a miniature mountain). A likely reason why myths tend to lack mountain references is that myths are generally set where the people now live; and as stated earlier, people do not, and did not, live on the small steep stony mountains of Pima-Papago country. They lived and live beneath and between them.[106] Thus the places of songs 2 through 8 are two great-houses, a witch's bed etched into the flat ground, a shrine where children were sacrificed (it is on flat ground by a water course), and a hill at whose base a battle was fought. These are all places marked by human presence, and more than that, they are all places with preserved artifacts: houses, bed, cemetary, battle debris. Finally, then, the significance of mountains is that they are islands of wildness standing around villages. And with their shape-and-texture-telling names—Broad, Greasy, White Pinched, Zigzag Connected—they conjointly identify villages in both the Ant songs and the Oriole songs.

---

[105] Sometimes called S-e'ehe and sometimes called I'itoi—the latter in song 18, which is the only Oriole or Ant song that mentions him. Pima and Papago mythologies generally say that he lived on Greasy Mountain during his active involvement in human affairs (mostly in the Hohokam era); and that after withdrawing from human affairs (after summoning the Pima-Papago from the underworld), he went to live at Baboquivari Mountain, on today's Papago (Tohono O'odham) reservation.

[106] The mythic references to Bent Remainder and Greasy prove my point. People fled to the top of Bent because the lowlands were flooded. The top was the only place left unflooded. Greasy on the other hand was the home of a man-god who, according to the stories, could not marry and live among people in the normal way. It is the same principle. The lowlands are for people, who live in society, and the mountains are for gods, who live alone.

One song in this series lacks the name of a mountain or watery place:

> 17. Many people gather there
>   While I here
>   Sorry nod.
>   This my feather tip,
>   Already dead.

In introducing the song Joseph said that the events took place "where a mountain stands." The tape interrupted his statement, but I know from him and Pablo that the mountain in question is Narrow (*Ajik*), on the Gila River a few miles downstream from Long Gray. There an Apache named Narrow Leg was captured and killed by the Pimas. He was so named because he was crippled and walked with a limp. (He normally rode a mule, it is said, and was a noted raider.) I assume that it is merely a coincidence that the narrow legged man met his end at Narrow Mountain.[107] The greater problem with this song is that Joseph all but said that the "I" is the Apache. In introducing the song he said that the mountain is "where an Apache spoke," and after singing it, in moving on to the next text, he said, "[thus] says this Narrow Leg song."

Now, there is no doubt that the text is a death song. I concede that the dying person *could* be an Apache, but I point out that the Apache has feathers. Moreover, the word for these feathers is *a'an* ("wing", "tail-feather"), not *siwodag* ("topknot," "warbonnet"), Thus, the Apache is birdlike, or, as I would prefer, this Oriole-person is *Apache*-like.

This preferred interpretation is bolstered in the second song following, the first of two on Broad Mountain, where a wing feather (*a'an*) drips in a drizzle:

> 19. Broad stands,
>   In front drizzle goes,
>   In front I go,
>   My wings already wet.

This is the same Broad Mountain where water endangered the Ant-person in the previous sing. In this song there is no hint of a human "I," Apache or otherwise. The "I" is a winged Oriole-person who skirts the edge of a squall, darts in, and gets its wings wet.

Such is Joseph's first Broad Mountain song, while Stepp's first was about finding songs. Joseph's equivalent, which is about *losing* them,

---

[107] I believe I understood Pablo, Joseph, and Giff correctly on the names, but I never asked about them.

comes twelve texts below. His second Broad Mountain song reiterates the wetness of the mountain, now in reference to a perpetual interior rain:

> 20. Broad Mountain,
>   Broad Mountain
>   Inside speaks windily.
>   Along behind
>   I slowly peep and listen.
>   Broad Mountain
>   Inside speaks rainily.

The Oriole-persons' westward journey has no more mountains, but it has two texts on waters. The first is about a hot spring along the Gila River. It is called Agua Caliente by whites (the same, *Ton Su:dagi,* 'Hot Water,' by Pimas). The second water place was said by Pablo and Joseph to be at the ocean shore, on the Gulf of California in today's Mexico, where Pima-Papagos went to get salt.[108]

As with the previous run of songs and also the next one, there is no obvious progression in the moods of this group. Death, dizziness, dancing in company, and delight alone in nature are mixed together in no discernable order. Geography takes precedence over emotions.

BIRDS

Now comes a run of songs that Joseph grouped together for the sole reason that they are about birds:

> 23. Look, this [previous string] we lined up, from here on are those [songs] that [are about what] you call birds. It says, "What kind of bird is it that goes low?" And it says, "It must be a pelican bird that goes low. Everywhere the land is made foggy." Fog exists there.

> > What bird goes low?
> > What bird goes low?
> > Must be a pelican going low,
> > Earth fogged.

---

[108] A good native-spoken, native-translated account of them is in Underhill et al., 1979:38–47.

It is possible that the "running path" in song 22 refers to an earth figure or geoglyph such those which Boma Johnson documented and described throughout the Lower Colorado and Gila Deserts (1985). Because of their fragility and mystical appeal (many are shaped like people and animals), Johnson did not state the precise locations of the hundred thirty-one that he drew. (The Witch's Bed of song 4 is one of them.) I would think that some, including the running path of this song, would be near the Gulf. I thank Gary Clyde for this suggestion.

24. Look, and this one which I will tell with them [bird songs], which is a bird flying. It [song] sounds as if a mother bird's children flew away somewhere, as [young] birds will do. Eventually they grow large and fly off.

> Oh! Oh! my children, where did you fly?
> Oh, oh, my children, where did you fly?
> So I just cry and wander below.
> Oh, oh my children,
> Each day filled with following you.

25. Of course it's true that it [previous song] is also [taken and used as] a God song,[109] but it belongs with the birds [too], since it says, as I say, "Oh, oh my children, where did you fly," for birds grow large and fly. It [also] says, "[I, the mother] cry and wander below you," for they [children] wander on high. "All day following [the children]." But it is a fact that you [Bahr] were told [this as a God song], but I still put it with the birds.

This [next] is surely an Oriole song, it is,

> Oh, oh, my children, what can I do to—
> Now, how does it sound? [He had made a false start]:
> Oh! Oh! my children, my children,
> What can I do to go high with you
> Now that my wings are shredded?
> My poor children,
> What can I do to go high with you?

26. This [last song] is an Oriole [not a Bird/God] song, because it means and says, "My poor children, what can I do and go high with you? My wing is shredded." Its feathers are ruined. It can't succeed in flying, to go with them [children].

Yes, then [next comes] the bird singing place. This one sounds, "Bird singing place lies," for birds sing there. "And I go to it. Here beside me a song stretches," like a rope. Look, "beside me a song stretches. And I grasp its middle, then coil it, then grab it up, then go." Heh, heh, heh, heh.[110]

> Bird singing place lies,
> Above it I go.

---

[109] I had commented that I knew this as a God, not an Oriole, song. It was absent from the Oriole songs that I had taped from Pablo in Joseph's company. Apparently Joseph learned it elsewhere, and he decided to treat it as an Oriole song.

[110] This song had tricky words, hence the chuckling.

Beside me songs stretch.
Oh, how I like it,
Take the middle,
Coil it,
Grab it,
And go.

27. It seems to say [in the last song], "Beside me there [a song] stretches. [I] like it, grasp its middle, grab it up, and go." This one now sounds as if it tells of night, of flying at night. "Night flying birds, and they go. During the night, topknots [or flames[111]] burn," they shine "the light [English]" towards them [other birds, or the Oriole-person].

Night fliers,
Night flying birds,
Away going.
Night following
Topknots burn.

28. Look, and this now is an [explicit] oriole bird [song], since it says, "Oriole bird, takes me to the sky. There brings me to Down [feather] Nested Medicine Man.[112] His soft down he clasps, covers my body, and lowers me home." As this song says,

Yellow Oriole,
Take me to the sky.
The down nested medicine man,
Bring me to him.
Very soft down will clasp,
Will cover me with and
Lower me home.

29. It [Oriole-person? the sing?] said and now says, since it says more, that something is a wren and this is a bird. It says it is "Gray Wren. Cholla [cactus] flower [the wren] makes into wine and [then] runs up to

---

[111] This is the same word, *siwoda*, that was discussed relative to songs 1 and 18.

[112] A god who lives in the sky in a feather-down nest. At the time of an ancient flood, he is said to have suggested that various birds save themselves by making nests from their own down. The birds did so, the nests floated, and the birds were saved. (Russell, 1908:211). Different versions of the story give lists of the birds, but they commonly include hummingbird, woodpecker, buzzard (I didn't expect this), and black phoebe. I am not aware of a mention of oriole in this context, although orioles make hanging, womblike nests of the sort that the Down Nested God seemed to have. Perhaps orioles are the latter-day descendents or associates of Down Nested Medicine Man.

me." It means and says "runs up to," [but this means] "summons me,"
[which is] the meaning of "runs up to me." "And I drink with him
[wren] and get drunk. I don't know [because I'm drunk], slantedly run-
ning." Heh, heh, heh, heh.

> Gray Wren
> Makes cholla wine and comes to me.
> I drink with him and, drunk,
> Alas for my knowing,
> Slantingly run.

This grouping was the most elastic of any in the sing. On the first
time that Joseph was recorded, he had all of the above songs but one
(24), but their order was different: 27, 23, 26, 28, 29. And 25 was
brought up as an afterthought after the performance was finished. The
third time that he sang, the run was as follows ("N" indicates a new song,
not previously sung): 23, N, N, 27, 24, 25, N, N, 26, 28, 29.

If fixity in sequence is a sign of poetic conviction, the bird songs are
low in conviction. Only one pair (the last two songs, 28 and 29) was re-
tained through all three sings and one other pair (24 and 25) was re-
tained though two. Of course conviction can be fugitive, and I made
much of the one-time poetry (for all that we know) of the Ant songs. The
problem is that I discern no poetry here. Fine though the bird songs are
individually, I cannot say that they make more than a miscellany on
birds, an opulent miscellany let us say.

CALAMITIES

First this is a death by water reminiscent of the logic of the Ant sing; then
the most remarkable song in either sing, on the cold, dark end of the cre-
ation of songs; then death by fire:

30. Look, and then there is this [song about] what happened, look, that
we [anciently] were drowned. The land everywhere bubbled water—
flooded, that means—when the water came out.[113] "Then the birds forgot
their flapping. Pitifully they huddled in a bunch." Since they gathered,
they couldn't fly.

> It will drown us,
> Earth everywhere floods.
> Just now the birds

---

[113] This flood was not from rain as in the European tradition, but from an abandoned
baby's salty tears (Russell, 1908:209–13).

Their flapping forgotten,
Pitiful feeling,
clingingly bunch.

31. Look, and then this one says the sun died. The other [previous song] said it flooded them [ancient creatures]. At that time the birds didn't know [forgot] their flapping, how to fly, "fly away" [English]. Look, and this one on the other hand says that the sun died. "Sun dies, sun dies. Just then every kind of bird dropped its cooing," it says.[114] Then it says, "the lying land nowhere echoes," "quiet" [English] is the land, "everywhere. Just the mockingbird pitifully speaks, but it just talks to itself." As it [song] also sounds,

Sun dies,
Sun dies,
Earth everywhere darkens.
Just then the birds stop their cooing,
Earth doesn't echo.
A mockingbird
Pitifully speaks,
Alone, distantly
Talks.

32. Look, and then it reaches this one [song], since before our drowning was told [songs 28, 30], and the sun also died [song 31]. Now here I say that it [sun] burned them. It says, just, "Alas, we burn. From every mountain top steam comes out," as does the "steam" [in English] or "boiling water" [English], and this is "steam." "From every mountain top steam comes out. It will burn us, and I already knew it," says this oriole [-person]. It says,

Oh! Oh! It will burn us,
Oh, oh, it will burn us.
All far mountains'
Edges steaming,
Oh oh, it will burn us,
And I knew.

---

[114] This is the "hoot/toot/coo" word discussed earlier, in reference to marching bands and musical instruments. The implication is that the birds had not been singing songs, but had only been making their wordless but musical calls; that they were birds, not song-speaking bird-persons. Still, their calls communicate, and their stopping would be a loss. The word "talk" at the end (ñiok) is normally confined to the human use of words. To say that the mocking bird talked, then, implies the use of words, which implies that the birds' coos were worded songs after all—since those coos are the implied sources of the mocking bird's talk. Thus, the text implies that both cooing and singing were at issue.

Song 31 is the answer back to the matter-of-fact creation of a new sun in song 2: what was easy to make is terrible to lose. This text also answers back to the miscellaneous bird series. Birds are the pre-eminent source of the social dancing songs of the Pima-Papagos and neighboring tribes (Maricopas, Yumas, Mojaves, etc.). Thus, the generic name for social dancing songs among the neighbors, although not among the Pima-Papago, is "Bird songs."[115] The Pima singers undoubtedly know of their neighbors' bird fancy. I suggest that this knowledge prevented them from singing generic Bird (as opposed to Oriole, Blackbird, etc.) songs among themselves. Their neighbors all spoke languages of the Yuman family while the Pima-Papago language is of the unrelated Uto-Aztecan family. Corresponding to the linguistic cleavage there is a cultural one: the two peoples have opposite death customs, distinct grand theatrical ceremonies,[116] different personality stereotypes, and of course different song nomenclatures. If the Yumans have Bird songs, the Pima-Papagos will not have them. And yet the latter surely do have them surreptitiously, as Joseph's miscellaneous bird category shows, and as is shown by the fact that most Pima-Papago social dancing songs are attributed to birds. Thus, the Bird song/not-Bird song distinction is a cultural nicety, an agreement on how to disagree in this situation of greatly similar cultural practice.

As an answer to song 2, song 31 says that at the sun's death all the birds stop their cooing, except for a mocking bird, a species that according to the Pimas never produces an original coo or tweet, but always imitates the calls of other species. Here then is the situation in song 31: all of the fresh calls (=songs) from the birds of the world have stopped with the death of the sun. Silence falls in the world. All that is left is a mocking bird who pitifully imitates the last call of the last original bird, equivalent to a tape recorder playing at the edge of the world, or a dream culture without

---

[115] There is a very short but very telling myth on the origin of these songs according to the Maricopa, who share the Gila River and Salt River Reservations with the Pima:

> The song set *ilyica'c* told how the little birds or animals of the air were preparing to go to a celebration [social dance] that was underway: how they got there [journeyed] and how they behaved [presumably, got manic, dizzy, and felt like falling in love]. "The middle part of the night" [portion of the story] told how they thought they should not spend the whole night there; how they decided it [would be] better to go home, and how they left the celebration. It [story] went on "to tell that toward morning" those [lady birds] who stayed all night were tired and sleepy; how their husbands and children starved in the morning, and how those who had returned had prepared breakfast for their families (Spier, 1933:256).

[116] Called the *wi:gita* (Pima-Papago) and the *keruk* (Yuman). I have written a long paper on these ceremonies, damned to be eternally "in press."

dreamers, or, more precisely, a dream culture without singing mythic persons, since the dreamers would merely imitate those persons.

SUNSET

Now there is a classic sunset song. Like Stepp, Joseph placed it in the middle of the sing. Unlike Stepp, however, Joseph deployed a *death*-of-the-sun song before it, with a double effect: the death is not a mere sunset because *here* is a sunset and the Pima words are different;[117] but neither is the death permanent because the sun must have risen again in order to set:

> 33. Look, then it says, look, "Sun now sets. Darkness comes from that, darkness, and it covers me"—it's still darker. "And then I sit down, and grasp my scraper [musical instrument]"—it means, "I do it, rasp and sit"—"thereby to tell you an Oriole song."

> > Sun now sets.
> > Darkness comes
> > Here covering me
> > As I sit down,
> > Grasping my scraper,
> > Oriole songs to tell.

This is the sing's first mention of Oriole songs. An oriole *bird* was mentioned earlier (song 28). Here, however, we should envision an Oriole-person settling down to begin a series for spirits to dance to. The person does not coo, but sings in Pima. If the songs are original, the future implied by the mockingbird scene is averted. In any case, this song in its time *is* original. The singing person is not a bird, but may be the same Oriole-person "I" who was taken to the sky by an oriole bird in song 28, a person more human than bird, but more oriole than the human dreamer who witnesses the scene and learns the song. The "I" may be the same person who took the dreamer to see the death of the sun and sang the frightening, now quieted, song 31.

Note the palpable, nearly tangible nature of the night in this song. It is something that comes and covers. I discussed another palpable night in connection with the first Ant song. There it was a question of whether the night, or darkness,[118] is something that can be "followed" as it moves

---

[117] *Tas mu:kig*, 'sun death;' and *Tas huduñig*, 'sun descent.'

[118] The same word, *cuhugam*, can be translated either as "darkness" or "night." Literally it means "blackness."

over the earth. Presumably it can, although the successors to that song imply a more conservative, metaphorical reading.

MEDICINE MEN

In the Ant songs the mythic "I" steers the dreamer's attention to "men," "women," and "whores," all spirits, or at least all visionary things (these include visions of the dreamer's future self). Here in the Oriole songs there is an additional kind of dreamed human, the medicine man, or, equally, "shaman," "doctor," "magician," or "seer."[119] If medicine men make a fourth kind of dreamed human, we can extend the roster still farther by mentioning the other kinds that occur in songs: cowboys, devils, angels (called "feathered men," *a'ancud o'odham*), certain individual gods (God, Mary, and I'itoi, the latter mentioned in 18), and of course the unlimited kinds of somewhat human mythic persons (Ant-persons, Oriole-persons, etc.) who guide dreamers and supply them with songs.

The Ant songs lack references to medicine men, but this is an exceptional lack. Most social dance sings have them, although not necessarily as a compact group, as in Joseph's. Furthermore, the lack of reference in the Ant-songs is more apparent than real because all dream songs are shamanic, or related to medicine men. Whoever dreams songs is likely to be a medicine person. Thus the whole of a sing from beginning to end is a recital of medicine man things or, if you prefer, of shamanic experience.

That association with shamanism makes singers reluctant to say whether they dreamed their songs or learned them from others (see chapter three). Whoever dreams songs for social dancing has probably dreamed others for curing the sick and divining the future, and that person can probably also cause magical harm. It is small wonder that the dancing songs, although used for entertainment, are about disquieting things.

In the following, then, the "I" and the dreamer visit a series of shamans:

34. Look, and next it [Oriole-person? this sing?] reaches the medicine men. This one [song] says that the "[On the] medicine man's stick

---

[119] All those have been used to translate the Pima-Papago word "*ma:kai*." I use "medicine man" because it is the word that Pima-Papagos use. Of course more important than the choice of word is one's understanding of the meaning. As I understand it, these medicine men do not so much administer ingestable medicines such as herbs, or ministrate with holy objects such as feathers or smoke (although they use both). Rather, they make contact with spirits, who give them mysterious assistance in their present and future activities. Both the contact and the assistance involve songs: singing to call on the spirits for help, and assistance in the form of new songs to call with. See Bahr et al., 1974, parts III and IV, and the appendix to this book for more on these matters.

[someone] four times cuts," cuts apart, and makes what is called a "scraper" [to accompany singing]. Using that, [someone] tells "nice sounding Oriole songs." As also sounds this song,

> Medicine man's stick
> Cut four times
> To make a scraper.
> And I, with it,
> Sound nicely singing.

35. Look, and this is also a medicine man [song], that "Earth [he] bumps [with the head] and comes out"—[or] molds it [with fingers], one might also say.[120] "Much cloud comes out with him. He stands it [cloud] and pulls it to bits and throws them." And of course he did it, and now there are clouds above us.

> Earth Medicine-man
> Earth bumps and comes out,
> Much cloud, too, comes out.
> Away off he stands it,
> To short bits he pulls it,
> World covering he throws it.

36. Look, this [song] as also [about] Earth Medicine-man. It surely says, "Earth Medicine-man has his own rock, has his own rock and makes stars. Tosses them to the front of the sky. They cover the sky and shine"—since they "twinkle [English]" like stars—and that is what this says. And it says,

> Earth Medicine-man
> His own rock does to and makes stars.
> Here above me tosses them,
> All the sky covers with them,
> Greatly they sparkle.

37. Now I've reached this one, and I'll tell it. "Pitifully it does to me. And I sink, here at the world beneath us I dwell. Oh, oh, pitifully it does to me." Thus said the one who died, was buried down there, and stayed there, and said,

---

[120] As the sung text says, this song is about the second most important character of Pima-Papago mythology, "Earth Shaman," "Earth Medicine-man," or "Earth Doctor." He created the universe, including clouds (this song), and people; and so was the first god. But he was replaced on earth by I'itoi, the subject of song 18, who more actively affected the Pima-Papagos' fate. See Russell, 1908:206–14.

Oh, oh, you do me ill.
Oh, oh, you do me ill,
So I sink.
The land below
Above I'll stay.
Oh, oh, you do me ill.

38. Look, and next is this, which is, "Silver lightning, there in a cloud met [me], and it killed me. I was four days dead, then I remembered [came conscious] again. Now you can call me 'Silver Lightning Meeter Man.'" Thus sounds this Lightning song,

Silver Lightning,
Silver Lightning
Met me in a cloud,
Four times killed me.
Four days dead,
Then thoughts came back,
So you can call me
"Silver Lightning Meeter."

39. This is that I tell with [the rest of] them,[121] which says, "What is the windiness?" This is [the same as to say] "What is the wind?" But it states, "What is the windiness that runs up there?" And it says, "It is the north windiness. Along its path, the land is spotted wet"—wet to a certain amount of spotting—then it [wind] stops, having wet enough.

What windiness ran up here?
What windiness ran up here?
Must be the north wind
In whose path
Land is spotted wet.

I didn't speculate on the order of the individual Bird songs, but considered them as an unordered mass—diverse birds, or more properly bird-persons—whose creation of songs would end if the sun died. The present group was more stable through the three sings than the Bird group, and I think I know why.[122]

---

[121] This text was not sung by Pablo as an Oriole song. Joseph added it on his own.

[122] The first sing had the first three Medicine Man songs in the same order as we have here. Then came Whore songs (the next group in this sing), then songs 37 and 38 together, and 39 was sung as an afterthought (along with song 25) after the main performance was finished. The third sing had the full group in the same order as we have it, but

The explanation involves a concept of sequential chaining or "clasping." Beyond the fact that all six texts treat medicine men, each text in succession has something to connect it to the one that comes before and the one that follows. These links are different for each pair of texts. There is no overall logic to them. It is as if each song holds hands with the one before and after it, but the reasons for the claspings are all different.

Thus, song 34 is linked to the Sunset song 33 by the idea of starting to sing. On the simplest reading, the sticks of 34 are the same as the "scraper" of 33, that is, they are a pair of notched sticks, a rasper and a rasped, the latter pressed onto a basket resonator; the rasping imparts growls to the singing. More complexly, and because song 34 says that the sticks are four rather than two, the things could be mnemonics for the songs, that is, things that approximate writing, being tangible, portable, and legible. As such they would be like the stickline objects set up by the man in Ant song 7, or the stretched, coilable, portable songs of Oriole song 26. And we will hear of such sticks as writing in the penultimate Oriole song, 46.

Song 34 links to song 35 by the idea of breaking ("cutting" in 34), of the stick in 34 and of a primordial, ancestral cloud in 35. In the transition the actor changes from the Oriole-person "I" in song 34 to Earth Medicine-man, the mythological creator of the earth, sun, stars, clouds, and people, in song 35. Next to I'itoi (song 18), he is the most important god of the mythology. He forms the link to song 36 which, like 35, is an outright creation song. As such, these songs might have come with song 2 on the sun or song 18 on I'itoi, except Joseph had other uses for those two songs: geography for both and mood setting as well for song 2. Thus Joseph filed this pair of creation songs under "Medicine Men."

Earth Medicine-man's mythic biography explains the placement of song 37. In the standard prose tellings, this god suffered abuse from I'itoi when the two recreated people after a flood that destroyed the previous humanity. Earth Medicine-man was disgusted and sank into the earth, never to return. Such I believe is *a* reading for this song. Some Pimas who sing the song today (I am not sure about Pablo, Giff, and Joseph) read the text in a different and contemporary context. Just as Paul saw the Ant song about the exploding heart as pertaining to a recent death, so these singers see the "I" of song 37 as a recent Pima speaking from the grave.[123]

---

the Sunset song (33) was placed in between 36 and 37. Thus, the inventory and sequence of Medicine Man songs were constant, but the group was interrupted by other songs in the other sings.

[123] Actually the song could refer either to Earth Medicine-man, who, according to legend, sank straight through the earth to the underworld after a quarrel with I'itoi (Bahr et

Actually both readings are needed for the chaining. Mine connects the song to its antecedent, the other reading connects it to its successor, which lacks the word "medicine-man" (as also did 37) but treats the death and resurrection of an Oriole-person who was struck by lightning. The resurrected person announces his new name, "Lightning Meeter." The word "meeter" is a standard Piman shamanic usage. People who dream of myth-persons are said to have "met" (*nam*) them. The Oriole-person says this more boastfully than most Pimas would do, but we understand that he is a spirit, and the boast is made to his pupil, a dreaming Pima shaman-to-be.

I see no good connection between songs 38 and 39. One could say that the wet-streaked land resembles sky lightning, but I am not sure that Pimas would agree. Nor are there obvious links on death or shamanism between the two texts. Thus, the transition is arbitrary. Song 39 does however lead perfectly into the first song of the next series, on Whores. I suspect that this is why Joseph put the song where he did, not so much to conlude the series on medicine men as to lead to the next series.

WHORES

The Wind Medicine-man song connects to the new series. As Joseph put it,

> 40. Look, and after those [medicine men songs] follows this one, which are their [whores'] songs, which you call "whore women."[124] [As this song says,] "There is a whore woman, and she runs up first to their [social dance singers'] songs." Then with someone's husband she runs singing eastward. He's not had [by his wife]. "Pitifully they do to me [the wife says], and they [good people] look askance in their midst."

> Whore woman, whore woman,
> First to run to our songs.
> With my husband
> Eastward runs singing.

---

al., 1994:78–80), or it could refer to I'itoi who was killed, then resurrected himself, then journeyed to the underworld by following the sun's path through the sky. In the latter case, the song would be addressed by I'itoi, impersonated by an Oriole-person, to Earth Medicine-man at the time of I'itoi's arrival in the underworld. See Russell, 1908:226, for a version of this meeting.

Emmett White, who now sings the songs, feels that the reference is to neither god, but is to some recent person who was poorly treated in life, who died, and was buried. I feel that while the song could refer to any of those, the speaker is an Oriole-person who calls all the others to mind.

[124] *Ce:paowi*, "whore," and *u'uwi*, "women."

I don't have him, ill he does me
Here in peoples' glances.

As the wind ran on the earth, so the whore blows through a dance. The first left a wet swath behind it, the second humiliates a wife. Such is the introduction of whores who, for this sing at least, are the female counterparts to male medicine men. This seems to be generally true. When songs use the word "man," the man tends to own songs, which makes him like a medicine man; and when "woman" is used, she tends to travel to men dance singers, which makes her like a whore. These are textual tendencies, not hard rules, but they describe all the social dancing songs that I am aware of; and they permit us to say that the heroes of the genre are medicine men and whores.

Those characters are not necessarily the "I's" of the songs, but sometimes they are. Thus in the previous group the medicine man was not the "I" in the first three texts, was the "I" in the next two, then was not again in the last text (that song, on the wind, actually had no stated "I"). There is a similar shifting in the present group.

41. Look, and this one then says, "Pitifully doing to me, are you making me a whore? Earth flower [you] wrap around my head"—threw an earth flower on her head—"therefore my heart feels like a whore," says this woman. These are womens' songs that I now follow:

> Oh are you making me a whore?
> Oh are you making me a whore
> You who earth flowers
> wrap on my head?
> Oh, oh, my heart
> Feels so whorish.

42. Now I've done the start [of women's songs]. Those [previous] two sound well together. Look, next it reaches one with a call to family, "My husband, my husband, I'm leaving you." She'll go alone in search of singing. "Here behind me, people bother me, 'whore' they call me. Oh, my husband, I'm leaving you."

> Oh, oh, my husband,
> Oh, oh, my husband,
> I left you and
> Ran alone away to sing
> Where people behind me
> Call "whore" and bother me.

Oh, oh, my husband,
I left you and
Ran alone away to sing.

43. This one next says, "Who is the woman? Who is the woman that clasps my hand?" They connected and ran to sing. "It's just the One Flower-having Woman, that clasps my hand and runs off to sing." Says this song,

Who is the woman?
Who is the woman
Who clasps my hand and
Runs far away to sing?
Must be One Flower Woman
Who clasps my hand and
Runs far away to sing.

44. Look, and this one also sounds like crying,[125] but now it says, "Who is the woman? She acts slightly whorish, there circling behind us. With her hair she hides her face. She acts slightly whorish, circling there behind us."

Who is that woman
Who acts so whorish,
Circling there behind us,
Hiding her face in her hair,
Acting so whorish,
Circling there behind us?

45. This now is the one with which it [the sing? the whore series?] closes, which is an oriole bird. "It [Oriole] does me ill. With a jimson-weed flower at the end of its wingtip, it offers me a drink and makes me drink it. And I drink it all and get dizzy"—that means "get drunk"—and "to standing sticks I cling."

White Oriole
So badly treats me,
Jimson-weed flower
Makes me drink from his wingtip.
Then I drink and get dizzy,
Slantingly run,

---

[125] The calling to the husband in song 42 would be interpreted as crying (*suak* in Pima-Papago).

> On upright trees
> Wavering cling.

The songs from 41 to 44 form a little drama. First a whore's "origin story" is told in the first person. It features the aphrodisiac earth flowers that were discussed in reference to Ant song 2. Then comes a first person confession that recapitulates the Whore myth as told in chapter two; then a man's tale of a woman who clasps his hand and causes him to run with her to or from a dance; then the voice of Society:[126] "Who is the woman who circles us covering her face with her hair?"

The series to this point is behaviorally reserved. The one narrated physical contact is a clasping of hands. The people at the start of the series merely glance at the unfortunate wife, the bad woman at the end has her face hidden by her hair, and it is the heart (="soul", too, in Pima-Papago, *i:bdag*) not any outward organs that feels whorish. For these reasons, "whore" may be too crude as a translation for the word *ce:paowi*. "Hellion" might be better, or "woman-who-leads-men-between-dances." And note that the last mentioned behavior makes whores resemble the myth-persons who lead dreaming humans on jouneys. Those guides give songs to the dreamers. The whores, I suppose, sing and make love with the men they entice.

There is a problem with song 45, which, to judge from his commentary, Joseph regarded as the culmination of the Whore series. Let us compare it with song 41. Both texts say that someone affects the "I's" mind with a potion. The affector in song 41 is the "you," so the song might be taken as an accusation leveled at the dreamer (since I hold that all "you's" are dreamers). The accusation would flatter a male "you," given that the potion is earth flowers, the naughty man's great sexual attractor. In the present text the naughty person is a white oriole, an "it," not the "you." The scene this time rivals Ant song 2 in manic antics. The bird or bird-person serves a jimsonweed (narcotic plant) cocktail off its wingtip. (Song 41's equivalent is earth flowers wrapped on the head, the same as in Ant song 2.) The effect of the potion in song 41 was a whorish heart. Here in 45 it is dizziness (=drunkenness), "slanted" running (=failure to remain erect), and tree clinging, all of which the unstated "you" watches and listens to silently—and *remembers*, so as to recall the drunk's text verbatim like the star pupil at a police academy.

Thus, this is not a Whore song, but a drinking man's parody thereof. As such it is a fitting transition from the whores to the concluding two

---

[126] Ant-person posing as such.

songs of the sing. Whores *are* dizzy (song 44), they infect men with dizziness, and they reduce them to the condition of the "I" of song 45. That person in turn reminds one of the moral debate surrounding the decline of Pima social dancing. The detractors hold that by dawn most of the participants at a dance are drunk. So they would be, according to this song: drunk, dizzy, clinging to trees, and unable to concentrate on anything. The unstated "you," however, remembers it all, is manic and not drunk, and is the hope of the art.

THE LAST TWO SONGS

The Drinking Man's song implies a dance, presumably in the land of spirits. Now the last two texts make the dance explicit. Moreover, they support my interpretation of the previous song, that if the drinker can't remember, at least the "you" stays alert; and finally these last two songs bring us to the same issues as those with which the Stepp sing concluded.

Before taking up those final matters, I want to review the ways in which Stepp's and Joseph's sings are similar: the westward journey, the monumentalization of the home village, the privileging of Broad as the last westward mountain, and the placing of a single sunset song in the middle of the sing. Here is how they differ: Stepp flanked his Sunset song with cycles of moods (Death and Dizziness) and Joseph flanked his with with groupings of birds and calamities before, and medicine men and whores after.

There is an additional difference between them, which paves the way to Joseph's final two songs: Joseph has a run of calamity songs in his middle part, while Stepp divides what is essentially the same theme, which I call apocalypse, between his westward songs and his conclusion. Surely, the key Stepp apocalypse song, his very last one, is not a world calamity or disaster, it is a world dance, an apocalypse in a "nice" sense. (To me, apocalypses are spectacularly revealed scenes. But what is revealed is not necessarily bad.)

Stepp's apocalypse first thunders with its dance, then shifts suddenly to the silentest of scenes, a down feather, a puff, and a cloud (no doubt small), all ambiguously related. It is a fine poem.

Joseph's conclusion is equally strong. He gives the following, his last two songs:

46. Look, and this says that they will stop singing. "And we stop singing. On top of our sitting place, our scrapers [instruments] lie. With song marks marked on them they lie." Says this one,

> And now we stop singing and scatter.
> Here on our seats our poor scraping sticks lie,
> With song-marks marked where they lie.

47. Well, and one [song] comes on top which is the very end, which says, "And we stop singing, go [away] various directions. Here at our singing place a wind jumps out. It runs back and forth. Peoples' traces"—since they have stepped and it shows—"peoples' traces it erases. They [traces] won't stay after the wind has run," it says. Well, thus this ends:

> And now we stop singing and scatter.
> Wind springs from our singing place,
> Runs back and forth,
> Erasing the marks of people,
> Nothing stays fixed.

The scene is a dance, whether in the spirit land or at a Pima village we really can't say. It is time for the dance to stop, or rather, this being the end of the sing, it is time for texts about the ending of songs. Hence these texts. (Stepp, it will be recalled, obstinately gave a text about the *starting* of songs at this point, his song 29.) Here is how I read these final Oriole songs:

Song 46 says that we will stop, our poor notched scraping sticks are not just notched as they were when we started, but their use tonight has imprinted them with "marks" (*o'ohon*, "drawing," "inscription," "petroglyph," "writing") of *this* sing. Thus the sticks are recording devices. *But,* song 47 says that as for the tracks of our dancing, the circles we have made in the earth (the same image is in Ant song 31), the wind will blow them away (there is a puff in song 31).

To which I reply on behalf of this book, "yes, this is so of tracks 'written' in the ground, and it's true of written-on sticks if they are left outside long enough, and it could be true of this poor book. Save them all! Save the poetry!" Yet as we know from all that has come before in this book, especially from Joseph's song on the death of the sun, saved songs are not new ones. We should wish for new ones, knowing however that few singers will admit to having dreamed them even if they have done so.

CHAPTER SEVEN

The Sing Loudly

Here I transcribe the Oriole songs in the same kind of Pima language that I used for the Ant songs, but with a different kind of translation and no accompanying ordinary Pima language rendition. The transcripts differ from the previous ones in small but significant ways. There are no beat marks, since the beats can be seen from the spacing; some syllables are capitalized to show loudness or pitch—discussed below; and the key metered zones are now shown by single asterisks placed above and below the onset of the zone in a song—previously the entire zone was marked with colons.

The key zones are marked in the same way in the translations. By that means and others, the translations are brought a bit nearer than those of the Ant songs to the sound of the Pima originals. Thus, each syllable in the original now has a counterpart in the translation. Also, the spacing of the syllables in a translation now corresponds to the duration of the syllable in Pima: a syllable held for half a beat has no space behind it, a syllable held for a beat receives one space, a beat-and-half syllable receives two spaces, and a two beat syllable is separated from the neighbor that follows it by three spaces. Those spaces are blank; the blank spaces show time.[127]

The translations use conventional English spellings. Once the English equivalent for a word or short phrase of the Pima was chosen, the pronunciation of the English was forced into the syllabic mold of the Pima original, generally by duplicating English syllables. The results will seem odd. They add loudness in the sense of semantically superfluous

---

[127] There is no durational significance to the space used to write the letters of a translation. In general, the syllables of a Pima language song have two sounds, first a consonant and then a vowel; and in the nicely rational way that I have learned to write the language (this applies to songs as well as speaking), each sound is written with one letter. This economy of pronunciation and spelling makes it possible to give a fixed typographic space to the beats of a Pima song transcript. This is not possible with the translations, partly because the phonemic shape of the English syllables is less regular, but also because the standard spelling (used here) of English words often requires more letters than the word has phonemes (for example, "feather," or "rough").

sound—noise in the information theory sense—to the translations. I do
not regret this, for Pima songs are noisier than Pima ordinary language in
the same way, that is, from the point of view of the everyday language the
songs have so many extra syllables that they are difficult to understand.

Since the translated syllables were selected for their meaning rather
than their sound (actually for the meaning of the English word of which
they are a part), there is only a chance correspondence between the
consonant and vowel qualities of a translation and those of the original.
Syllable number per line and per word unit, and syllable duration, corre-
spond to the Pima as I have explained, but not the sounds themselves,
that is, the selection of consonants and vowels—not even approximately.
Being unrelated languages, the words for the same meanings have noth-
ing in common phonetically. From this unrelatedness comes a difference
in aesthetic noise between the Pima songs and the translations. The Pima
songs have rhymes and alliterations—euphonies—which are unmatched
in translation. If one of these loud translations reads euphonically, that is
just good luck. In general, they read cacophonically—noisily.

Finally, on the subject of sound, the transcripts and translations use
capitalization to register either raised loudness ("stress") or pitch. Lower
case is used for syllables judged either as soft or low pitched. This method
is crude, with its mere two values and its confounding of stress and pitch.
But granted that the method fails to make the texts satisfactorily singable,
at least it establishes that the songs as songs are not meant for calm con-
templation (Joseph's prose and my quiet translations are for that[128]), but
rather are for singing and dancing; and, importantly, for the remembering
of dreams. Songs are dreamed in the loud, not the soft, mode.

There is at least one other loud translator of Pima-Papago songs,
Philip Lopez of Santa Rosa, Arizona. Here is a song from him:

*

DAñegeWAI	noMI	ye				
dañegewai	nomi	ye				
dañegewai	nomi	ye				
dañegewai	nomi					
cPI	he	dai	wo	ha	so	ñju
dañegeWAI	nomi	ye				
dañegewai	nomi.					

*

---

[128] The sound that they give is that of free verse ("poetry that is based on the irregular
rhythmic cadences of the recurrence, with variations, of phrases, images, and syntactical
patterns rather than... conventional... meter"—Holman, 1981, "Free Verse" entry).

He sang the English as follows (his English is written here with the same letters and sound values as are used for the Ant and Oriole songs):

```
            *
AI    meLUmineME    e
ai    melumineme    e
ai    melumineme    e
ai    melumineme
eNO    ba    di    ka    nduNEtin    tu    i
ai    melumineME    e
ai    melumineme.
        *
```

Quietly translated this is:

```
I'm aluminum.
I'm aluminum,
I'm aluminum,
I'm aluminum,
And nobody can do nothing to me.
I'm aluminum,
I'm aluminum.
```

The Pima-Papago word Lopez translated as "aluminum," *wainom*, normally means "iron." There is no special word for aluminum. His choice of English "aluminum" rather than "iron" is fortunate because the former word fits the song's sounds better and also is better for conveying the song's word picture. The song is from a Lizard-person whose supple and shiny skin is more like aluminum than iron.

The translations given below are not as singable as Lopez's, but they are methodical, they give the impression of loudness, and they make nice visual shadows to the Pima originals.

```
1.                                    *
                    ku   ñi  mo   NA   NA   hi  wa
               MU   mui  yo  tame ñi   ya   ce
WE  se ke WI  wi ne SI   wone ka  ce   ÑI   ya   ce
               WO        sa  po   ma   ma   sim
            i  dame ñe   ñe   ka  ce   mune weme da
                                     *
```

```
                         and i'm here SI I i ting
                         MA ny pe eopleto me stick
ALL   o ver DOWN  fea ther TOP knootwi ith TO me stick
                         ALL    nice ly ma an ner'd
          the esemyso ongs wi ith waaaaver.
                                             *


2.                                    *
     TA    sai wa    YE       moi ye NA         to
ga hu wa SI  ya      li    ma so  wo NAni to
                     A  boi wa CE   sa CE  ke
       Je  wene  WE       si  ko tone li  da
          I    yeñe DA mai wo hi    me  kai
     GA  mu    wa     hunu ni ko  wa ñu   piñ him
                                   *

          SU   u un NE   ew ly MA    ade
  a way to EA ea east fro ont will TOSSaway
              a gainst will CLI i IMB    and
          la aandEV   ry where makeitli ight
          he remeA bove will tra vel and
          A wa ay weee est will si i ink.
                                   *


3.                              *
                    DO       mi kya ÑEI        na
    Ga hu siya line ma sone tone tome wa ki  ke      e he  ke
       ke de  ge  NA NA  koho MA  ma sii ÑE        ñei
                    ku  ñame ku u     u pi
                    ku  ñame ku   ku   pyo ke
                    wa  ñiki ÑE      e i   DA
                                   *

              WHO    o o SI   ings?
  a way eeeeastfro onttheshiiininggreat house sta aands
          in side the VA RI iousKINDSoofSO  ongs
              in sideareloo oockt
              and ithenun  lock them and
              then iiSE    ee E.
                                   *
```

4.   *
  ba me TOI ñi bei   cu kim
  ba me toi ñi bei   cu kim
    ga mu we YO o ke NA toi kune je wene
  ga mu cu mo ÑUA pa
        YO ho ke WOI ku ne
    da mai **na** je we ne ha mo **s**a nana wai ke
        *
where yo OU are ta king me
where yo ou are ta king me
    a wa ay WI i tch's MA king plaacela aand
  the er try to TAKE me
        WI i tch's BE e ed
    upon the gro o ound ve e ry spaaar kles.
      *

5.   *
    YA a al HI YA hiñim
    ya a a hi ya hiñim
  ku ñe ge ye e da mo me lhi wa
  a no ñi we wega ñi ME liho
        ge YO o si ke yone mai sim
  ku ñe ge i ye heda mo me lhi wa
      *
    CHI iil DREN'S BU rial
    chi iil dren's bu rial
  and i it ju uust thencome up on
theer me round about meO coti-
    llo FLO oow ers makeafence there
and i it ju u uust then come up on.
      *

6.   *
    weg YOmi YONA i KA wu li ka
    weg yomi yona i ka wu li ka
    ku ñege WE gace miñe mime tam
    a mo yaa WE we ga ñi
    ga ga te ME me tame wi pi kame we we ce
    ku ñame ñei no ke
  ni moi dan si wo pi A po ta hame tam

```
                        *
          re EedROO ockHI i i ill
          re eedroo ockhi i i ill
        and iitBE hiindciiiircle
       the e eerBE e hind it
      bo   o ows BU u uurntcru u umblingli i ie
         and iisee   ee it and
   my he eart   ve ry hur TING ly fe ee els.
                        *
```

```
7.                      *
          SI  WA  ÑI  WA  awa  ki ke e e  ke
          si  wa  ñi  wa  awa  ki ke e e  ke
     ko ñe ge ye da  mo wa wake
     ke da na si wai ñi wa siba mo ka a a   ce
     ku ña ma i  yo  ke NA wamo
          mu mui wo ñe heta
                        *
          CHI I IEF GRE eeat  house sta aa    ands
          chi i ief gre eeat  house sta aa    ands
  and i it in side there en terand
   in side the chi i ief dri inkthe er li ii    ies
  and i then dri ink and GE etdrunk
          ma ny will si iing.
                        *
```

```
8.      *
    si WAñe wa        wa ki
    ke dane si        wai we   ye we    he  li nai   wo ñe
       ya         hai be  no    no ta
       KYO hone we  po  ma   si mai  we   na naiwe no no ta
  ga hu TA  te  kame no  wane ga muwe kune wu pa
       *
    chi IEiefgre     eat house
    in sidethebi     i ter wi i i ind ju umps out
       back    and forth sta ger ing
       RAI ainbowin the ma a ner of a croosstu u urn
  a way FE e elermo ountaina waaycometoa stop.
       *
```

9.   *
cuku MA   **S**U dani ka   ce   e
          ke dene yu   hu   wi ñei   yo   pa
                 i   ya   ta wui   wa   woi wan hi me
                 WE   SE   ke yone wage ya   hak ni ni kwa
ce   doni wa ñi   ce ce no
      a   ba cume na ha tam
                         *
    blaaACK WA tererli   i ies
         just theenwo   o men ju ump out
                   he   ere us twar ards they're ru u u ning
                   A   A all caattaaillea eaf cro o ownd
gre een dra a gon fly y y
         up on trytosi i it.
                         *

10.   *
  to   HAI WE ÑI wu   li ke
  to   hai we ñi wu   li ke
  ke done tone tome kyo hote wu **s**a ñe he   na   na we no no ta
          mo   dani ka wu   li ke da mowa ku**n**e wu pa
                      *
      whi   I ITE PI i i inchd
      whi   i ite pi i i inchd
  in sidetheshiiniingrain boowju umps out and back and forth tu u urns
         gre eeyhi i i ill top oofstooo ops.
                      *

11.   *
        ju ÑUla ÑI ÑI   ka
Ku ñe**n**e na mena ñu   li na
   i ne wa ÑII yu   gi na   me
CU   cu ke CE wa**n**i ju ñale hi me ta
WA   ña si YO   hoi wo ñei   ta
                   *
        zig ZAagCO NE ect'd
    i theero oonre   e est
        he e ere MEEa long side of
      BLA   a ack CLO ooudzig zaaggo o oes
      OH   how so PLEA   sant to wa   atch.
                   *

12.   *
WE   GYU mi   NA ko na ke
we   gyu mi   na ko na ke
    ke da ga ÑE   ñei wo kai na ke
    wa ñi ni SOI gai ñi WA a   a   ta
    we ga ñi ya hai cu mo bi ñim him
        hai ya sa ñui ñi ju he
        ke damo WA we kai   ha
    mu mui wa ñe ñei wa ñi ki ma ma ce
                     *

        RE   E ed BE e e ent
        re   e ed be e e ent
    in side the SO   ongs will so o ound
        and i so PI ti fly do oo o
        be hi ind back-forth try to ci ir cle
            oh oh, what can i do o?
        just no owE en ter   and
            ma a ny so ongs will i just kno o ow.
                    *

13.   *
        ce wesi KO mani we   come ñe he te
we ma ka li   GA huwe me   ne ta
        i   ya wo me   li wa
    ga wañe WE wui cune wu   da
        ke name ku hu   na
        cene WE weme ÑE ñeiwo ya na hi
             *

        lo oongGRA aaybe neeathsi i ings
co om pan ion DIS tantlyru   u ning
            he ere will ru u un
    the enmeT'WA wards daaan ces
            just theenhoo o ting
        andmeWI iithso ongswillte e ell.
             *

14.   *
        WI   KA me NA ko na ke
        wi   ka me na ko na ke
    ke dene   tone dome kyo hote wu sa ñe
        WA ÑU PI ÑU hi ne wu wikoi ñi wañe me da

ke da   mañ wa   a   a   pa
              pya mi   ki   ye   dai wo ñe hita
              pya mi   ki   ye   dai wo ma ma   ce
              *
              RE   MAIN der BE e e ent
              re   main der be e e ent
        in sidetheshiiinyrain boowco omes out
              O RI OLE BI i ird to itwill meleaee ead
        in side ie een ter
              no thing and no one will see eee
              no thing and no one will kno o ow.
              *

15.   *
        WI   KA   me NA ko   na   ke
        wi   ka   me na ko   na   ke
    ke de ge ÑE heñei si WA haha mo kai na   ke
        ku ña   mi ka kai yo ke we   hewi no nei me ta
           do   ki YO NAI YO nam
        ke no   ki WA haha mo KAI hita   mo ñe he ta
              *
              RE   MAIN der BE e e ent
              re   main der be e e ent
in side the SO oongs soEX cited lysou ou ound
        and i then he ear it and to oit therego to sing
           must be STO ONE PEO ple
        must be e EX cited lySOUN diing lysi i ing.
              *

16.   *
           wai NOMIDO   an
           wai nomido   wa ne
    do wa pyai YA boi   ta ÑI wihi   mo kai je
        he we   lano me ne   ke
        ya toi   ke   ke
        KE nawe ku hu ke
           *
           i ROON MOUN   tain
           i roon moun   ta in
  i is not A gainst ap proach able theresoun ding
           wi i indtheerru uns and

```
                        wi  il sta    and
                        THE eenhoo oo oots.
                             *


17.                 *
        mu MUI  YO name wa  suwa ye    e  ma  pa
 ku ñe se ga   YE     da
                 SO      I  ga   mu  mu  kya
     i  dawa ya hane ku  ku   nan
                 HE      kyu wa   mu  mu  ku
                     *
        ma NY  PE eop plea waayga  aa ther
    bu ut i i MEAN     while
                 PI   TI ful di  i  ie
        thi iisfea eatherend ti ip on
                 AL   rea dy y y ing.
                     *


18.             *
 mua DAni  WE conal i  toi wu sa  ñe
 ga  mu  WAa ku   ku ka  no na  hi wa
         MA   a  a  si  U   u hu wa we pene ka
 ga  mu  si  wo   da ne  to ne  da
                 *
    gre EAsyBE lowsmalli toi co omes out
      a way THEer'edge a long there si i its
             MO  oor ning STA  aaris li iiike
      a way fla a a ame shi i ines.
                 *


19.             *
    ko me  NA ko ke    ka
      a mai BA   so na HI ku  sa pi wo hime da
 ku ñe ge  ma so ñi ka hi me   da
 i  da we  ÑA    ha ne he kyu WA o  U  pe
                 *
      bro o O ad sta   ands
   there in FRO   ont the dri i i zle will gooo
   and i in front al so go o o
   thi i is MY fea ther 'lrea dy WE e E et.
                 *
```

20.   *

```
              ko    meNA   ke    no    no   wa
              ko    mena   ke    no    no   wa
       me dawai   si    YEWE   de    dame kai    je
          a     moiye WE    wega    ñi
  gesi BA a ba    ni   KWA   cine     ko kai    ham
              ko    meNA   keno no    wa    ne
       me dawai   si    ÑU    keda      mo kai ñe te
```

                    *

```
              bro   oOA  admo oun tain
              bro   ooa  admo oun tain
         in siide  soWII indilyspe   eaks
         the erinBA  aa ack
       verySLO oow lyPE  epin andlis ten
              bro   oOA  admo oun tai in
         in siide  soRA  ini  lyspe e eaks.
```

                    *

21.   *

```
              TO    ñi   wi  SU        na   ni
   ga me ko si    KA    kai  da amo ka    ha   ce
       ku ñege NA    mane ñi ñi   wia  ake ñee hi da
     A  mi we   NA    mai  ge NA nako ma  masi
       wa  ni  CE   CE   no opi yane ge   wa
       wa to   YAne ge   wa       ha  ka ha   ce
              *
              HO  o ot WA   a ter
   off fa ar so NO o oi silyli i ies
         and iitO overar ri i iveandloookat it
       the e er A bove the VA riouslo oking
         dra a A A gon fliiesbeeeat wings
         wi il BEeeat wi   ings ly y ing.
              *
```


22.   *

```
     mama KA ÑIme SU nani Ka    ce e
   ku ñege NA mane mui ho   cu me ñi ñi wia
   a  no  YA we  ña yi
       YO o   ta me   me li ku do ma    ma si
       *
```

```
    spooON gyyWA aterli   i ies
and iitO veerfre quent mere ly co o ome
  the e ER a rou ound
           PE e eo ples' run ning pa a a ath sho   o ows.
        *


23.                   *
           HA cune U  hine kame juma lano hi   me      ta
           ha cune u  hine kame juma lano hi   me      ta
   do ki WA KA wa   U      hi  ne  kane juma lame hi me ta
           je wene WE si   ko   mai wa   ke
                   *
        WHAT istheBI iirdanditloooowgo o oes
        what isthebi iirdanditloooowgo o oes
   must be PE LI can BI   i ird anditloooowgo o oes
           e earthALL o ver fo o o gy.
                   *


24.                   *
    hai ya   ñe   MA  ama   ne ba  towa ÑE  ene
    hai ya   ñe   ma  ama   ne ba  towa ñe  ene
        kuñe si   SUA kena  ce we  cume YOI mena
        hai  yañe ma  ama
   we si ta   sai  YOI meKAI ji moi nahi me
                   *
           oh oh my CHI iil drenwhere doyoufly yy?
           oh oh my chi iil drenwhere doyoufly yy?
           soiIjust CRY yy  and be loowWA ander
              oh ohmychi ildren
         ev' ry da ay THRO oOU ughfol lowingyou.
                   *


25.                 *
  hai YA ñi   MA MA    da ñi  ma       ma  da
     sañ hiñe YU hame  we weme yu   kane yoi me da
     i   dañe YA hane  ya moi cume YA   wo  ke
  hai ya ñe   ma ma    de
     sa  ñiñe ñu haime we weme yu   kane yoi me da
                *
```

oh OH my CHI IL dren, my chi   ildren
what caniDO andyouwi iithhi iighwa an der
the esemyFEA etherstru ly justareshre ed ded
oh oh my chi il dren
what canido andyouwi iithhi iighwa an der?
                    *

26.   *
u   HI ge Ñei   ku   ne   ka   ce
     ku ñege NA ma   ñi   kya hi me ta
  i no wañi YU ki   naa na a ÑE ñei wa wa ñe
 wa nii si YO   hoi
             SA ñine bei hime ke
             YA kwa to   oke
             ÑI ña   hime ke
             NA mowa HI   me   ta
                    *

  Bi   I ird SING   ing place li   ies
       and iitA bove i there go o o
  the e eremeBE si iiiideSO ongs stre e etch
    how iiso LIKE   it
             MI iddleta aakeand
             COIL it a roundand
             GRA a abitand
             THe eenGO o o.
                 *

27.   *
   cu HUke ÑE ñe da a   ame
   cu huke ñe ñe da a   hame u   hi ne
   ga muwa hi   me da
   cu KAni yoi me kai
 si si WO   hote me me him
      *
   ni IightFLI i   iiiers
   ni iightfli i   iierbi   ir ds
    a waaygo o o ing
   da ARKnessfol lo wing
 to op KNO ootsbu u urn.
       *

28.   *
    wa   hame WA   ÑU   pi   ñi
          da   MAI ka   cime wui koñe bei   cu   kim
    gu   mu   WI   wini ko   **s**e   kame MA   a   kai
    kume seke WU   wiwo ÑUA   aha pa
ge wee   sa   MO   moi   ka   wi   wi**n**i gi   **ni** to
    he   koñe yona gewe cuke
                YU   pame ñu   ñu   ñi   ta
                    *

    ye ellowO RI o ole
        sky Y y yyto willmeta   a ake
      the er DO oownne est havingMED 'cin man
    andyouhiimTO ooBRI   iing me
    the veeerySO o oft do oowncla a asp
    with itmecooooverand
                HOme waardme lo o wer.
                    *

29.   *
    ko   ko MA   gi   WA wa cus
         ha na   mi   YO si ke   na wai to ke i   yañe meli wi ta
         ku ña   ma   WE ma ci   i   yo   ke na wa mo
    hai ya wañe piñe ma ma ce
         ga mu   **s**a   ka la   no me   ne ta
                    *

        gra a ay WRE e en
      cho o lla FLO o wer make wine from and he ermeruunup to
      and i then WI ith him drink up and ge et drunk
    oh oh soidonotkno o ow
            a way slan ted ly there ru un ning.
                    *

30.   *
    wa   to te   WI   pi   no   ke
          je wene WE   si   ko wa   pa   wa
    ke   da ge   WE   sai cu yu   hine
          ke dane YAne **ne**   wa   pi ma   ma   ce
    wo hi **ni** **S**O   hi   **n**o   TA hane ta
          kane NA   name cume i   yane cim
                    *

```
it   will us DRO o own and
         wo oorlALL    ov er flo o ded
just   now the  ALL   kinds of bi iirds
      just nowtheirFLAaa ping wo on't kno   o ow
will then so PI ti ful FE eeel
              andsoBU uunchtrytocli iiing.
                  *


31.               *
      ta       SAI waha mu      mu kim
      ta       sai waha mu      mu kim
      je wene WE  si   ko  cu ka ke
ke   da  ge  WE      sai cu yu hine KU kuiwe da ni to
      je wene KA     cim    ga mu   pi sa    mu ñe
 su HU  ge  YU   u  hi      ne
     soi newe KAI     je
he je li  GA      nu
      we ñe ño   ke
              *

      su   Un theendi   i ies
       Su   un theendi   i ies
      la aandEV ry where dar ar ark
 just   the en ALL   kinds of bi iirdCOO ooingsto o op
       ea aarthLY  ing    a way no e cho ing
   mo OCK ing BI  ii  ird
      pit iflySPE    eaks
      a lo one A    way
          just ta a alks.
              *


32.            *
      HAI ya WA to te me   me    him
      hai ya wa to te me   me    him
   ga nu wa WE si to wa   ne
ku ku ka ne KU ñu ñei kane wu   wa     ke
      hai ya wa to te me   me    him
      he kya ÑHU si ma ma   ce
              *

      OH oh IT will us bu ur urn
      oh oh it will us bu ur urn
```

```
         a wa ay A all moun tai ins
     e e ends at STE e eam theerco omes out
             oh oh it will us bu ur urn
         al read Y i knew ew it.
                     *
```

33.   *
```
       TA     sai we    YE        mei wa    hu  nu ke
   a bi YOI ne ku    ne    CU ka    NI  ba    hi  me kai
                     ha     hi  yeñe mai  sa pa
             ku  ñe    ke ye    na  mo    na  hi wa
             hi  kañe HI hiwe ku    ne    SA  se ku
       he  WA ñu  piñe ÑE ñei    wa    ñiki MA  ni ta
                                         *
```

```
              SU     u un NO    o ow se e ets
       ri ight NO o o ow DAR ark ness here co omes and
                            he er ermeco o vers
                  and i just no ow then si it down
                  thi ismySCRA aaa per GRA a asp
              O ri oolSO o ongs itoyouTE e ell.
                            *
```


34.   *
```
      ma    kai YU se    ga      he
      mowe nawe GI  ni    ko wa HI   ku    myo
            ka   HI hiwe ku de NA   to
  ku ñe    ga    YE ga    no
            SA  a    po we KAI    hi da    mo ñe he da
                  *
```

```
      doc tor's STI i i    ck
      theertheenFO o our times CU u ut
          and SCRA aaa per ma ake
        and i it U u use
              NI i i i ce SOU  oound ing si i ing.
                  *
```


35.   *
```
      je    he WE DE   MA          kai
      je       WE ne   MO    ke    no  ke WU  sa ñe
      mu mui  CE wani we    weme wu  sa ñe
```

```
ga mu wa   ke ki   wa
   so so   po li   wañe ku   mio
   je wene CE moka ñe   ñei   cu
           *
       e  eEAR EARTH DOC   tor
       e   EAR earth BUMP with head and CO ome out
     mu uch CLO ooudwi iithco ome out
     a wa ay stand it up
       sho o o ort breakita part
   e earearthALL overthro o ow.
           *
```

```
36.                 *
je  he WE de   MA      kai      i
he     JE li   YO nai  ya  a     YUu  u   sena ge  na to
     i  yeñe DA   he mai be   nane gyo
da     mai we  KA      ci      me   ce       mo
           ta WA   SA NAne wai  ke
           *
   e   eEAR earth DOC   to   or
       o   O own RO ock wi ith STaa  aarsjustma ake
          he remeA   boov there throoow
       sky  y y Y   y   y co   ver
           they VE RY SPAaar kle.
           *
```

```
37.                  *
hai YA wame tine SOI geñe do     o  da
hai ya wame tine soi geñe do   o   da
    ku  ñine ñu pi  ñi        me
    i  na  ta  WE co  ka  cime je  we
    ku  ñege NA  mane ñuli NA      he
hai ya wame tine soi geñe DO        DA
           *
   oh OH, youuumeI illmedo  oo
   oh oh, youuumei illmedo o o
       and ithensi i i  ink
       he ere us BE low ly yingla and
       and ithereON toopihaA   ang
   oh oh, youuumei illmeDO   O.
           *
```

38.   *
         tone TOme WUI   ho   mi
         tone tome wui   ho   mi
         gan hu   CE wani CE   doni na me kim
gi   ni ko   beñe MUM wa   him
kuñe ni ni   ko   TA   se kaje mu   mu ku
yu   pa moi iñe CE   ni to
         kuma seke YE   ka   no
tone tome name kame WUI home ña   a   ga
                    *
         shiiNIingLIGHT   ni ing
         shiiniinglight   ni ing
             a way CLO uudIN siideme e et
    fo ur times thermeKI i ill
         andifo u ur DA a aysamdea a ad
    back a gain ismyME mo ry
         andsoyoucanTHE er for
    shiiniingmeeeterLIGHT niingme ca all.
                    *

39.   *
         has PEne yewe line GA tune meli na me
         has cune yewe line ga tune meli na me
    dok yale WI ñime hewe li   ga
                  meli kune yoi ne   kai
                  je   wene KA ka   wide WAO si me
                    *
         what ISthewiiiindA waayruuu uns
         what isthewiiiinda waayruuu uns
    must besmallNO oorthwiii ind
                  paaaathfol low ing
                  la aandspo o otyWET e et.
                    *

40.   *
ce   PAwi YU   huwi ce pawi yu   hui
i   yate ñei yate we pege me   li wa
ñe   KU   na   wa   we weme
ga   muwa siya like we wiwe ÑEI me da
wañe pi   yune ni   no   soi ga ñi WA.a a da
yo   TAme sa   nine YA hai   cume ñe no ke

    *
 who OorWO oman, who Oorwo oman
here atourso oongsfi iirstru un up
  my HUS ba and wi iith
 a waayeeeeastwa aardRUN to sing
soidon't haaave him i ill me DO oo o
   pe EOplemi iidstBACK forth juustgla a ance.
     *

41.   *
     hai YA   name toñi CE pawi cu
     hai ya   name toñi ce pawi cu
     ku   mene je wene YO   si   ne
i yañe mo mo   dam aiwo ÑI ni ta
        hai yaa ÑI moi ta
sa si CE pa wi   mo TA hane ta
             *
    oh OH willyounowmeWHO oormake
    oh oh willyounowmewho oormake
   so youtheea e eearthFLO wer
 he eremyhe ead o onwillWRA a ap
        oh ooh MY he eart
 sure ly who or ish now FE eeels.
           *

42.   *
     hai YAñe KU   na
     hai yañe ku   na
     da ñeme DA ni to ke
     he ñeli GA   mu   we ñei me da
ano wani we weGA ñi YO   ooo da   ha me
cee pawi ña ñeNA a   ci ÑUna weke
     hai yañe ku   na
     ña ñume da ni to ke
     he ñeli ga   mu   we ñei me da
        *
     oh OHmyHUS   band
      oh ohmyhus   band
   here iyouLE e eave and
     a loonA wa ayrun to sing

```
        heeermea aRO   oundPE eeee   ople
        whoooorme eCA all  andMEbooother
                oh ohmyhus    band
              here iyoule e eave and
                 a loona    wa  ayrun to sing.
                          *


43.        *
 do WUne YU      u vi
 do wune yu      u vi
 he goñe ma  we  sa ke
 ga muwe ñei me  da
 do ki  HE  ma  ko YO si kame YU   hu
 he goñe ma  we  sa
 ga muwe ñei me  da
              *
who IStheWO  oman
who isthewo  oman
she whomeclasps the hand and
   a waayruns to sing
 must be O o one FLO wer havingWO   man
she whomeclasps the hand and
   a waayruns to sing.
            *


44.             *
    do    WU ne YU      WI      i
 sa    wa si CE pa   wi   mo  WA     dam
     I  ma te WE gace miñe ñime ta
     he je li MO mo   ka   ce  WI ho wa   sa mai sa pa
  na   WA si CE pa  wi   mo  WA     da
     i  no te we gace miñe ñime ta
              *
   who   IS the WO  O   man?
rea   ly quite WHOR ish ly there ACT    ing
 back there us BE hiindciiiircling
      her o own HA air wi ith FA a a ace co vers up
rea   LY quite WHOR ish ly there ACT    ing
 back there us be hiindciiiircling.
            *
```

45.   *
        towa HAne WAa nu   pi ñi
    si wo   ho   **S**OI geñe Do   da
    ko te   NEmi YO   **s**ine
       he   ÑEli YA   hane KU gane WA si pe ko ÑI   cu
       ku   ñame I   yo ke   NO NO te
    sa KA   LAno ME   NE   te
       yu   u   HU   si   CU ci   me
    ya HAI   ceme TAI **S**AI wu pa
                        *
        whiiIitOori o ol
      so tru ly I illmeDO ing
    jim son WEeedFLO ower
           its OownWI iingE eendOF fer dri ink and I   drink
        then ithereDRI ink and GET DIZ zy
      sla AN TIingRU U un
           tre e E es so STA an ding
back FORTH trytoCLI I i ing.
                    *

46.   *
    ku ti no ÑEI do   ke   na mu   we   ya hai wa   hi   me da
    i ya ta NA nai kune da mane **s**o   hi**n**e te hiwo kude we we ce
    ñe ñei YO hone kace ño hone kame we   we ce
                *
and we now SONGS stop and a wa ay here and there go o o
  he er our SI i tiingson tooppo oorlyour scraaapersli i ie
    so ongs MA arkingswiithma arkedlyyli i ie.
                *

47.   *
    ku ti yo ÑEI to   ke   na   mo we YA hai   we   hi me da
    i ya te ÑEI kune ce   nawe he weli DAI wu   ñim
                                 YA haipe meli no ke
               yo   tame CUI ñi kune ya haiya wi   yu me
               ga   mu pi MA si   ma   pa yu li na
                             *

```
     and we now SONGS stop and a wa ay HERE and there go o o
e ere our SING ingplacein sideofwi iindJU umps out
                                   BACK fo orthruuuns and
                      pe oplesTRA a acesback foorthe e rase
                           a way not VI si ble there sta a ay.
                                         *
```

CHAPTER EIGHT

Conclusion: On Criticism

Having been interested in Pima-Papago songs for twenty years, and having known several singers and written papers on their work, I decided to write a book incorporating the Ant and Oriole songs that would be a summation of what I had learned, a mature statement. Maturity was needed because I had not met Stepp and was not sure at first which side of the tape of him represented the beginning of his sing. And this fact might make the book seem deficient in background, a half baked white chatter on an unmet man's art. It was a test of whether an acquired feeling for the well-formedness of sings, or actually for novelty within well-formedness, would make one of the two possible orderings of the tape light up, and the other not. This book has described the light of the one ordering only.

I hope that various ideas employed in this study may be of use elsewhere, most especially in the study of other poetries of small nations.

Texts that need to be written both loudly and quietly

English song lyrics are generally written, for example in album-liner notes, with the same spelling and punctuation that is used for English prose and poetry. When the poems are songs, these are quieted writings, although we usually don't think of them as such. The songs as sung have a precise apportionment of syllables to beats which our English quiet writing conventions don't show, and the songs probably have syllables which the quiet rendition lacks, and vice versa.

There is no special reason to write the syllables of English songs onto their beats, but there are good reasons to do so with Pima and, I suppose, other poetries. Pima song stands at a farther remove from their quiet language than does English song, as evidenced by the difficulty that Pimas have in stating their songs quietly. Also, their songs are probably more packed with poetic nuance than the average English one, song being their sole form of lyric or verse. And it seems that their poetry actually lives, breathes and is born, in song. It is not that they get poems first in quiet form and then set them to music, as often happens in English. The poems begin as sung words. When such things are true, and when one wishes to enter the works into the record of poetry, both forms, loud and quiet, need to be given.

Quiet language, the language of criticism

People the world over clarify their thoughts in *quiet* language. This is the preferred medium for exchanging and clarifying thought, and, I believe, for *certifying* thought between people. ("What do you mean?" "I mean and say *this* [quiet language].") For example, the reader of the loud English translation of the Oriole songs clarifies their meaning by rendering them into quiet, conventional English. Thus, "and i'm here SI I i ting" (Oriole song 1, line 1, translated into the loud) becomes, "I'm seated".

Literary criticism is written in quiet language. This is as it should be. But is all quiet language about songs or other forms of literature considered criticism, and if so, what is special and beneficial about the criticism practiced in this book?

Why have criticism for the poetry of tribes and small nations?

There are many ways to define criticism, including the following, which have been used in this book:

(1) My paraphrase of Liu's purpose discussed in the introduction: "the definition, by the critic, of a particular art, and the examination of a few good examples."

(2) The particular agenda set in the introduction: to inquire into the expressive qualities of individual songs; into the principles of the whole sing; to trace suggestions of story through whole sings; and to consider the origin of songs in dreaming and their use in dancing.

(3) As I would now put the general task: the study of the time, uses, devices, and meanings of an art.

All of these are acceptable. But why have criticism for the poetry of small nations? The Pimas did not write. They had their own criticism, which was oral and in quiet language. It was mainly concerned first with stating in quiet language what their unquiet poetry says ("This means..."), of which criticism Joseph was a master; and, second, with discussing the uses and observed associations of songs ("The old people used to..."). All of the vexing and demanding technical matters discussed in this book were not discussed, so far as I know, by the Pimas. Let us call those matters "technical" criticism. One can have poetry without taking them up, for the Pimas surely had poetry, and one can have an appreciative criticism, as they did, which is not technical.

Technical inquiry concerns the parts of things, for example, of sentences (subjects, predicates, nouns, verbs) and poems (key zone, segment) and sings (starting, middle, and ending); it seeks regularity; it compares by analogy (songs are filmic and are like postcards and monuments, sings are like M. Rosenthal's and S. Gall's poetic sequences). These are the principal technical concerns in this book.

Supposing it is true that the Pimas lacked technical criticism, why should their poetry be subjected to it? As I stated in the introduction, I believe that poets like to have their works noticed and thought through. Technical criticism does this. It caresses, it takes care, it proceeds from fascination, it is love-struck—or so I believe. Surely, just as there are clumsy, dishonest, and feeble lovers, there are counterpart failures in criticism. But I see nothing wrong or damaging to poetry in the ideal. On the contrary, the ideal of technical criticism seems good.

If it is good, why didn't the Pimas have it? It is unacceptable to think that they had to wait for a white to bring it to them. One must dissolve the question into many strands, all analytical and vexing: the importance of writing, the social role of the critic, the love of mystery, the joy of having poems of great playfulness while failing to state the rules. Conceivably they had "it" but wouldn't say so, even to themselves. Criticism after all is that which is published, or at least is quiet language which is clearly enunciated to someone. Conceivably they had it but never quite spoke it.

Criticism as new thoughts

Criticism of any sort has nothing to recommend it apart from the questions that it asks and answers. It should continually answer those questions afresh, and continually revise and deepen itself. Writing, not to mention speaking, surely helps in this. Now, there is a large field for the criticism of the poetries of small nations insofar as good questions remain unasked and unanswered.

Note how criticism differs from collecting and translating, which do not say anything new in or about art, but merely get art and display it, albeit in translation, by switching the language. The merit of criticism is that the critic must add new thoughts to the world, thoughts about poetry, not actual poems.

Translation, Criticism, and Song dreaming

I took moderate pains with translation in this book for two reasons, to secure a base for a criticism that was conducted in English, and to establish that the quiet verse that English readers might expect is not the mode of the dream or the sing. I wish now to draw an analogy between what takes place in the English of this book and what seems to take place in a Pima dream. I, Bahr, am analogous to the spirit who sings songs in a dream. You the reader are analogous to the dreamer whom the spirit takes on a journey and sings to. The song texts of this book are not analogues to the songs of the dream—my *criticism* is analogous to the dreamed songs. The book's song texts are analogous, rather, to the scenes witnessed by the dreamer and spirit during their journey. Those scenes are things that the dreamer and spirit share, and things that the spirit's songs provide poetic mementos about. The scenes ground, or give rise to, the songs. There would be no songs if the scenes had not stimulated a spirit to sing them to the dreamer.

You are less fortunate than the dreamer, for the dreamer sees landscape and events (although apparently does not enter or affect them in any way) and hears songs. You "see" texts and read criticism. And I am freer than the spirit guide because in translating I can manipulate the text/scene that you read/see. This is one point. Translation is power and creation, but it is, or should be, a kindly service. Hence I was attentive to translation in this book, marking this loudly, that softly, signaling the key zone, etc., all to tie the text/scene to something external, namely its source in a real (if I may use that word) auditory "vision." I would like the translations to be pictures of mountains. The other point is that which was made in the previous section. The criticism, not the poem texts, is what I made for you.

The Central Illusion

A final remark on this book's criticism and also on how Pima singing has changed. I say on the basis of the Pima appreciative criticism that the "I's" of song texts must be read in the first place as "I the mythic person spirit who now sings in your dream." But I noted the uncanny similarity of interest and mood between this mythic person and both the Pimas who dream songs (their shamans if you wish to put it that way) and those who participate as adults in the old way of social dancing. These last two similarities, or readings, I call overtones (or "subtexts" one could say). Such is the ambiguity of the "I's." This ambiguity, endlessly played upon, is the central illusion of social dancing sings.

The illusion stands beside the various other principles which are advanced to explain song form and sing organization: the filmicness of songs, the ephemerality of story (although one could say that the ambiguity of "I's" is a part of that ephemerality), the starting and ending conventions, and the principle of discontiguous songs "answering back." Those others are true regardless of the merit of the claim of the central illusion.

That is good. The other principles, I believe, are true of more than social dance sings. They may not be true of all Pima or Pima-Papago song poetry (some sets are fixed, at least for a time, and are therefore solid rather than ephemeral), but they apply more generally than does the claim of the illusion. The merits of this claim are, first, that it has served well in interpreting *these* sings, so it works; and second, it identifies something that has changed between the old and the new way of using social dance songs. Simply, the new way breaks the illusion. Adult dancers are being replaced by children, and dreaming is giving way to the wakeful, reverential learning of songs, even to fictional creation. Thus, the literary illusion is no longer supported by practice or, if you please, by reality.

I do not say this to demean the present, but to distinguish it from the past. I have heard young Pimas say that the old timers are harsh to them. I don't know if this judgment was true of Stepp and Joseph, but I believe it is true that those men were good poets who wondered whether the poetry they loved would survive them. So I read their sings as implying a fear that their art was dying.

That reading can be questioned. If it is accepted, there is still the interesting possibility that such sings are not new. Stepp and Joesph learned most their songs from other singers. Thus, the separate ingredients for their laments are old. For all we know, singers constructed the same laments when traditional social dancing was thriving, say in 1920. And surely it is not beyond Pimas to lament the future of something that they hope to maintain. Unfortunately, we have no sings from fifty or a hundred years ago to compare with these two. We have these sings, and a criticism of them, but not the history. I do say however that the central illusion describes a reality that was more prevalent than it now is.

Three Pagago Airplane Songs and the Dreaming of Ancientness

This paper is a response to two evocative phrases used by the linguist-ethnomusicologist George Herzog more than a half century ago.[129] With the first phrase, "mythic dreamt song series," he gave a name to a singing tradition that must have been widely spread through the New World, as widely as songs were sought and received in visions and dreams (1928). But the dream songs that interested him the most, no doubt partly because they were part of a still living tradition, were those of Uto-Aztecan and Yuman language speaking peoples who lived from Sonora, Mexico, up the Gila and Colorado Rivers, and north through the Great Basin to southeastern Oregon and Southwestern Wyoming.

It is possible that it was not just the vitality of this region's tradition that drew Herzog. Perhaps these peoples made more of dreaming and singing and myth, or of the combination of those (in Herzog's ordering, "myth," "dreaming," and "song,"), than anyone else in the New World. I must say, this is possible but uncertain. The present paper will not establish the region's uniqueness, it will simply delve into the local practice so as to make it better understood.

All of the peoples of the region claimed to know songs which were preserved from the time when the universe was new. They also all claimed to obtain songs in current, dreamed encounters with spirits and gods. A handful of the peoples, however, including the Mojave, Yuma, Cocopa, and Maricopa, claimed the above and something more, namely that they could and did dream ancientness itself, that is, they dreamed of visits back to the time when the universe was founded. The most tangible results of those visits were songs which they heard from the gods and which they could sing with perfect accuracy.

---

[129] A version of this paper was published in the *Journal de la Société des Americanistes* under the title "Native American Dream Songs, Myth, Memory, and Improvisation." My thanks to the Journal for permitting its republication here.

Here is how Alfred Kroeber expressed the matter concerning the Mojave:

> Not only all shamanic power but most myths and songs . . . are dreamed. Knowledge is not a thing to be desired, the Mojave declare, but to be acquired by each man in accord with his dreams. . . . Nor is this a dreaming by men as much as by unconscious infants in their mothers or even earlier when their . . . shadows stood at Avikwame or played at Aha'av'ulypo [mythic places]. "I was there, I saw him," a myth teller says of his hero. . . (1925:754).

Unlike these four peoples the others had the same attitude toward documents and gods as a conservative Christian. The past is knowable through preserved documents and perhaps through latter-day divine revelation. This revelation is doubtful, however. If a Christian wished for additional information on the origin of the universe or the era of Jesus, he or she would usually seek that information in the world, and not ask God for it, notwithstanding God's omniscience. Even Joseph Smith, the founder of Mormonism and an ardent searcher for new information on ancient history, received his revelation in the form of ancient artifacts, tablets which were supposedly written at the time he was interested in. The location of the tablets (they became the Book of Mormon) was revealed to him by an angel.

So it was for the unexceptional native peoples of the region and is also, I suspect, for humans generally. Speeches of admonition, blessings, and prophecies are heard from gods, but the voice of history is not. Historical documents are only found as preservations, that is, as things which were made before the inquiry. The exception of the four peoples is that they acquired history "live," and not from a god's telling them from on high, but from a god's taking them back to the past and showing and telling them there.

This paper deals with the normal more than the exceptional. The norms for the region can be stated as follows:

> People greatly valued songs as exact, memorized preservations of language.
>
> They also valued stories of the ancient past, that is, myths; but except for some old mythic songs which they memorized at the level of the individual sound,[130] they could only remember their mythic

---

[130] These songs are considered to be handed down, through memorization, from the moment of their enunciation. They are preservations from mythic times, not visits back into those times. No one dreamed them; they were heard and remembered and passed

past in prose—oral prose—stories that they memorized at the level of the episode.

They dreamed new songs, but not new prose stories.

They did not dream songs of, or from, the events they narrated in their prose myths.

The exceptions that I discuss concern the last two points, in fact only the last one.[131] I suspect that this was the sole way in which the exceptional peoples differed from the others.

The second of Herzog's evocative phrases, the discussion of which will underline the importance I attach to memorization, is "the music of song versus the music of speech" (1934). With it Herzog called attention to the ever interesting question of the debt that a people's singing tradition, for example their melodic preference, owes to the prosody and phonemics (system of significant sounds) of their spoken language. I will deal with a special aspect of that debt. In the pages that follow I will treat a set of three Pima-Papago (southern Arizona) dream songs in some detail, but with the greatest attention to the songs' grammar and syntax, and to the stories told in the texts, and with lesser attention to the songs' melodies, intonation, rhythm, and phonemics. I make this selection in order to stress that literature is a means by which people preserve spans of meaningful language. Among oral peoples, this preservation must be in memory. And the oral peoples we are concerned with used song for such preservation.

In taking this approach I don't wish to dispute the influence of speech upon song. To me, however, this influence is less a matter of aesthetics than of practicality. Songs, I hold, at least *these* songs, exist to store knowledge in language. Song is, as it were, a way of writing, a way of transforming speech into something keepable.

This bears on the problem of the dreaming of ancientness in that it was only *song* that the exceptional peoples' dreamers brought back new from their travels to the origins of things. I want to show what the nature

---

down by waking adults. No one knows how long ago these times were. They may not be as long ago as a Westerner would think, just some time before the life of the oldest of peoples' actual known ancestors, perhaps only a century ago.

[131] George Devereux's book *Mojave Ethnopsychiatry* (1969) is silent on these matters. He reports many Mojave dreams but these lack songs and myth witnessing. He found the Mojave to be interested in dreams as clues on forces acting in their present and future personal lives. Thus, for example, in summarizing their fetal dreaming (alluded to in the passage quoted above from Kroeber), Devereaux reports Mojaves as saying the fetuses reluctantly look forward to being born, not backward nor around themselves into the time of myth (p.344. See also p.58).

of these songs is, especially what their narrative nature is, their power of narrative, their ability to say what was what way back when; and I want to demonstrate the relationship between those precious revealed songs and the pasts told in prose which the dreamers already knew.

SONG AS LITERATURE AND AS MEMORY

I propose that tribal peoples, that is, oral peoples, peoples without writing, set some of their literature to music because they want to remember what the literature says, and they find that thoughts set to music are highly memorable. If this seems like an origin story of music, I accept that and will now modify it just slightly. It is not that there was first literature (discourse, story), and then some of that literature was set to music for safekeeping in memory. Rather, slightly differently, there were first thoughts and utterances that pleased and moved people, and oral *literature*, including song, arose as a means to fix those thoughts in memorable, recoverable, keepable forms. Thus I am giving an origin of literature, but of literature in a certain sense, namely "stretches of language (discourse) kept in memory or (later) in writing;" or more simply, "kept language." Song, I propose, is the most rigorous way for oral peoples to memorize stretches of language.

Before discussing the rigors of memorization I should note that this definition excludes two types of language art from literature: completely improvisational, ephemeral statements, that is, statements that are not really meant for keeping;[132] and statements that lack or are perceived to lack meaningful words, for example, orchestra music or voiced works consisting entirely of "vocables" (meaningless sounds). I don't exclude them haughtily, but from a desire to focus on this nearly banal quality of most of the things that we call literature, that they are intentionally kept stretches of meaningful words.[133] What is banal for us, however, with our power of writing, is precious to people where everything, and the only thing, is memory.

In Native America generally, songs usually occupy the highest of three levels of rigor in memorization. This is the level of letter perfect (sound for sound) recall. Not surprisingly, the works committed to this most rigorous memorization are short. Thus, the songs of this dream tradition are typi-

---

[132] By "keeping" I mean "keeping for *reenactment*," including retelling and rereading. At the end of this paper I argue that the dominant patten of dream song series performance is of this ephemeral nature, the ephemeral combination of individually fixed texts.

[133] But should one wish to memorize a meaningless text, there is no doubt that a text fit for singing would be better than one without meter, melody, and rhyme.

cally about half a minute long, but they are repeated several times in each singing. They are never sung singly, but always in series (hence Herzog's term, dreamt song series). They seem to be designed so an audience will readily know if the singer has memorized them properly. They are "tricky" in execution, with syncopation and odd turns of pronunciation, and whoever stumbles in a repeated singing has failed the test of memorization.

A memorization level slightly lower than songs is occupied in Native America by texts that we call chants, prayers, spells, recitatives, and orations. These attain either word-for-word (less rigorous than sound-for-sound) memorization, or they exhibit what Milman Parry and Albert Lord called "oral formulaic" memorization (for example, Lord, 1960), a semi-improvisional manipulation of stock phrases.[134] Such texts typically range in length from five minutes to half an hour.

Below that level are the longest and least rigorously memorized texts, which I call "prose." Here we find the bulk of what are conventionally called "myth" texts. They are told in an ordinary speaking voice, not sung or chanted. They can last for over an hour, and they may be parts of an organized whole tribal mythic history that would reach book length if fully told. Such texts are memorized at the level of the episode: the teller is sure to give the essential narrative facts, but there is no guarantee, or even intent, that the teller will repeat exactly the same words that were used in a previous telling. The texts are paraphrased on each performance. One must say that this is a kind of memorization, but of episodes not of words or of sounds.[135]

Implicit in the fact that the principal genres of Native American oral literature fall into a scale of memorization is the idea that literature is precious. Only a small portion of what people in oral societies know and say is committed to literature. One wonders, "why those things?" I have no answer, only an approach to the problem: studying the levels in interaction and aking "why is this in song and that in prose?" and, in this case, "what has dreaming to do with it?"[136]

---

[134] This form of analysis was convincingly applied by Michael Foster to Iroquois Longhouse speeches in a 1974 publication.

[135] The oral aspects of such works have been well discussed by Dennis Tedlock (1977), Dell Hymes (1981), and Paul Zolbrod (1995). Tedlock calls them "oral poetry," Hymes calls them "verse" (in a specific sense), and Zolbrod classifies them as the "colloquial," as opposed to the "lyric" voice of "oral poetry." I don't dispute those designations, and my calling such works prose is not to deny their poetic qualities.

[136] We can understand something here about why Native Americans feel their literature to be sacred: because the literature has been handed down *with effort*, by memorization. It is not handed down on paper (externalized), but through memory (internalized);

JOHN LEWIS'S AIRPLANE SONGS

The key documents relative to the exceptional time voyaging of this dream culture are certain very long series of songs with accompanying prose. There is only one complete written version of such a text, that is, a version with both the songs and the prose. It is a Yuma myth called Lightning that was taken down by A. M. Halpern and excerpted for publication under the name of the singer, William Wilson (1984). Before I discuss that text and others like it (Halpern kindly gave me a copy of the full version), I wish to introduce and analyze a very short series from the Papago or Tohono O'odham singer John Lewis, of Gunsight Village, Arizona.

I will pay particular attention to the way Lewis's songs tell a story. They leave the story to the imagination of the hearer, or reader. I believe that this was the norm for the region, which raises one more issue on norms and exceptions: whether and why a dreamed song series would have accompanying prose. I will explore this by contrasting the Airplane and Lightning sets at the end of the paper.

The Airplane songs are said to have been dreamed from (overheard from) an airplane in the 1940s. Mr. Lewis did not dream them himself, but learned them from the dreamer while they both worked at farms near Gila Bend, Arizona. Gila Bend is mentioned in the first song, for there was a small Army Air Corps training field there, which supposedly attracted the plane.

The songs were from modern times, but their use was traditional. They were danced to. On weekends the Indians in the farm labor camp would sing the songs and dance to them. The Lightning songs were also danced to, as I believe were all dream song series.[137] We will discuss these dances as narrative or literary performances at the end of the paper.

At intervals during the Airplane dances, Lewis said, the song dreamer passed out chocolates to his helpers. These were snacks; the occasion was lighthearted. The idea was to imitate pilots who were understood to eat chocolate while flying, for alertness. Lewis said that there were many more songs than the three he remembered. The three do, however, suggest an ordered whole.

---

and while paper can easily be kept, memorized texts must be constantly tended to, called up and dusted off so to speak, to establish whether one still "has" them. Native Americans can resent the ease with which writing preserves their memorized texts.

[137] More precisely, all peoples who dreamed song series danced to some of those songs. But they also had dream songs that they didn't dance to, primarily songs used for curing. See Bahr, 1987, for the distinction between social dancing and curing songs.

THE TEXTS

The songs are rendered according to the procedures used in the body of this book: song transcripts with beats and key metered zones shown; ordinary, spoken Pima renditions with literal English equivalents (this time the "auxiliary" is marked by the expression "Aux," and the information it carries on person, number, and aspect is enclosed in brackets); and free translation (here completely capitalized). The next section, on interpretation, and two appended Supplements (numbers two and three) discuss technicalities. A standard musical notation by Richard Haefer is in Supplement One. I thank Haefer for that and for his consulations on the musical contours of the key metered zones.

SONG 1.
(Song Language Version)

```
 /    /    /    /    /    /    /    /    /    *    *    /    /    /    /    /

                              Da  ñai yu  huke hi  me  da         he
                         Ku   nya ñai yu  huke hi  me  da
Ga  mu  ka  li  fo  na  je   je  we  ame jede hi  me  da
Ga  mu  ka  li  fo  na  je   je  we  ame jede hi  me  da
    Ga  mu  hi  la  wine je  je  we  da  mane yu  nu  ke
    Ga  mu  hi  la  wine je  je  we  da  mane yu  nu  ke

 /    /    /    /    /    /    /    /    /    *    *    /    /    /    /    /
```

(Native Ordinary and Literal English Renditions)

Dañ   u:g   himdam,
Am Aux[1 sing, imperf] high goer,

Kuñ   a:ñ u:g   himdam.
Aux[1 sing, imperf] I   high goer.

Gam hu Kalifona   jewed amjed him,
Away   California land from go,

Gam hu Kalifona   jewed amjed him.
Away   California land from go.

Gam hu Hila:wi   jewed da:m hud,
Away   Gila Bend land above descend,

Gam hu Hila:wi   jewe**d** da:m hu**d**.
Away   Gila Bend land   above descend.

(Free Translation)
I'M AN AIRPLANE,
AND I'M AN AIRPLANE.
AWAY FROM CALIFORNIA GOING,
AWAY FROM CALIFORNIA GOING.
AWAY ON GILA BEND DESCENDING,
AWAY ON GILA BEND DESCENDING.

SONG 2.
(Song Language Version)

′	′	′	′	′	′	′	*	*	′	′	′	′	′
Ku	ñia	wu	**s**a	nye	ke	ju	ju	male	hi	me	da		
Ku	ñi	wu	**s**a	nye	ke	ju	ju	male	hi	me	da		
	Ga	mu	ya	ho	no	wa**n**e	da	mane	si	kole	hi	me	de
	Ga	mu	ya	ho	no	wa**n**e	da	mane	si	kole	hi	me	de
′	′	′	′	′	′	′	*	*	′	′	′	′	′

(Native Ordinary and Literal English Versions)
Kuñ   i:ya i wu:**s**k   jumal him,
And Aux[1, sing, imperf] here come out and low   go,

Kuñ   i:ya i wu:**s**k   jumal him.
And Aux[1, sing, imperf] here come out and low go.

Gam hu Aho du'ag   da:m sikol   him,
Away   Ajo mountain above circling go,

Gam hu Ajo du'ag   da:m sikol   him.
Away   Ajo mounatain above circling go.

(Free Translation)
AND I COME OUT AND LOW GO,
AND I COME OUT AND LOW GO.
AWAY AJO MOUNTAIN ABOVE CIRCLING GOING.
AWAY AJO MOUNTAIN ABOVE CIRCLING GOING.

SONG 3.
(Song Language Version)

′	′	′	′	′	′	′	*	*	′	′	′
Mu	ku	li	do	wane	je	wene	yoni	nane	ke		ke
Mu	ku	li	do	wane	je	wene	yoni	nane	ke		ke
	Sa	poi	ku	ku	na	he	si	wode	me	me	he
							Ku	ñege	yai	hi	me
	Sa	poi	ku	ku	na	he	si	wode	me	me	he
							Ku	ñege	yai	hi	me
′	′	′	′	′	′	′	*	*	′	′	′

(Native Ordinary and Literal English versions)
Mukul du'ag   jewed hogid an   ke:k,
Mukul mountain earth edge   there stand,

Mukul du'ag   jewed hogid an   ke:k.
Mukul mountain earth edge   there stand.

S-ap   o i   ku:g ab siwod   mehe,
Nicely Aux[3, sing/plu, imperf] end at flaming burn,

Kuñ   g ai.
And Aux[i, sing, imperf] it reach.

S-ap   o i   ku:g ab siwod   mehe,
Nicely Aux[3, sing/plu, imperf] end at flaming burn,

Kuñ   g ai.
And Aux[1, sing, imperf] it reach.

(Free Translation)
MUKUL MOUNTAIN AT THE WORLD'S EDGE STANDS,
MUKUL MOUNTAIN AT THE WORLD'S EDGE STANDS.
GOOD, ON ITS TIP A FIRE BURNS,
AND I REACH IT.
GOOD, ON ITS TIP A FIRE BURNS,
AND I REACH IT.

INTERPRETATION OF STORY, ANALYSIS OF MEANS

I discuss here how the three songs in sequence assimilate a modern airplane into an established dream song rubric on shamanic journeying. After that narrative analysis I discuss the role of the key zone in the songs, to show that it corresponds to a single grammatical (adverbial) and syntactic (penultimate) category, and that it has a musical (meter, rhyme, and tone) identity.

As I stated earlier, the song set originated in farm labor camps near Gila Bend, Arizona, during the Second World War. Near Gila Bend was an air field where, as the first song says, planes landed on flights from California. (The field still exists by this small desert town—see Map 2 for the route). Forty miles south of Gila Bend is the mining town of Ajo, Arizona, and fifteen miles southeast of that town is a large mountain also called Ajo (*Aho* in Pima-Papago). The mountain name probably preceded the town, which dates from the turn of the century. Lewis's home is near the mountain, and so perhaps was the home of the dreamer. I have heard the mountain mentioned in Pima songs, dreamed from birds rather than airplanes, but the Pima singers were unfamiliar with the actual mountain.

The "I" in this set is an airplane that starts from California, flies to and descends at Gila Bend, and then flies to and circles above Ajo Mountain. Finally, in the last song, the plane flies to a destination which I believe no waking person has seen, and whose very name, *Mukul,* I have not heard interpreted in Pima-Papago or translated into English. According to Lewis the destination is a mountain at the edge of the world in a southeasterly direction from Ajo Mountain. This puts it in roughly the same orientation to Ajo Mountain as that mountain is to Gila Bend. The song says that a fire burns at Mukul's tip, and the plane arrives there. The fire, Lewis says, is an airplane beacon.

Each line of each song is a complete sentence, simple or complex. The set has a total of sixteen lines, but there are really only eight different ones, because each line is sung twice. Almost every line ends in a verb. The exception is the duplicated first line of song 1 whose verb is in the first word and is "am" (the copula, Pima-Papago *wud,* here contracted to D-). There is one more verb out of the final position. The duplicated first line in song 2 is a sentence with two clauses. The line ends with "go," but begins with a clause whose verb is "come out." The eighteen verbal positions are filled with just seven verbs: "am," "go," "descend," "come out," "stand," "burn," and "reach." "Go" is the most frequent, and all except "am" and "burn" are what one could call "travel words," that is, words about bodily movement. Margot Astrov long ago noted the prevalence of such words in Native American literatures (1950—her special interest was the Navajo). Note also that the exceptional first line of song 1 ends with a play on the verb "go." "High goer," the standard Pima-Papago expression for "airplane," is built from a verb and occurs in the expected line final verbal position.

Immediately before the final verb comes the key metered zone. It is regularly filled by an adverb. Some of these are paired with nouns to form adverbial phrases (the adverbial words are then called "post positions"— Zepeda, 1983:46–52): "earth *from*," "earth *upon*," "mountain *upon*," and "earth *beside*." One adverb is hidden but implied in an auxiliary plus a pronoun (song 3, roughly speaking "and-I-*to-it*"). And four are normal, simple adverbs: "high," "low," "circling," and "flaming".

Prior to the adverbs come nouns or noun phrases: "high goer" ("airplane"), "California earth," "Gila Bend earth," "Ajo mountain," "Mukul mountain," and "earth end-at." Deviantly present in this syntactic position is one verb ("come-out-and") in song 2; and the expected noun position is empty in the repeated short final line of song 3. There is one more syntactical position in this set's formula. Prior to the noun phrase and at the *start* of each line is an auxiliary, either a "subject complex word" (see Supplement 2, "On Translation") or a "locative auxiliary." Roughly translated, the subject complexes are "I-am," "And-I-am," "And-I-here," "Nicely it-will," and "And-I-to-it." There is just one recurrent locative auxiliary, "Away." One duplicated line has nothing in this slot: song 3, lines 1 and 2.

This syntactic pattern is not required by Papago ordinary language. In fact, the one strict rule that has been formulated for ordinary Papago word order is that a subject complex auxiliary must always occur in second position in a sentence (Zepeda, 1983:7–9). The set's formula violates that rule. When its sentences have auxiliaries, they come in the first position. This is surely not the only syntactic pattern that occurs in Papago and Pima song lines (these are the same people linguistically and musically), but the range of these patterns is not known. The sole clear general principle of the people's songs is that lines tend to end in verbs.[138]

---

[138] The songs do not fit very well the formula given in the section discussing filmicness in chapter three. Actually, song 3 fits it perfectly: (1) there was a mountain; (2) at its tip a fire burns; (3) and I reach it. But song 2 has only two of the requisite three sentences: it has good examples of the formula's last two, but it lacks an expression or realization of the formula's first. Song 3 is hopeless as far as the formula is concerned. It has three sen-

Also, leaving aside what the song lines regularly include, they are notable for what they leave out. They tend to leave out the grammatical subjects of their sentences and therefore the identities of the actors or heroes of their stories. Thus, although these three songs are heavy with nouns, the nouns are not the subjects of sentences or the doers of actions. Rather, the nouns name things or places that the actor, an "I" (signaled by a single sound in the auxiliary), comes upon. Song 3 is a partial exception. It has a substantive noun ("Mukul mountain"[139]) as the subject of its first line. To this mountain comes the "I." Finally, if the majority of nouns are not subjects, neither are they direct objects in the strict sense. Almost all the verbs are intransitive, thus they lack direct objects. The nouns are more loosely objects, however, being the travel destinations of the "I."

These syntactical tendencies combine to produce a subjective, action oriented, pictorial and shamanic poetry. The "I" is like a camera recording what it sees. The point of the song set, I think, is that the plane is like a shaman or medicine man because it reaches the edge of the world and finds something burning there. Thus it is the last song that transforms the set from a merely amusing piece on airplanes into a piece on shamanism. The songs used by Pima-Papago shamans for divination and curing generally feature first person journeys, and the journeys commonly involve flight (Russell, 1908:302–06; Underhill, 1946:272–77; Bahr, 1988 and 1991). Here is an example, also preoccupied with flying, from John Lewis:

> It is little winged turtle and here descends.
> It is little winged turtle and here descends,
> Here to me stretches, away eastward leads me.
> Here to me stretches, away eastward leads me,
> Here to me stretches, away children's burial inside I enter,
> Several shinings cover me.

tences, but contrary to formula it starts off with its "I." And its second and third sentences (each repeated once) are close variants of each other. Clearly, the formula is an impressionistic quasi or pseudo statistical, abstracted profile. It is not so much wrong as squinty-eyed.

[139] The nouns in this line are interestingly ambiguous. From the text, one cannot tell who or what is standing where: Mukul mountain at the edge of the earth or an unnamed something at the edge of Mukul mountain's land. In speaking about the song, Lewis opted for the first interpretation, which makes the mountain the grammatical subject and actor and locates this mountain at the edge of the world. The alternative interpretation, equally valid in terms of grammar and vocabulary, is that the mountain might be anywhere. The "edgeness" is that of an unnamed stander to the land of the mountain, not that of the mountain to the land/earth. This is possible because the grammar is ambiguous and so is the word translated "land" and "earth" (Pima-Papago *jewed*).

The "east" refers to the land of the dead, the children's burial is the place of a mythic child sacrifice. The "I," either a ghost or a shaman, is illuminated after entering that underground place (Bahr, 1988:74–76).

I turn now to the music, with special attention to the key zones. Metrically this zone approximately corresponds to the instances where three syllables are apportioned over two beats (full beat, then two half beats). There are twelve such instances within the zone (four times the zone has exceptional four syllable apportionments: lines 3 and 4 of song 1, and 1 and 2 of song 3); and there are twelve occurrences outside it. Eight of the exceptions are contiguous with the zone (songs 2 and 3), and we may say that they mimic it. I cannot explain the other four.

The key zone comprises a column of controlled phonetic variation, in other words, of rhyme. There is no doubt that the words that occupy the zone have been modififed from ordinary speech for the sake of rhyme. The key zone of song 2 is the clearest example.[140] The first syllables do not rhyme, but the last two do. The second syllable is a stack of "ma"-s. and the third has the constant vowel "e" with differences in consonants. Thus,

```
ju   ma  le
ju   ma  le
da   ma  ne
da   ma  ne.
```

The ordinary language sources of these words are *jumal* and *da:m*, a two- and a one-syllable word. The initial syllables of those words retain their true sounds, but the final syllables are rhymed. I suspect that the key zone the prime locus for rhyming, but only in a statisical sense: modifications from ordinary language to singing will be more frequent in the key zone than outside it, and these modifications will be in the direction of consonance with other occupants of the song's key zone.

Now tone. More often than not, the key zone, if of three syllables, has the tonal configuration Hi Lo Hi; and if the zone has four syllables the configuation is Hi Hi Lo Hi. Although the absolute pitch values vary from line to line (see Haefer's musical notation in Supplement One), the Hi's in each instance are of the same pitch, so the configuration is a pitch,

---

[140] And this example is not perfect. I have located the key zone of the second pair of lines on the adverbial word "above," but the following adverb, "circling," is an equally good candidate. The rhyme is better for the "above" word than for "circling." If I may say so, this line pair has a doubled key zone, "above" and "circling," the first for rhyme and the second for syntax.

a drop, and a resumption of the original pitch. This pattern holds for twelve of the sixteen key zones, and it occurs four times outside a zone.

If the key zone is musically distinct, it is also pinpointed. Therefore we should not expect it to capture the full play of linguistic meaning in a song. As we have seen, the key zone consists of adverbs, but these are not what make the narratives interesting. In my opinion, the narratives are interesting because of their concealed first personness, their supression of grammatical subject nouns, and the suggestion of shamanism. Those complexities are not contained in the key zones. Nor could they be. The key zones, while meaningful, are not poems. They attest to memorization but they do not hold the secret of a text.

LIGHTNING

Lightning is the story of one hero's journeying, usually in the company of three other individuals, one of whom dreamed the songs. The dreamer was the singer William Wilson's father. He is not mentioned in the text. Wilson explained to Halpern that his father was present as a silent witness and overhearer of the songs. Wilson's prose then is a paraphrase of his father's prose account of what happened, but the songs that Wilson sang are taken as the exact words sung by the mythical hero, named Wonder Boy (who beomes thunder and lightning at the end of the story). Also present during parts of the journey, but silent, are Coyote and Marxo Kwave (untranslated), the orignal ancestor (not creator) of the Yuma.

Each of the 118 songs in the series supposedly originated in the journey. Thus the text qualifies as an exception by the fourth norm stated at the beginning of this essay—new songs—but not by the third—new myth. I say this because Wonder Boy observed and sang about mythic events that the Yumas already knew; he came upon them and burst into song. In doing so he was as much an observer as the dreamer whom he guided and sang to. He did not affect the events, or analyze them, but simply acknowledged them, as the following example from lightning will illustrate. An important event in Yuma mythology is the death and cremation of a creator god named Kukumat. Here, with brackets by me and parantheses by Halpern, is a part of the event as rendered in Lightning. First comes prose, then a song:

> Thus saying [by the dying god Kukumat], "I have finished the story" he is saying. Now he is really about to take a turn for the worse [die], and as he [Wonder Boy] is looking at him there, "Well, I will (admit my)

fail(ure)," he [Kukumat] said, then the sick man [K] said, "Well, I am about to pass away. Come really closer [K said to all the creatures assembled, including the journeyers], surround me and look at me!"; and these people moved over there and surrounded him and looked. And he [WB] stood there describing it again [singing the following song for the dreamer to hear].

> I [K] am passing away, he tells himself
> He [K] describes his failure [to live longer]
> They [onlookers] surround him
> He [WB] sees them surrounding him
> He describes them surrounding him. (Halpern, n.d.:15–16)[141]

The Lightning text is not a new myth in the sense of a new or revised insight into the foundation of the Yuma universe. It is an old myth revisited and commented upon by Wonder Boy for a Yuma dreamer's benefit. The text's plot as a whole is like the much shorter Airplane series: a guiding spirit (Wonder Boy, or an Airplane-person) and an entourage (a single Papago dreamer in the the airplane songs[142]) travel, and the spirit sings songs in the process. The prose parts (lacking in the Papago) mostly tell where the hero moved next.

CONCLUSION: MYTH AND DREAM SONG

I close with observations on: (1) how the Lightning songs, while giving testimony of a dreamed visit to mythic time, necessarily deliver that testimony in a mixture of prose and song; (2) how the Airplane songs tell more of a story in pure song than the Lightning songs would, were they taken "cold" without any prose explication; and (3) what the Airplane song practice implies about the improvisation of myth.

To begin I will review the extent of ancient myth dreaming in the region. Besides the Mojave, Yuma, Cocopa, and Maricopa, the practice is reported from practically all the peoples of southern California (Diegeno, Cupeno, etc.) and adjacent Lower California, Mexico. It is not reported elsewhere, and I doubt that it has been missed. Kroeber published the prose portions of many such Mojave myths, but he omitted the

---

[141] Halpern does not give the music for this text, and his translation obscures the fact, or apparent fact, that most of the most of the song lines end in verbs.

[142] I assume that Lewis thought the original dreamer accompanied the Plane-person on this trip. Otherwise it would be a matter of the Plane-person coming to the dreamer as the latter lay in sleep, or perhaps buzzing him somewhere.

songs (1948, 1972). William Kelly published the prose but not the songs of a Cocopa myth of this sort (1977). As for dream songs of the normal sort, from peoples other than the above, the best publications are by Larry Evers and Felipe Molina of Yaqui Deer songs (1987), by Judith Vander of Shoshone Ghost dance songs (1986), and by me and several other people of Pima-Papago songs. It is difficult to tell where the dream song tradition stopped or where it was absent in the American and Mexican west. It probably existed throughout northern Mexico, but may not have existed, at least may not have been important, among the Navajos, Apaches, and the Pueblos.

Comparing Lightning and the Airplane songs, it is evident that Lightning is prose and song and Airplane is pure song. The songs of Lightning however do not make a story. The four songs that follow (with prose intervals) and the one quoted above defy narrative sense.

> He [who?] stands there weeping
> He sees him weeping
> He describes weeping.
>
> He digs up the ground.
>
> It [what?] is high.
>
> He takes it [what?] and stands it up
> He stands it up, it is high, he takes it and stands it up
> He describes his standing it up (Halpern, n.d.:16).

However, the Lightning text is not faulty because its songs make no sense on their own. Rather, it is extravagant. To understand the sequence one needs to know that the songs came from an eyewitness to myth, and one also needs to know the myth.

The dances in which dream songs were used were held out of doors in the night and were intended to last a full night. They were held at village ceremonial grounds, or at convenient places between houses (the houses were dispersed among fields and scrub), or at houses. They were communal, that is, attended by a throng, not merely by members of one family. They were held for mourning, for girls' puberty, to await the return of ghosts (the Ghost dance of the Shoshones and Paiutes was of this tradition), to celebrate good harvests and war victories, and to celebrate paydays (Airplane songs) and American holidays such as Memorial Day or Fourth of July. As Kroeber remarked, the same series could be sung at any such event (1925:756). These were generalized celebrations like the American "party." They celebrated something that had been accomplished, not something that lay ahead.[143] The dancing was sometimes in circles and sometimes in straight lines, but it was always popular, mass dancing.[144] It included both men and women. Whoever came could dance and could join in the singing while dancing. There was teasing and lovemaking.

If public speaking occured at a dance, it was admonitory on behavior, not explanatory on the stories behind the songs. One did not receive such explanations at a dance, but later at the singer's house. In fact, private houses are where all prose mythology was told. There was no central authority over mythology and in reality no institutionalized public prose. Songs and the middle memorized range of chant were used in public, prose in private.

Few social dances have been observed by anthropologists. I know of just four published observations of actual dances of this tradition, two of Yaqui Deer dances (Wilder, 1963; Evers and Molina, 1987) and two of Pima-Papago Circle or Skipping dances (Haefer, 1980. Kozak, 1992). Those four contain lists of the songs sung at the dances.

The story told in the Airplane songs is of a single hero, an "I" who is an airplane who mimics a shaman. Now, one can say this story requires background knowledge equivalent to that required by the Lightning songs. For example, one must know that medicine men seek light and must be familiar with the mountain locations. I grant this, and yet I hold that the Airplane songs are a complete, solvable puzzle-poem, while the Lightning songs by themselves are no poem or solvable puzzle at all. They are exaltations uttered upon walking in on a live, independently known story. I never saw an Airplane dance but I am sure that the three songs we have discussed would not fill a night of dancing. As noted earlier, Lewis said that the dreamer knew many more songs. What we have from Lewis, then, is a selection, a picked medley, and one picked I am sure for their rhyme and reason as one poem.

Now, if the three songs are too few for a dance, the 118 Lightning songs are too many. My experience from a handful of Pima-Papago dances suggests that from twenty to fifty songs would fill a normal night's

---

[143] According to Vander, the Shoshone Ghost dance grew out of such a celebration, and it reverted back to it once the expectation of the millennium had past (1986).

[144] An exception is the Yaqui Deer dance whose songs fit the regional tradition in that they are dreamt, they are sung in series through the night, and the series tells a story. Evers and Molina (1987) give the best collection and analysis of them. The Deer dancing is exceptional, however, because it is not done by the masses of adults who attend, but by expert solo performers. Those in attendance watch. The daytime Pima dances discussed in the body of this book are also performed in like manner.

program. Wilson told Halpern that he regularly sang the first thirty-seven songs in summer dances and the first sixty-four in the winter when the nights are long. These were for dances at funerals. This implies that lightning was a fixed sequence that he could never complete, except at home. I have written about a similar person, a Pima singer, Manuel, who knew upwards of 250 Swallow songs (dreamed from that bird-person). The singer was repeatedly recorded during three-hour "sings" at an Indian nursing home where dancing was only a memory. The average session included about 30 songs. The paper analyzes this singer's eternal tinkering with his sequences (1986).

For the Pima singer there was no underlying myth. Rather there were *topics* for songs: the beginning of singing, sundown, going west, water, rocks, medicine men, whores, nice women, birds awakening, dawn, and the ending of singing. Only a few categories were sung on a given night, often only one. The singer liked to summon his materials on a topic ruminatively and slightly differently each time. The only constant songs were a series of three at the beginning *on* the beginning of singing, and two at the end on the ending. His ruminations were not trivial. "Beginnings" had overtones of mythic origins in some medleys, "endings" hinted at the end of the singing tradition and the universe. There were strings on sex, war, and loneliness. Each song was perfectly memorized and supposedly orginated in a Swallow, but one felt that the singer, Paul Manuel, used them to address almost anything.

Kroeber said that Mojave singers varied the number of songs at points in their series (1925:757), but he implies that the order of events in the prose story—the dreamed itinerary—prevented wholesale rearrangement such as Manuel practiced. Manuel may have been unusual, perhaps unusually restless, but I have found identical songs in Pima-Papago series that were supposedly dreamed from different sources (Swallow and Owl from Manuel, Ant and Buzzard and God and Oriole from others). Thus songs are somewhat freely appropriated from their original dreamed journeys, and are used as by Manuel to constitute new virtual myths.

Singers do not talk freely about this. They like to serve up a sequence as if it came from one actual dream. I am sure that they know what they are doing, that through selection and recombination they create illusions of story, more or less fixed, of which we have just analyzed an example, the Airplane songs. For them to admit that they do it would probably strike them as too boastful. They pretend to remember their combinations of songs, which in the Airplane case is not a Great Myth but a very modest one, the myth of the first airplane that acted like a medicine man.

Musical Notation

By J. Richard Haefer, Arizona State University

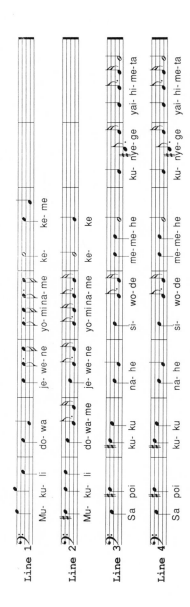

Song 3

On Translation

Most people who read a translation do not know the language that is being translated. They take the translator's knowledge on trust. My method tries to anchor the trust. This is not only a matter of literalism. I give a literal and free version like everyone else, but because songs stand at a remove from the spoken native language, there is also a problem of having something to be literal to. The proper anchor, I believe, is a native, ordinary language version of the song, a version that is itself a kind of translation, or at least an interpretation. Such is needed because the hearers of dream songs do not know what songs say when they first hear them. Through processes that remain mysterious to me even though I have developed a certain facility with them, one eventually arrives at a satisfactory ordinary language interpretation, that is, an interpretation that comprehends every sung syllable. Analogy certainly plays a role in this task. A word or word form that was clearly present in one song illuminates a difficult passage in another. The singer's authority also plays a role. An interpretation can be confirmed by asking the singer. (Singers tend not to volunteer interpretations. They prefer to judge the interpretations of others).

Literal translation proceeds on that base. My preference here is to match each Pima-Papago word with a word or phrase of English, in the hope that the result will be readable as a stream of actual but awkward English. There is but one recourse. When a Pima-Papago word is judged to be too exotic for an ordinary English equivalent, one can define the native word within brackets. In so doing, one shifts from English ordinary language equivalents (which are always suspect and always imposters) to metalanguage analysis (equally suspect, always an imposition). In these texts, there is only one type of Pima-Papago word where I take the metalanguage recourse. This is the word called the "auxiliary," actually the "subject complex auxiliary" (Zepeda, 1983:7–11;

Mathiot, 1983:202).[145] This word carries information, first, on the person and number of the grammatical subject of the verb (that is, the persons or things who do the action that the verb refers to); and second on the aspect (perfective or imperfective) of the verb. The information is coded in single sounds. Thus, the auxiliary is a very short but semantically dense word. In principle, each clause must have an auxiliary, but in fact, the clauses in songs sometimes dispense with them. When the auxiliary occurs, I do not attempt an ordinary English equivalent, for there is none, but use the bracketed label "aux" with abbreviated information on person (1,2,3), number (sing., plu.), and aspect (perf., imperf.).

The "literal" word sequences are barely readable in English. Maddeningly ambiguous, they point in several connotative directions at once, and one can say that they point nowhere in concert, that is, they are not tuned to guide the reader to a particular reading of a poem. They are *pre-poems*. The free translation, simply, aims to come closer to polished English poetry. The goal is to stay true to the original, but to convey that original meaning and feel into good English.

In this procedure, free translation departs from the literal in the direction of a more beautiful English. There is another possible direction for a post-literal translation, namely towards the syllabification and music of the original song. One can only make this move after determining what the song says in native ordinary language and after determining the literal English equivalents for that language. Then, instead of moving towards acceptable English poetry, the translator reverts to the native language of song, as follows:

> i-i'm   A-A-AIR pla-a-ane-uh,
> and i-im A-A-AIR pla-a-ane.
> a-way ca-li-forn-ya la-a-and   FRO-O-O-OM go-o-o,
> a-way ca-li-forn-ya la-a-and   FRO-O-O-OM go-o-o.
> a-way gi-la be-end la-a-and   ON TO-OP de-e-scend,
> a-way gi-la be-end la-a-and   ON TO-OP de-e-scend.

The key zone words are capitalized and aligned. Thus capitalization does not mark accoustic volume or pitch as in the loud rendition of the Oriole songs, it simply marks the zone of most careful metric control.

---

[145] Mathiot (1983:203) calls it the subject complex auxiliary, noting that there are other forms of auxiliary in the language, namely demonstrative, locative, indefinite quantifier, and indefinite manner qualifier.

On the Study of Individual Songs

The body of this essay ended with the nature of multisong sets. Here I review how the present study of Airplane songs pertains to the study of individual dream songs. This topic is farther advanced with the Pima-Papago than with the other peoples, but the Pima-Papago yield is still slight. The concept of the key metered zone awaits application beyond the Pima-Papago. I consider it a subtle part of the design of their songs, one that serves the practical purpose of attesting to proper memorization. In the Airplane songs this zone is a narrow column of versification where meter, rhyme, and tone are brought under a particularly tight discipline. It remains to be seen how generally and clearly such intermittent versification occurs. On the other hand, the ending of song lines with verbs seems general through the region; and the practice of loading songs with nouns that are not grammatical subjects may also be so.[146]

The challenge of coordinating Herzog's two "musics" is largely unmet. A desirable project along those lines would start with the facts that (1) the songs of this tradition are fully texted, that is, they contain no nonsense syllables; and yet (2) the sung words differ considerably from the words as pronounced in ordinary language; and (3) only a small portion of the words of a given spoken language are prominently used in songs. Working in the reverse order of those points, one could develop an inventory of the favored words of the songs of the several different dream song peoples; one could note the sung manifestations of those favored words (a word is manifest differently depending on its melodic and rhythmic context); and one could then make observations on regional

---

[146] In a suggestive study of the syntax of about twenty-five Pima-Papago songs, David Shaul (1981) observed the line final position of verbs, but he also marked many if not all song clauses as having subjects. He does not give the texts, but I suspect that many of these subjects are pronouns or subject complex auxiliaries rather than freestanding substantive nouns. Still, there certainly are substantive noun subjects in many song clauses. The interesting question is their role in the song-poem as a whole. Is there also an "I" in the song? If so, what is the relation of the "I" to the substantive noun?

unity versus diversity relative to song music and sense (lexicon). This project will not be accomplished until the tradition's participants take up scholarship or alternatively until outside scholars take up the translation practices discussed in this appendix.

References

Astrov, M.
1950   "The Concept of Motion as Psychological Leitmotiv in Navajo Life and Literature." *Journal of American Folklore,* 63:45–56.

Bahr, D.
1986   "Pima Swallow Songs." *Cultural Anthropology,* 1(2):171–87.
1987   "Pima Heaven Songs." In B. Swann and A. Krupat, eds. *Recovering the Words, Essays in Native American Literature.* Berkeley: Univeristy of California Press.
1988   "La modernisation du chananisme pima-papago." *Recherches amerindiennes au Quebec.* 18(2–3):69–81.
1991   "A grey and fervent shamanism." *Journal de la Société des Americanistes,* 77:7–26.
1994   "Native American Dream Songs, Myth, Memory, and Improvisation." *Journal de la Société des Americanistes,* 80:73–94.

Bahr, D., J. Gregorio, D. Lopez, and A. Alvarez
1974   *Piman Shamanism and Staying Sickness.* Tucson: University of Arizona Press.

Bahr, D. and J. Haefer
1978   "Song in Piman Curing." *Ethnomusicology,* 22(1):89–122.

Bahr, D., J. Giff, and M. Havier
1979   "Piman Songs on Hunting." *Ethnomusicology,* 23(2):245–96.

Bahr, D., J. Smith, W. Allison, and J. Hayden
1994   *The Short, Swift Time of Gods on Earth.* Berkeley: Univerity of California Press.

Bahr D. and V. Joseph
1994   "Pima Oriole Songs." In B. Sawnn, ed., *Coming to Light,* pp.541–63. New York: Random House.

Densmore, F.
1929   *Papago Music.* Bureau of American Ethnology Bulletin 90. Washington, D.C.: Smithsonian Institution.

Devereux, G.

1969   *Mojave Ethnopsychiatry: the Psychic Disturbances of an Indian Tribe.*
        Washington, D.C.: Smithsonian Institution Press.

Evers, L. and F. Molina

1987   *Yaqui Deer Songs, Maso Bwikam.* Tucson: University of Arizona Press.

Foster, M.

1974   *From the Earth to Beyond the Sky: An Ethnographic Approach to Four Iro-*
        quois Longhouse Speech Events. National Museums of Canada, National
        Museum of Man Mercury Series, Canadian Ethnology Service Paper, 20.

Giff, J.

1980   "Pima Blue Swallow Songs of Gratitude." In F. Barkin and E. Brandt, eds.,
        Speaking, Singing, and Teaching: A Multidisciplinary Approach to Language
        Variation, pp. 127–39. Arizona State Univesity Anthropological Research
        Papers, 20. Tempe: Arizona State University Department of Anthropology.

Haefer, J. R.

1980   "O'odham Celkona: The Papago Skipping Dance." In C. Frisbie, ed.
        Southwest Indian Ritual Drama, pp. 239–73. Albuquerque: University of
        New Mexico Press.

Halpern, A. M.

n.d.   [Yuma] Lightning [songs]. Unpublished manuscript, a copy of which is
        in Bahr's keeping.

Herzog, G.

1928   "Musical Styles in North America." *Proceedings.* Twenty-third Interna-
        tional Congress of Americanists, pp.455–58.

1934   "Speech-Melody in Primitive Music." *Musical Quarterly,* 20(4):452–56.

Hill, J.

1992   "The Flower World of Old Uto-Aztecan." *Journal of Anthropological Re-*
        search, 48:117–44.

Holman, C.

1981   *A Handbook to Literature.* Indianapolis: Bobbs-Merrill.

Hymes, D.

1981   *In Vain I Tried to Tell You.* Philadelphia: University of Pennsylvania Press.

Johnson, B.

1985   "Earth Figures of the Lower Colorado and Gila River Deserts." *Arizona*
        Archaeologist, 20. Phoenix: Arizona Archaeological Society.

Kelly, W.

1977   *Cocopa Ethnography.* Anthropological Papers of the University of Ari-
        zona, 29. Tucson.

Kozak, D.

1992   "Swallow Dizziness, the Laughter of Carnival, and Kateri." *Wicazo Sa Re-*
        view, 8(2):1–10.

Kroeber, A.

1925   *Handbook of the Indians of California.* Bulletin 78 of the Bureau of American Ethnology of the Smithsonian Institution. Washington, D.C.

1948   "Seven Mojave Myths." *Anthropological Records,* Univeristy of California, 11(1):1–70. Berkeley.

1972   "More Mojave Myths." *Anthropological Records,* University of California, 27:1–160. Berkeley.

Lewis, O.

1961   *The Children of Sanchez: Autobiography of a Mexican Family.* New York: Random House.

Levi-Strauss, C.

1966   *The Savage Mind.* Chicago: University of Chicago Press.

Liu, J.

1962   *The Art of Chinese Poetry.* Chicago: University of Chicago Press.

Lord, A.

1960   *The Singer of Tales.* Cambridge: Harvard University Press.

Mathiot, M.

N.d.   *A Dictionary of Papago Usage.* Language Science Monographs, 9(1,2). Bloomington: Indiana University Press.

1983   "Papago Semantics." In W. Sturtevant, ed. *Handbook of North American Indians,* v. 10, pp. 201–11. Washington, D.C.: Smithsonian Institution.

Mesa Public Schools

1978   *Our Town—Mesa, Arizona, 1878–1978.* Mesa: Mesa Public Schools.

Rosenthal, M. and S. Gall

1983   *The Modern Poetic Sequence: the Genius of Modern Poetry.* New York: Oxford University Press.

Russell, F.

1908   *The Pima Indians.* Bureau of American Ethnology, Annual Report 26. Washington, D.C. Republished 1974. Tucson: University of Arizona Press.

Salt River Project

1970   *The Taming of the Salt.* Phoenix: Salt River Project.

Saxton, D. and L. Saxton

1969   *Dictionary: Pima and Papago to English and English to Papago and Pima.* Tucson: University of Arizona Press.

Saxton, D., L. Saxton, and S. Enos

1983   *Dictionary: Pima/Papago-English, English-Papago/Pima.* Tucson: University of Arizona Press.

Shaul, D.

1981   "Piman Song Syntax." *Proceedings.* Seventh Annual Meeting of the Berkeley Linguistics Society, pp. 275–83. Berkeley, California.

Spier, L.
1933   *Yuman Tribes of the Gila River.* Chicago: University of Chicago Press.

Tedlock D.
1977   "Toward an Oral Poetics." *New Literary History,* 8(3):507–l9.

Underhill, R.
1946   *Papago Indian Religion.* New York: Columbia University Press.

Underhill, R., D. Bahr, B. Lopez, D, Lopez, and J. Pancho
1979   *Rainhouse and Ocean, Speeches for the Papago Year.* Flagstaff: Museum of Northern Arizona Press.

Vander. J.
1986   *Ghost Dance Songs and Religion of a Wind River Shoshone Woman.* Monograph Series in Ethnomusicology, No. 4. Los Angeles: Univeristy of Californian at Los Angeles, Dept. of Music.

Wilder, C.
1963   *The Yaqui Deer Dance.* Bureau of American Ethnology, Bulletin 186. Washington, D.C.: Smithsonian Institution.

Wilson, W.
1984   "Excerpts from the Lightning Song." In L. Hinton and L. Watahomigie, eds., *Spirit Mountain: An Anthology of Yuma Song and Story.* Tucson: Sun Tracks and University of Arizona Press.

Zepeda, O.
1983   *A Papago Grammar.* Tucson: University of Arizona Press.

Zolbrod, P.
1995   *Reading the Voice.* Salt Lake City: University of Utah Press.

Index

Traveling: in Ant songs, 83–92. *See also* Geography; Journey

Underhill, R., 127n.108
Uto-Aztecan language family: and Herzog's study of dream songs, 171; and Pima-Papago language, 132

Vander, Judith, 186, 187n.143
Villages: names of in Ant songs, 94n. 70

War: and Pima social dances, 30
Water: and death in Ant songs, 101n.78; and journey in Oriole songs, 127. *See also* Agriculture; Drowning; Floods; Rivers
Water rights: Pima agriculture and Salt River community, 7, 10–11, 17
White, Emmett, 138n.123
Whores: in Ant songs, 29, 93; curing songs and, 66n.31; in Oriole songs, 29, 138–42; in Pima mythology, 29

Wilson, William: and Lightning songs, 176, 184, 188
Wind/wind-person: in Papago myth, 117n.96
Wonder Boy: and Lightning songs, 184, 185

Yaqui Deer songs and dances, 186, 187
Yavapais, 7
Yuma: dreams and ancientness in song traditions of, 171–74, 185; Lightning songs and, 184–85; mythology of and names of mountains, 85n.57. *See also* Yumans
Yumans: birds and social dancing songs, 132; dream songs and, 171; song myths and, 71–72, 73n.36. *See also* Maricopa; Mojave; Yuma

Zolbrod, Paul, 175n.135
Zones: as phenomena of sound, 72; transcription of Pima songs and theory of, 41. *See also* Key zones
Zunis, 24